T · H · E

7th

GARFIELD
TREASURY

T·H·E 7th GARFIELD TREASURY

BY: JIM DAVIS

THE RANDOM HOUSE PUBLISHING GROUP • NEW YORK

A Ballantine Book
Published by The Random House Publishing Group

The Sunday strips appearing here in color were previously in black and white in
GARFIELD BY THE POUND #22, GARFIELD KEEPS HIS CHINS UP #23,
GARFIELD TAKES HIS LICKS #24, and GARFIELD HITS THE BIG TIME #25.

www.ballantinebooks.com

Library of Congress Catalog Card Number: 93-90045

ISBN: 0-345-38427-X

Manufactured in the United States of America

First Edition: November 1993

20 19 18 17 16 15 14

T · H · E
7th
GARFIELD
TREASURY

STRANGE *but weird!*

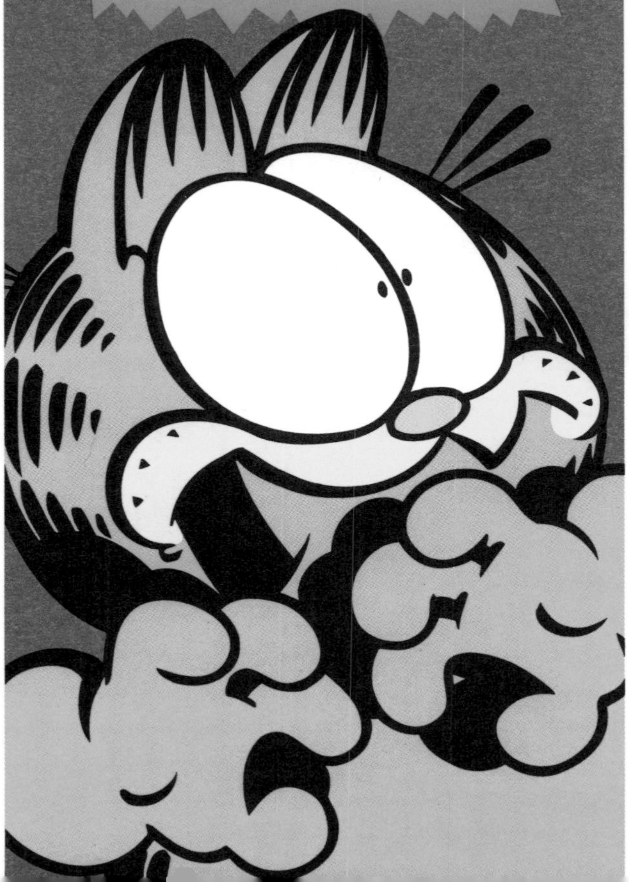

ODIE MOONLIGHTS AS A CHIA PET!

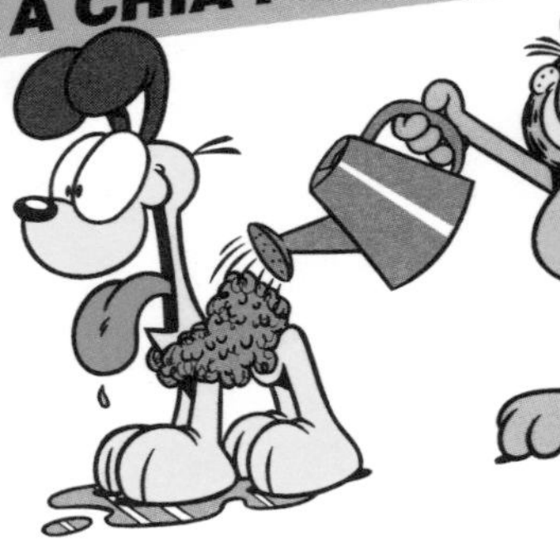

GARFIELD LOVES CHOCOLATE MOUSSE... EVEN THE ANTLERS!

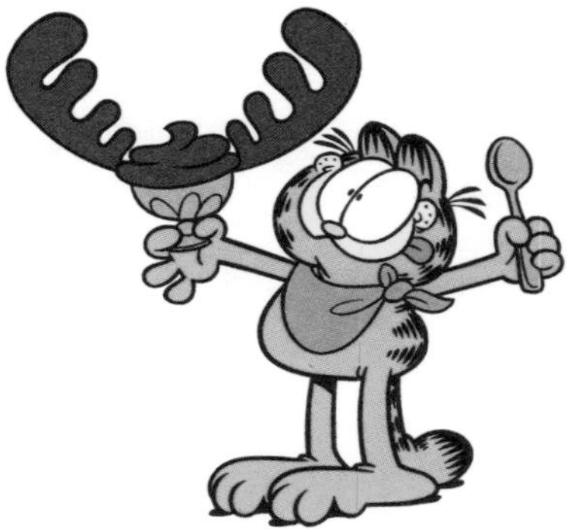

GARFIELD ONCE SWALLOWED AN ENTIRE MAILMAN!

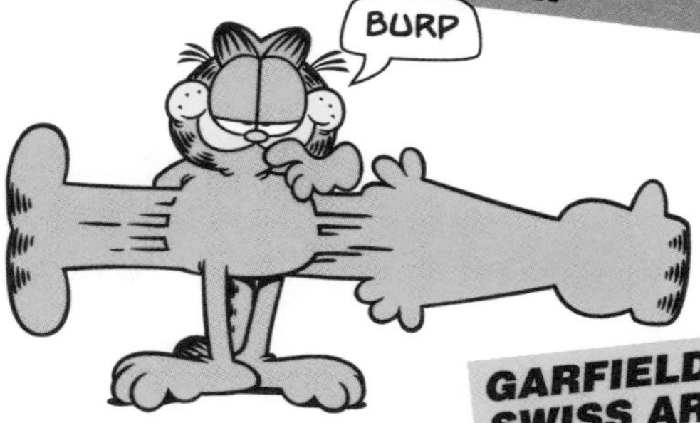
BURP

IN A FORMER LIFE, JON WAS THE VILLAGE DWEEB!

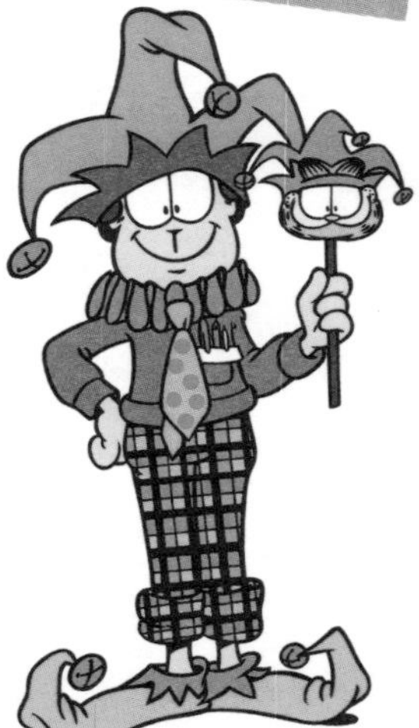

GARFIELD HAS SWISS ARMY CLAWS!

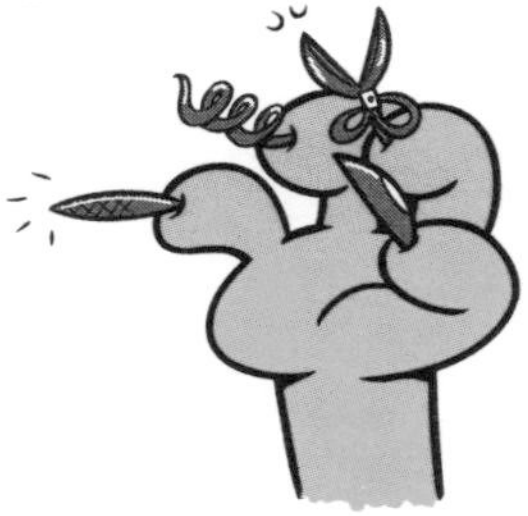

JON MAKES LAMPS OUT OF CAT HAIR!

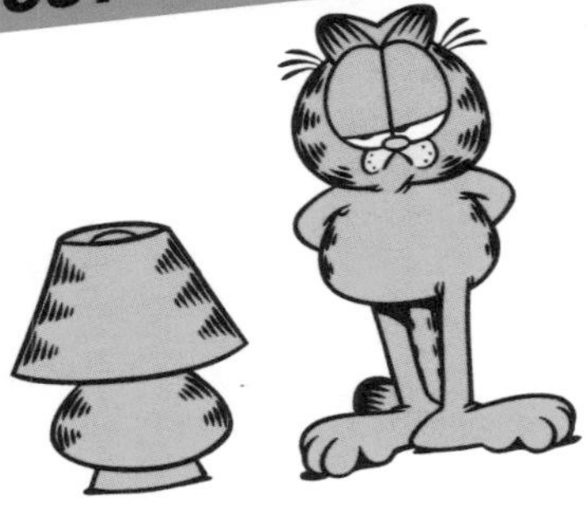

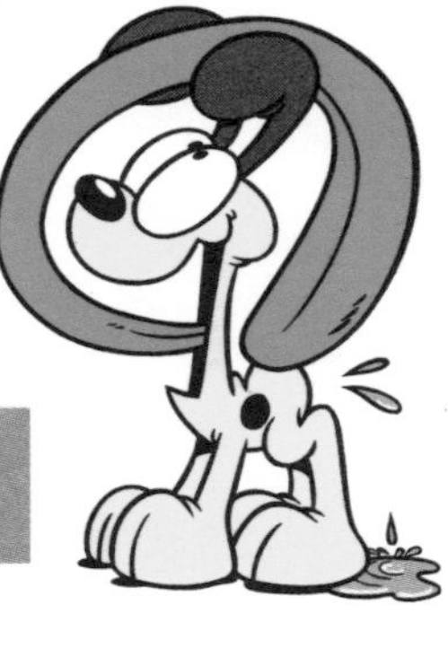

ODIE CAN LICK HIMSELF ON HIS BACK!

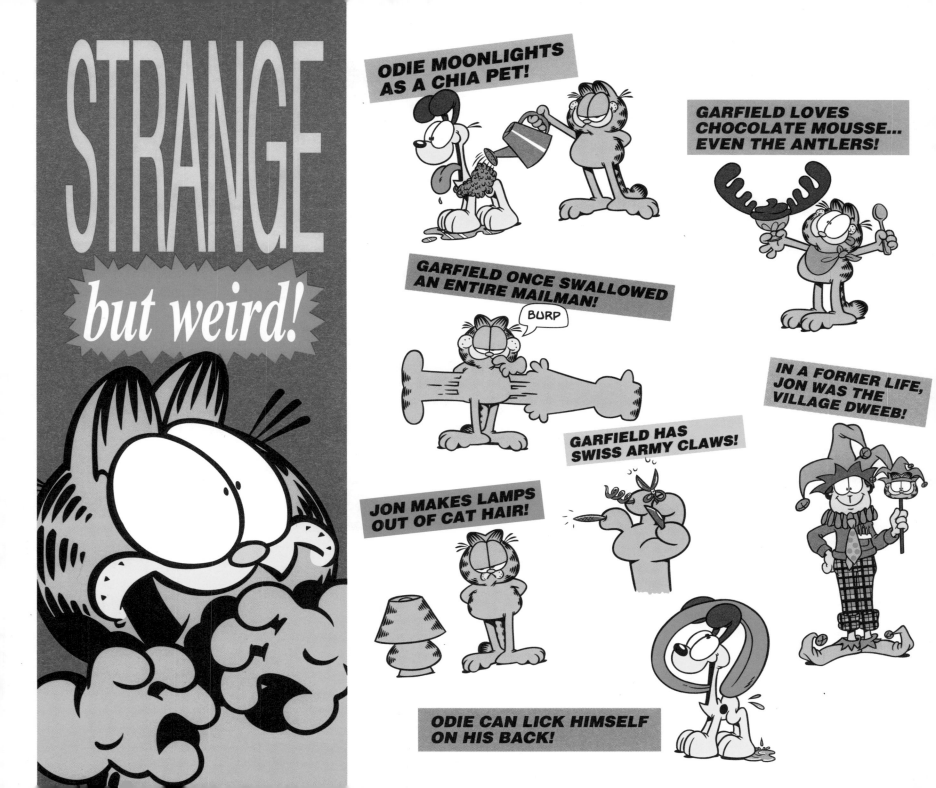

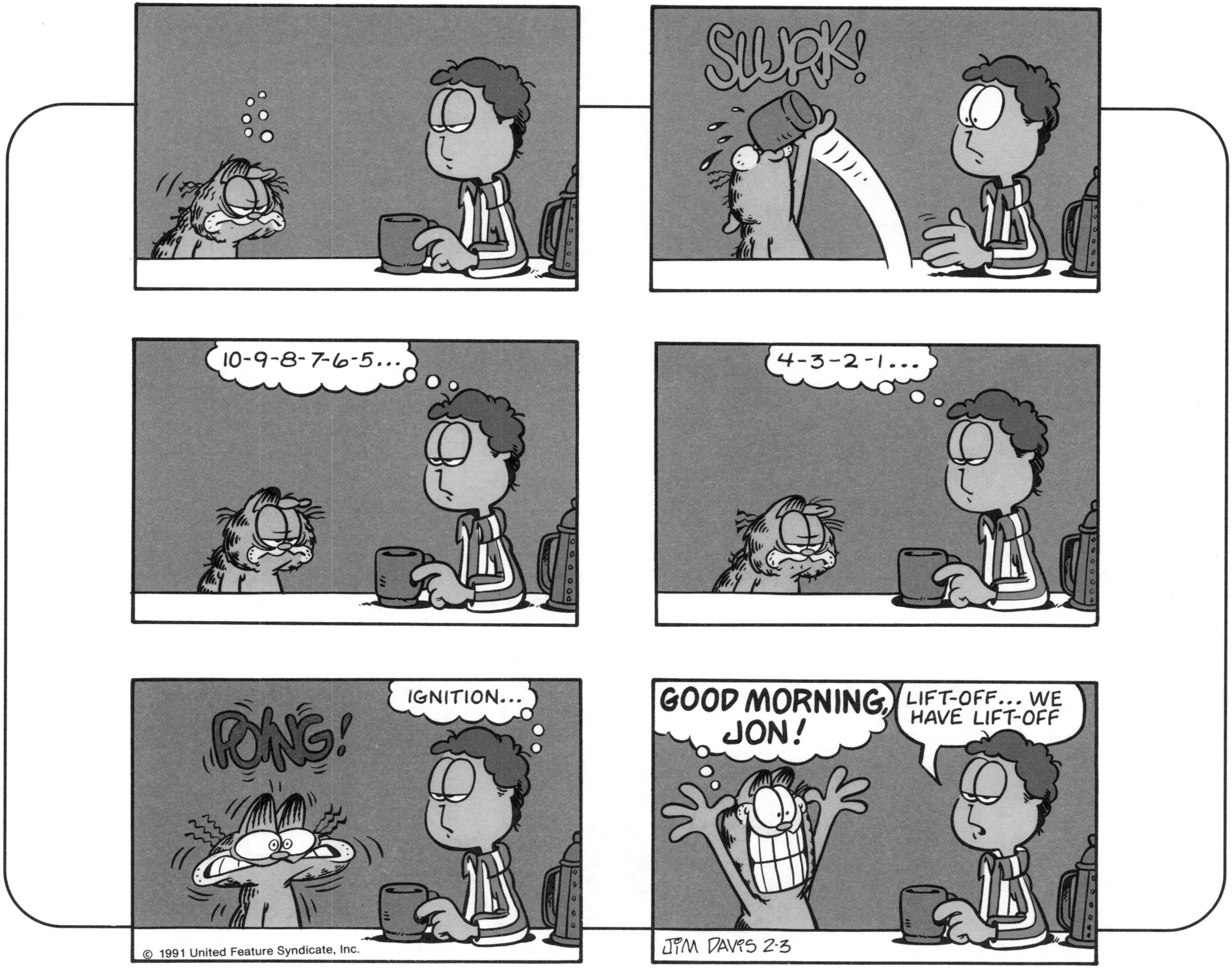

SLURK!
10-9-8-7-6-5...
4-3-2-1...
PONG!
IGNITION...
GOOD MORNING, JON!
LIFT-OFF... WE HAVE LIFT-OFF
JIM DAVIS 2-3

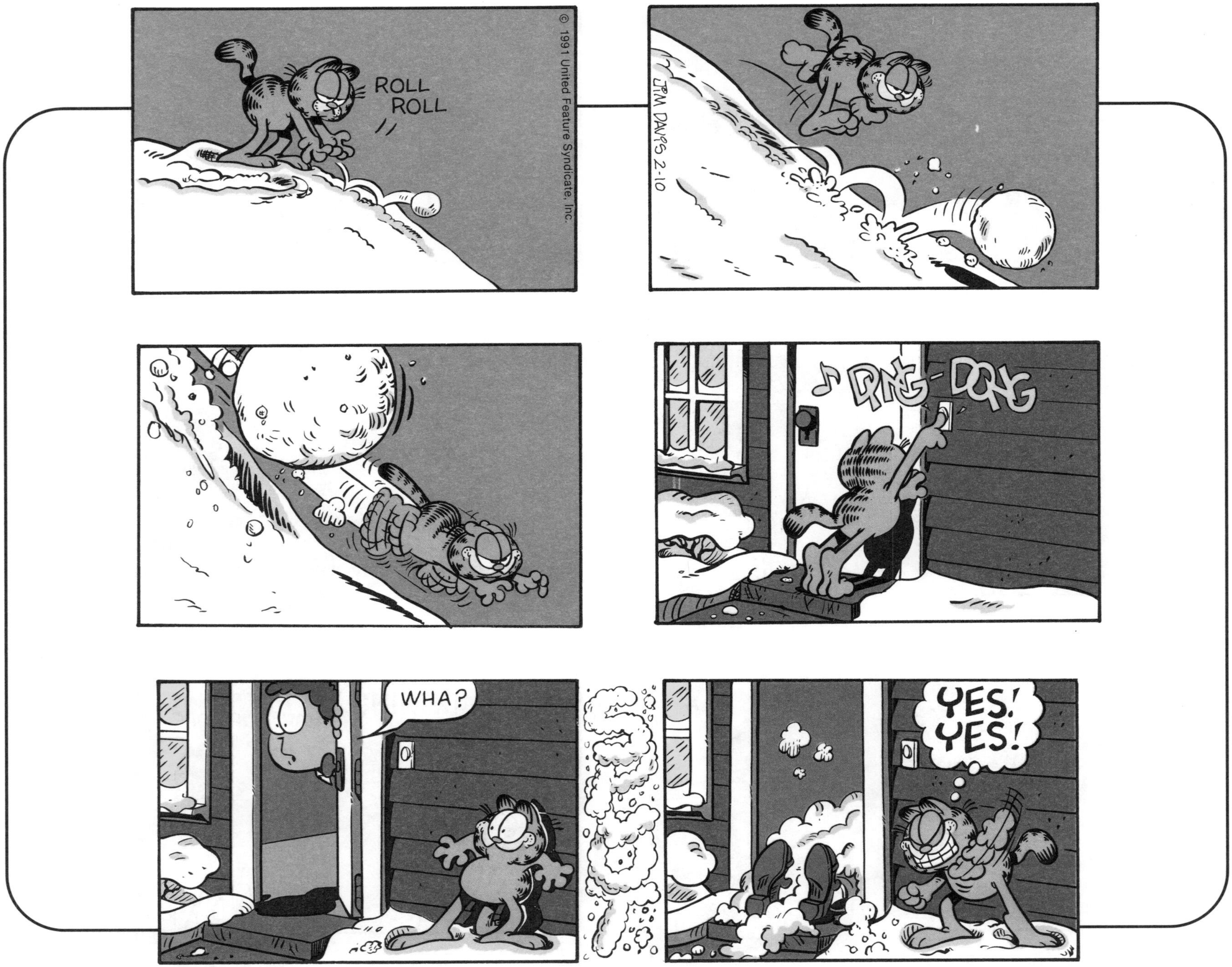

© 1991 United Feature Syndicate, Inc.
ROLL ROLL
JIM DAVIS 2-10
DING-DONG
WHA?
YES! YES!

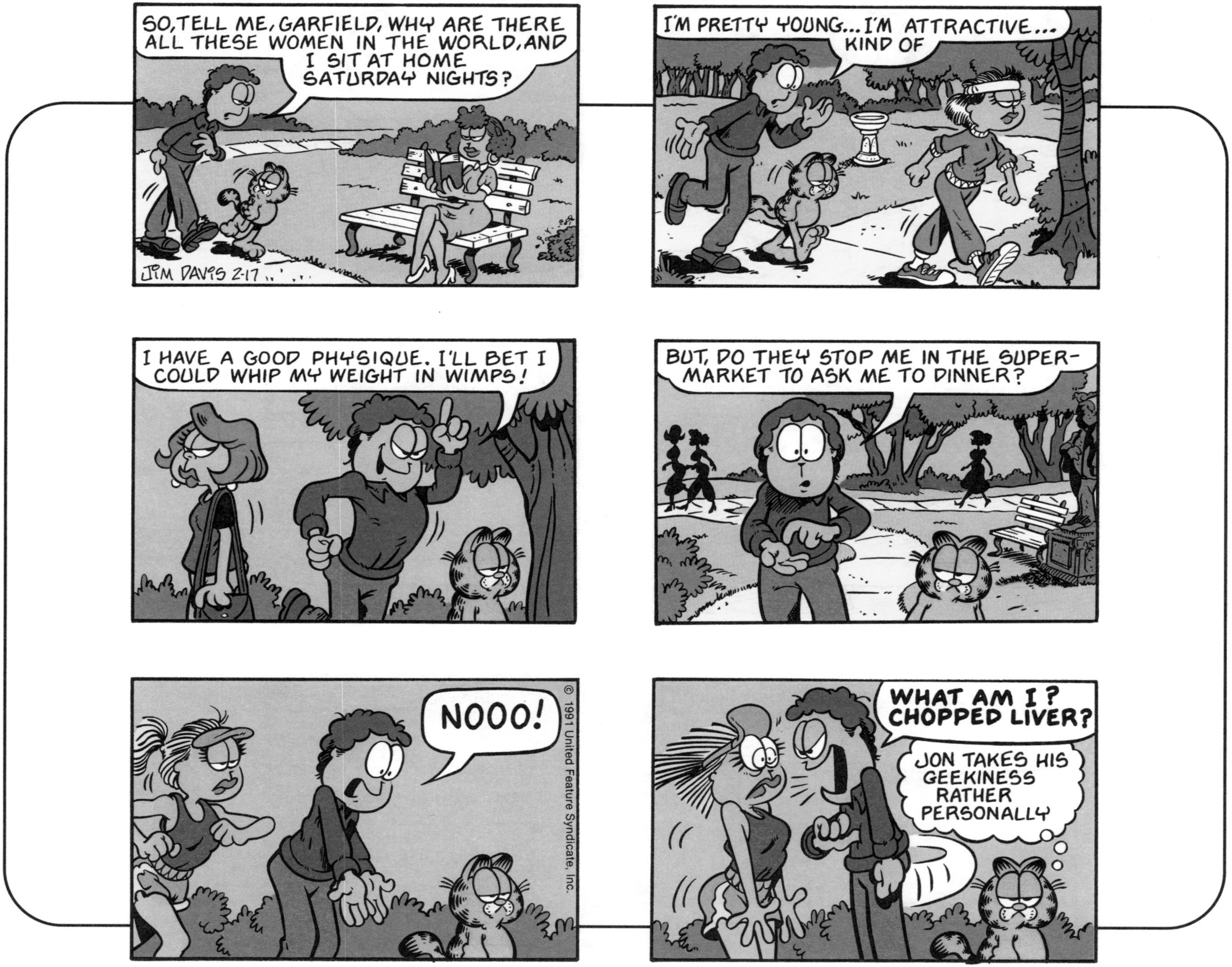
SO, TELL ME, GARFIELD, WHY ARE THERE ALL THESE WOMEN IN THE WORLD, AND I SIT AT HOME SATURDAY NIGHTS?
JIM DAVIS 2-17
I'M PRETTY YOUNG... I'M ATTRACTIVE... KIND OF
I HAVE A GOOD PHYSIQUE. I'LL BET I COULD WHIP MY WEIGHT IN WIMPS!
BUT, DO THEY STOP ME IN THE SUPER-MARKET TO ASK ME TO DINNER?
NOOO!
© 1991 United Feature Syndicate, Inc.
WHAT AM I? CHOPPED LIVER?
JON TAKES HIS GEEKINESS RATHER PERSONALLY

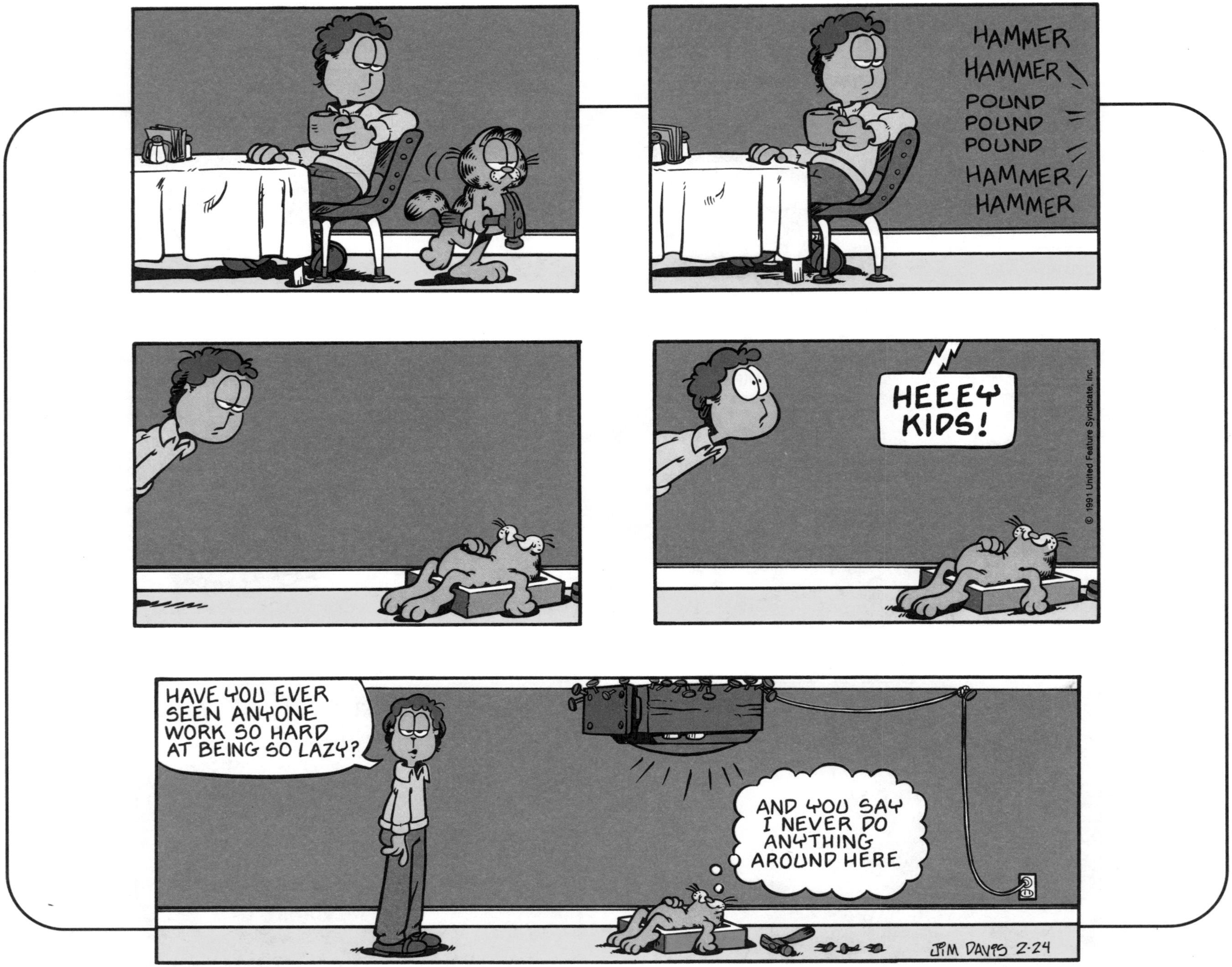
HAMMER
HAMMER
POUND
POUND
POUND
HAMMER
HAMMER
HEEEY KIDS!
© 1991 United Feature Syndicate, Inc.
HAVE YOU EVER SEEN ANYONE WORK SO HARD AT BEING SO LAZY?
AND YOU SAY I NEVER DO ANYTHING AROUND HERE
JIM DAVIS 2-24

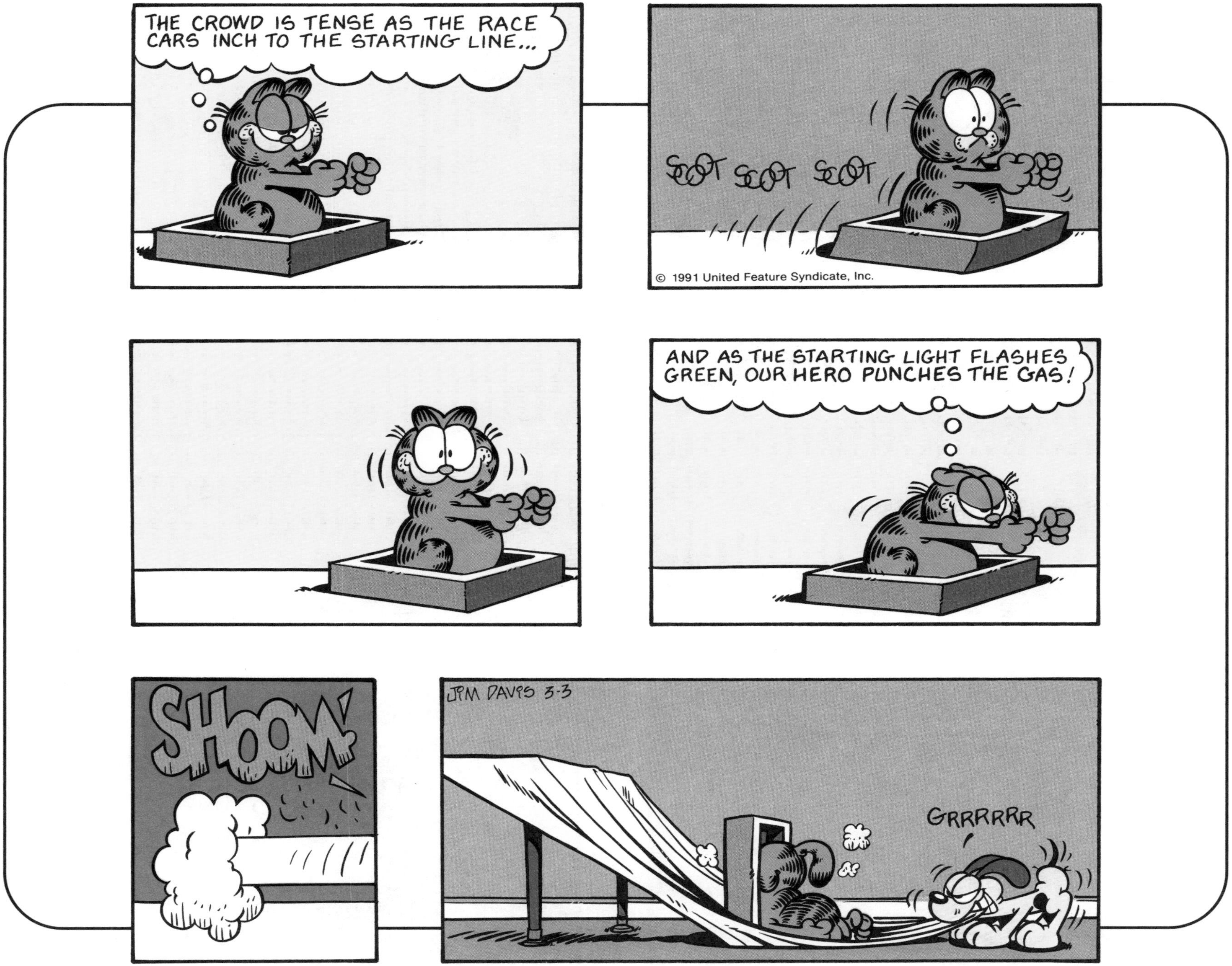
THE CROWD IS TENSE AS THE RACE CARS INCH TO THE STARTING LINE...
SCOOT SCOOT SCOOT
© 1991 United Feature Syndicate, Inc.
AND AS THE STARTING LIGHT FLASHES GREEN, OUR HERO PUNCHES THE GAS!
SHOOM!
JIM DAVIS 3-3
GRRRRRR

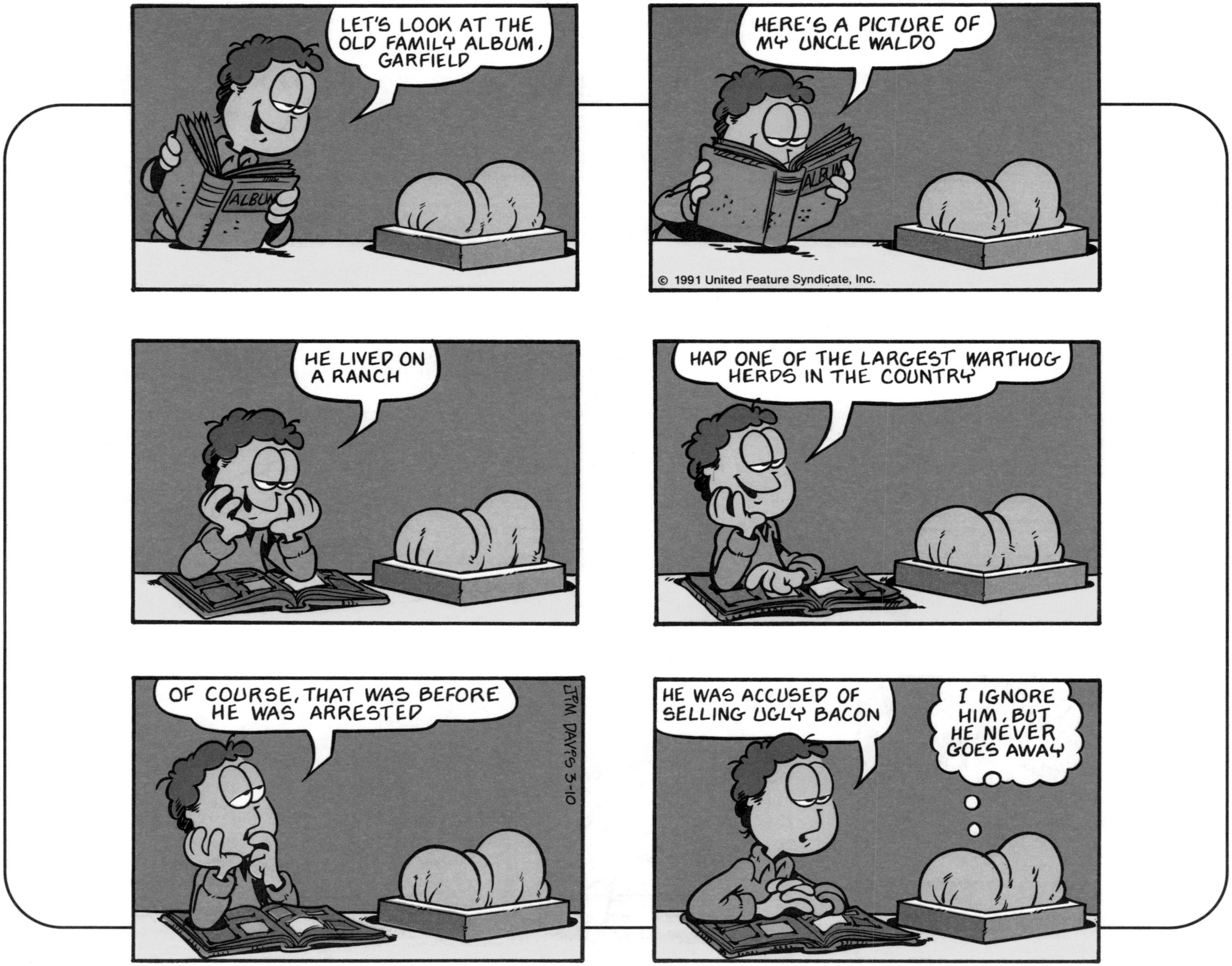
LET'S LOOK AT THE OLD FAMILY ALBUM, GARFIELD
ALBUM
HERE'S A PICTURE OF MY UNCLE WALDO
ALBUM
© 1991 United Feature Syndicate, Inc.
HE LIVED ON A RANCH
HAD ONE OF THE LARGEST WARTHOG HERDS IN THE COUNTRY
OF COURSE, THAT WAS BEFORE HE WAS ARRESTED
JPM DAVPS 3-10
HE WAS ACCUSED OF SELLING UGLY BACON
I IGNORE HIM, BUT HE NEVER GOES AWAY

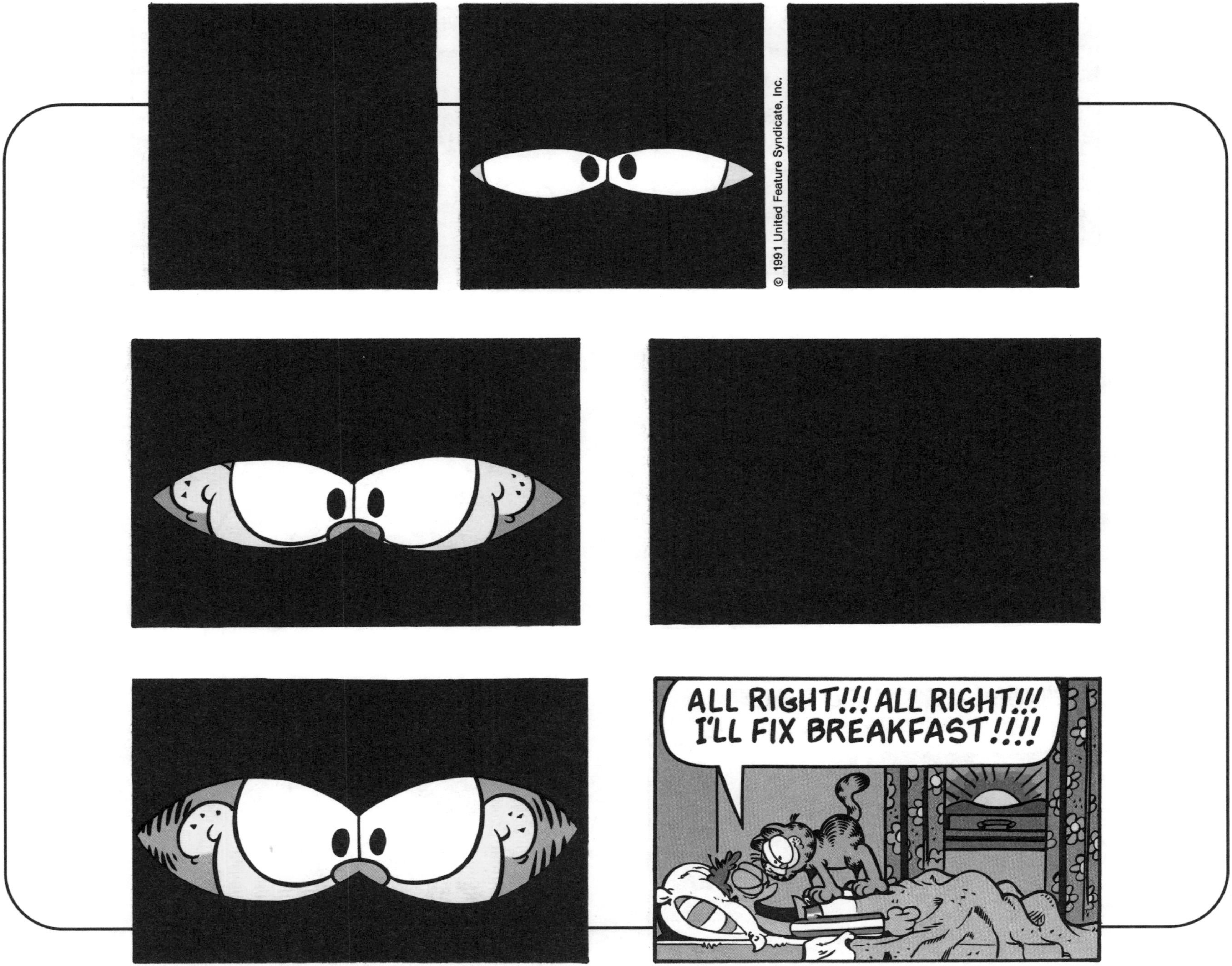
© 1991 United Feature Syndicate, Inc.
ALL RIGHT!!! ALL RIGHT!!!
I'LL FIX BREAKFAST!!!!

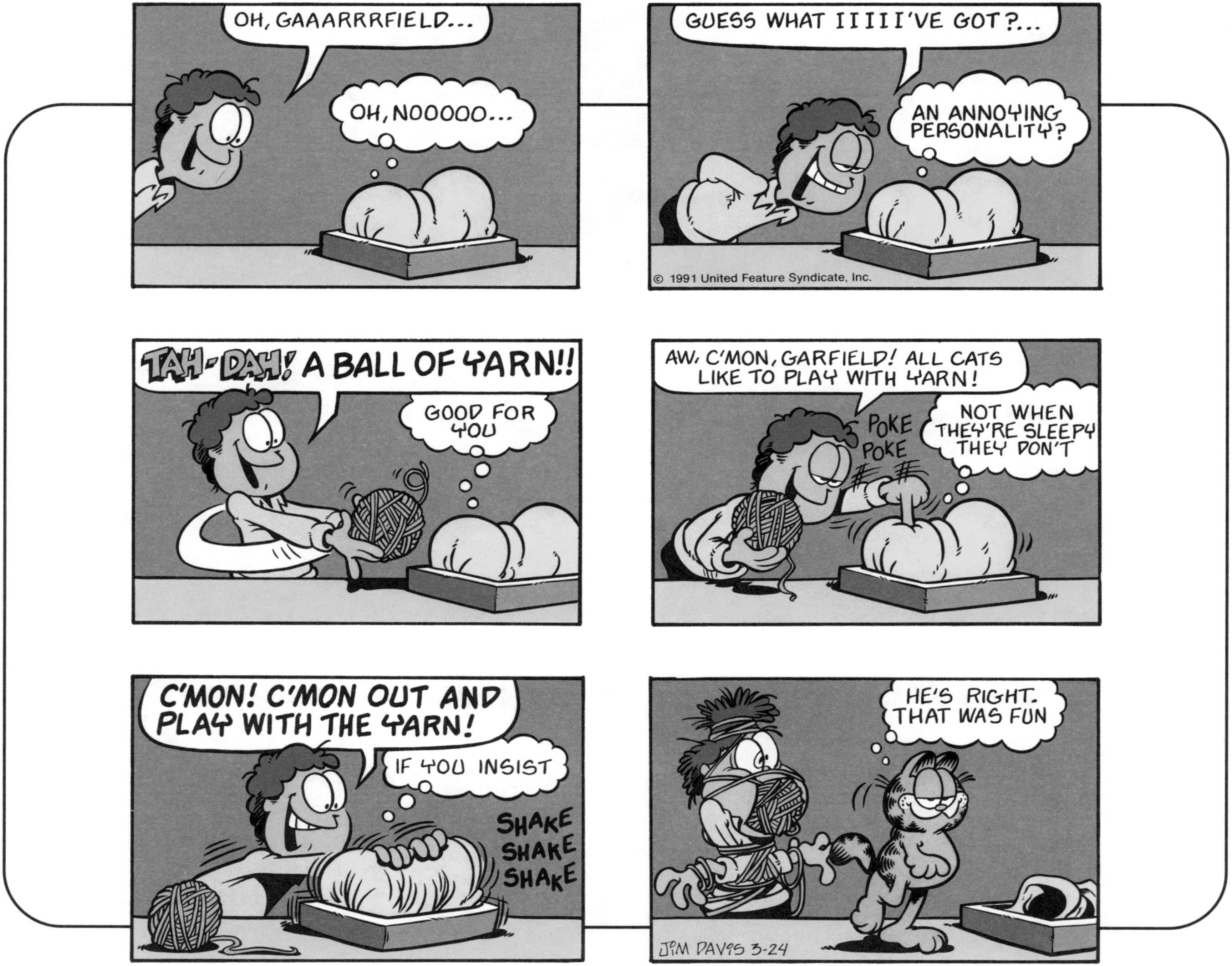
OH, GAAARRRFIELD...
OH, NOOOOO...
GUESS WHAT IIIII'VE GOT?...
AN ANNOYING PERSONALITY?
© 1991 United Feature Syndicate, Inc.
TAH-DAH! A BALL OF YARN!!
GOOD FOR YOU
AW, C'MON, GARFIELD! ALL CATS LIKE TO PLAY WITH YARN!
POKE POKE
NOT WHEN THEY'RE SLEEPY THEY DON'T
C'MON! C'MON OUT AND PLAY WITH THE YARN!
IF YOU INSIST
SHAKE SHAKE SHAKE
HE'S RIGHT. THAT WAS FUN
JIM DAVIS 3-24

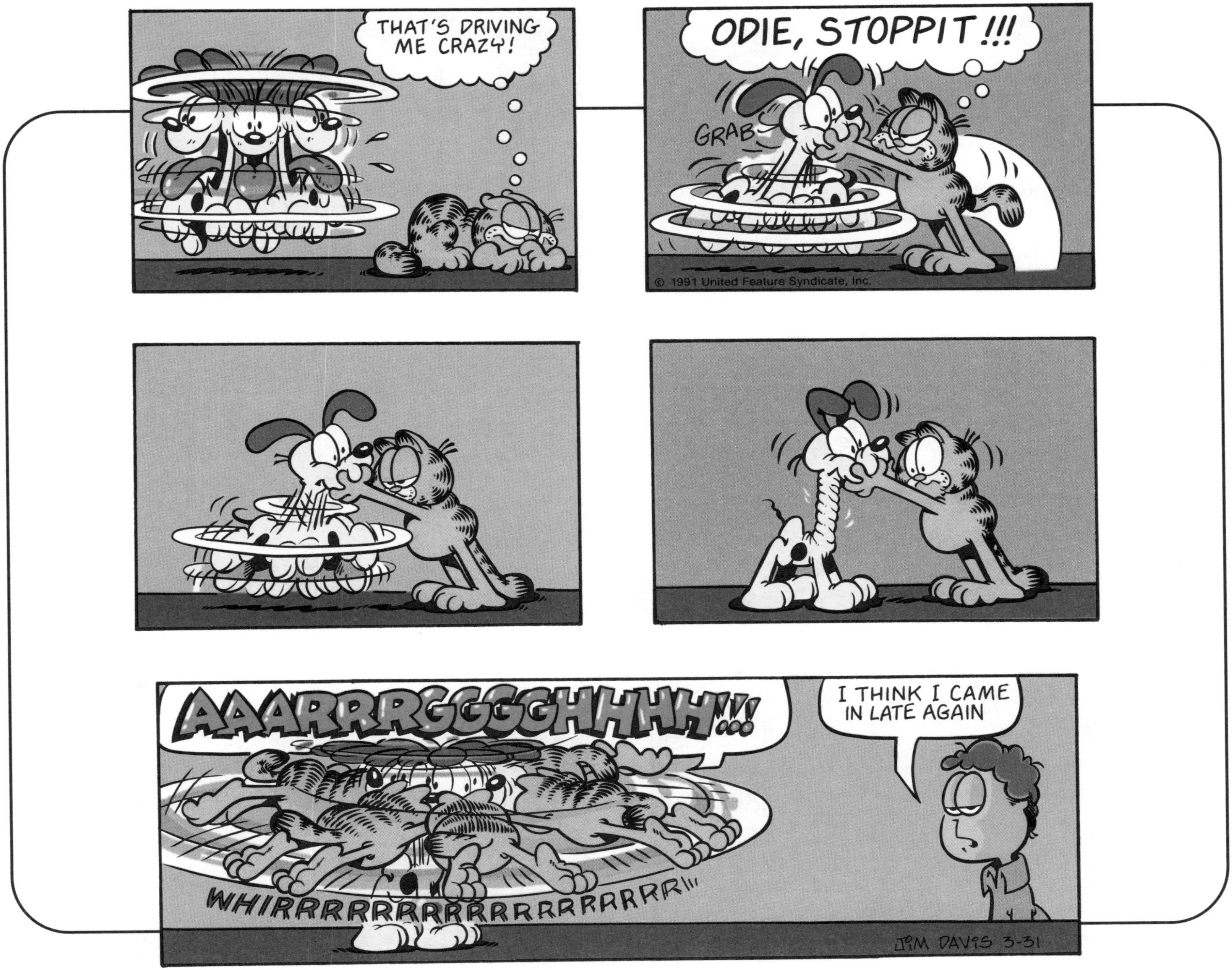

THAT'S DRIVING ME CRAZY!
ODIE, STOPPIT!!!
GRAB
© 1991 United Feature Syndicate, Inc.
AAARRRRGGGGHHHH!!!
I THINK I CAME IN LATE AGAIN
WHIRRRRRRRRRRRRRRRRRRRRRRR
JIM DAVIS 3-31

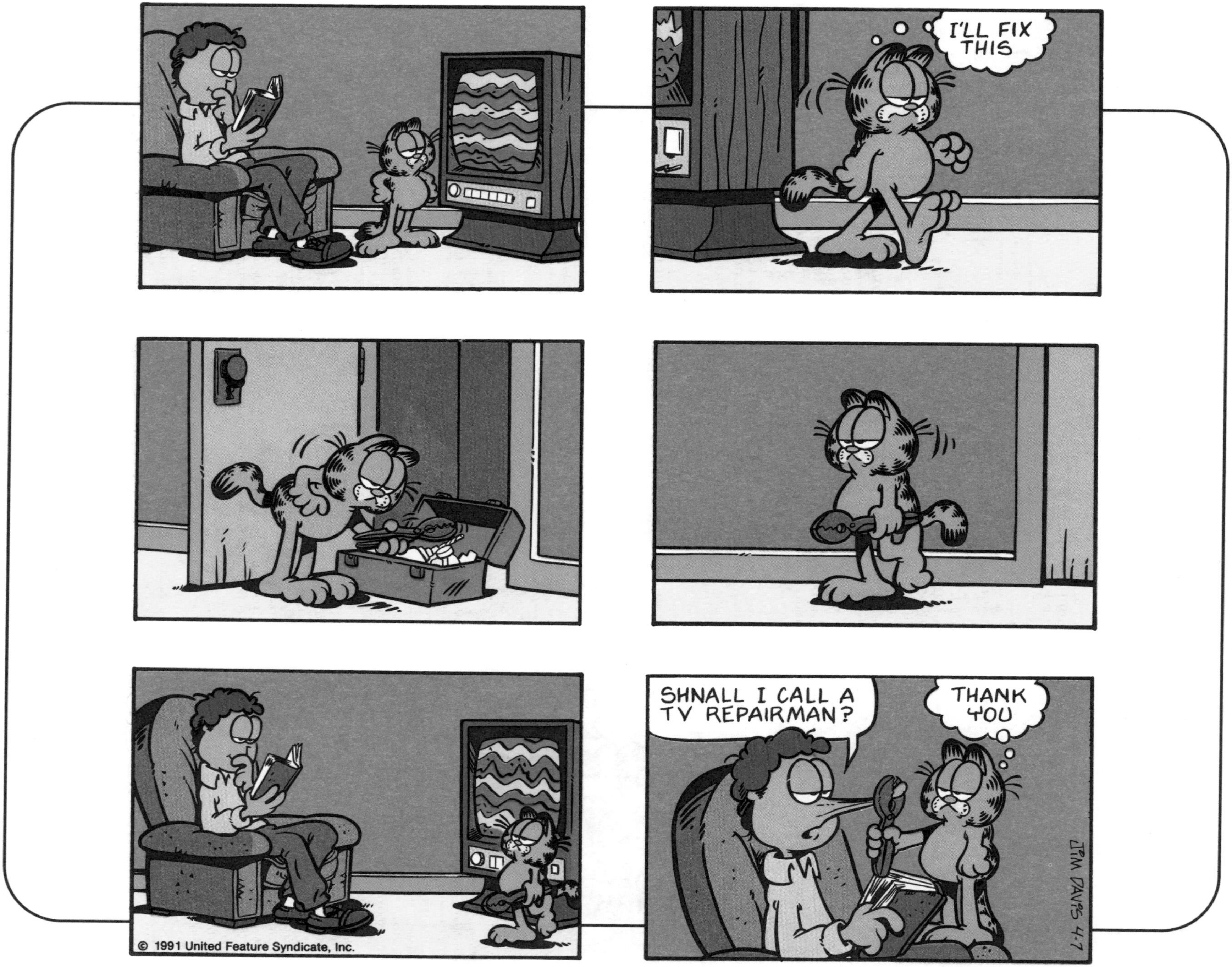
I'LL FIX THIS
SHNALL I CALL A TV REPAIRMAN?
THANK YOU
JIM DAVIS 4-7

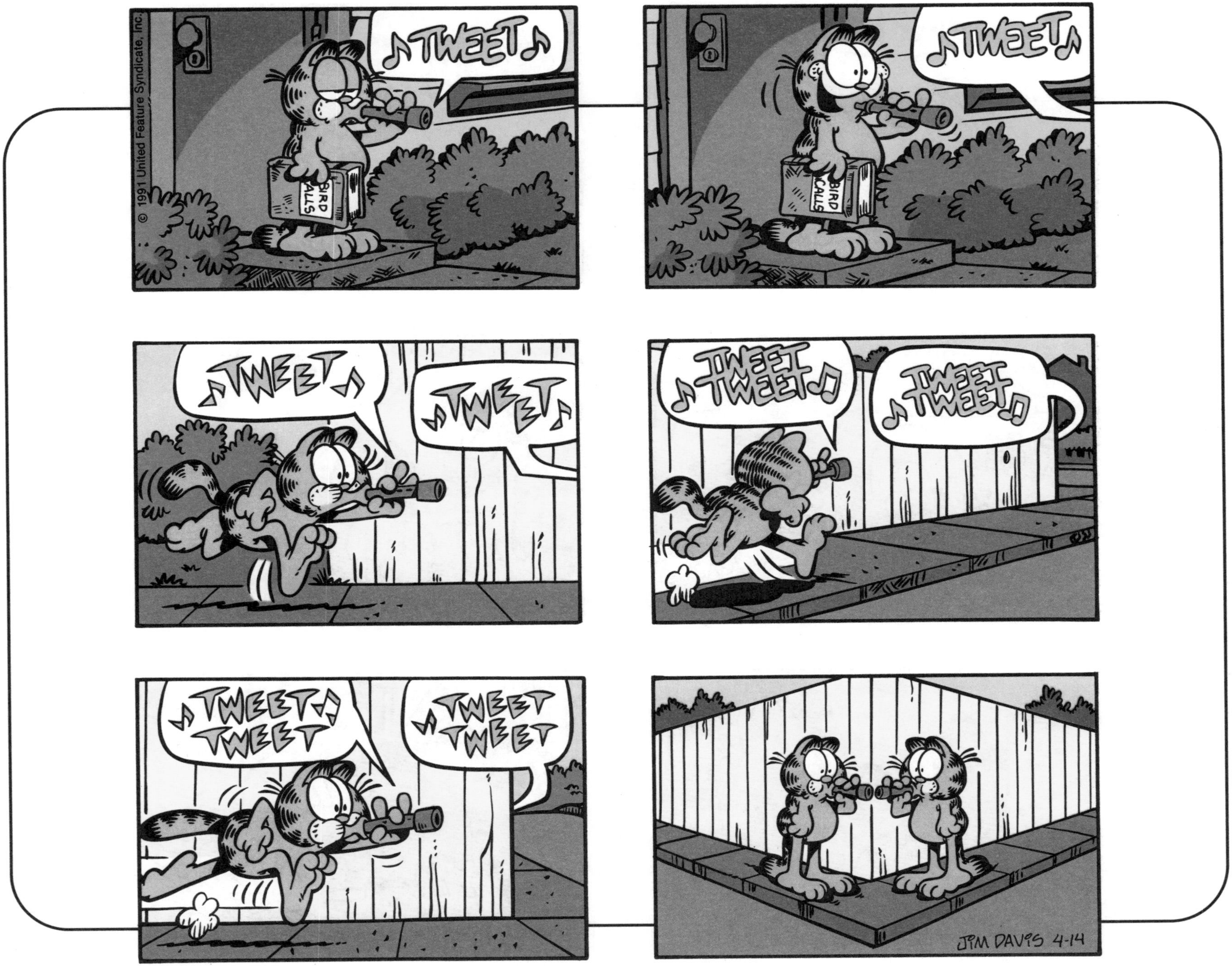
© 1991 United Feature Syndicate, Inc.
♪TWEET♪
BIRD CALLS
♪TWEET♪
BIRD CALLS
♪TWEET♪
♪TWEET♪
♪TWEET TWEET♫
♪TWEET TWEET♫
♪TWEET♪ TWEET
♪TWEET TWEET
JIM DAVIS 4-14

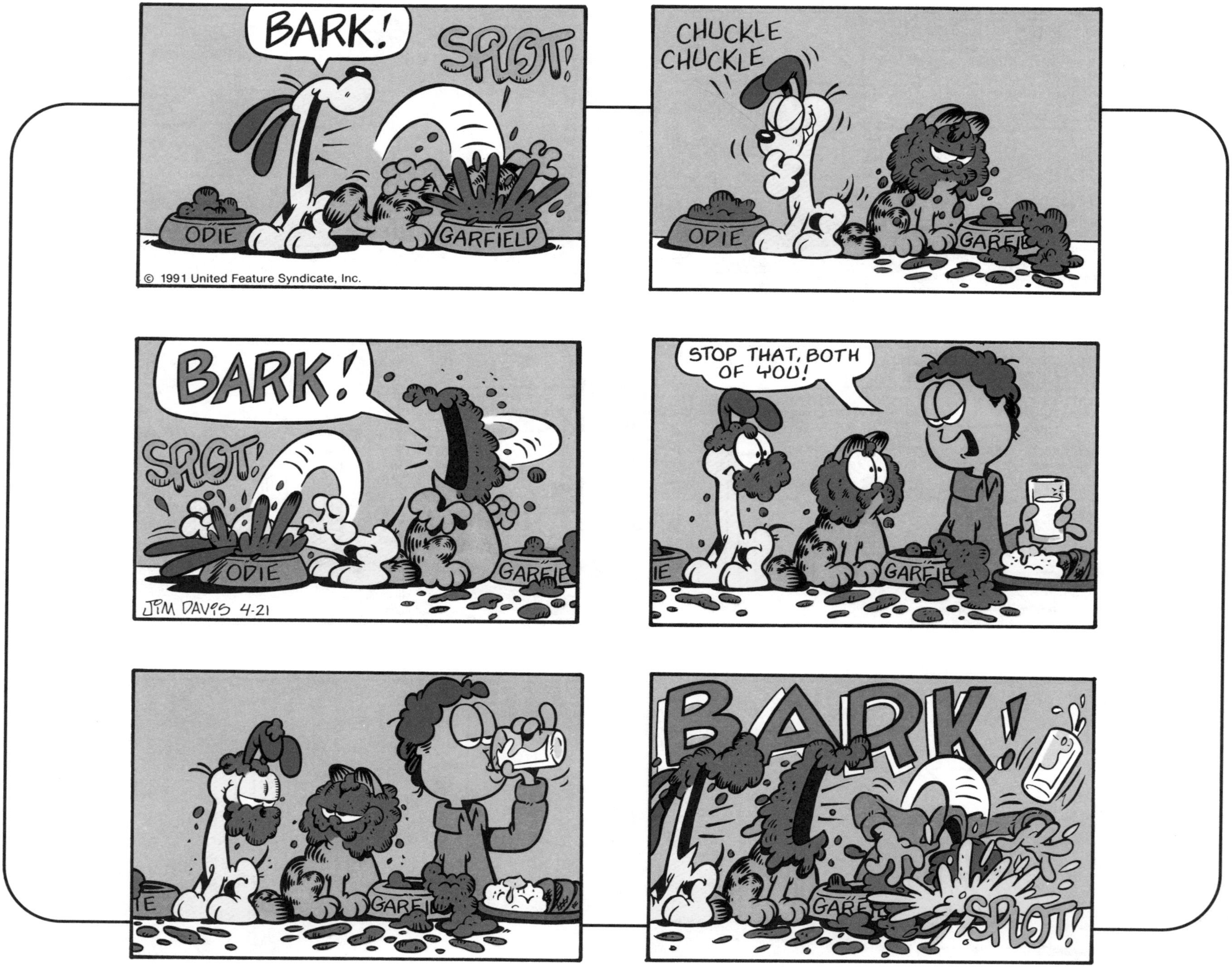
BARK!
SPLOT!
ODIE
GARFIELD
© 1991 United Feature Syndicate, Inc.
CHUCKLE CHUCKLE
ODIE
BARK!
SPLOT!
ODIE
JIM DAVIS 4-21
STOP THAT, BOTH OF YOU!
BARK!
SPLOT!

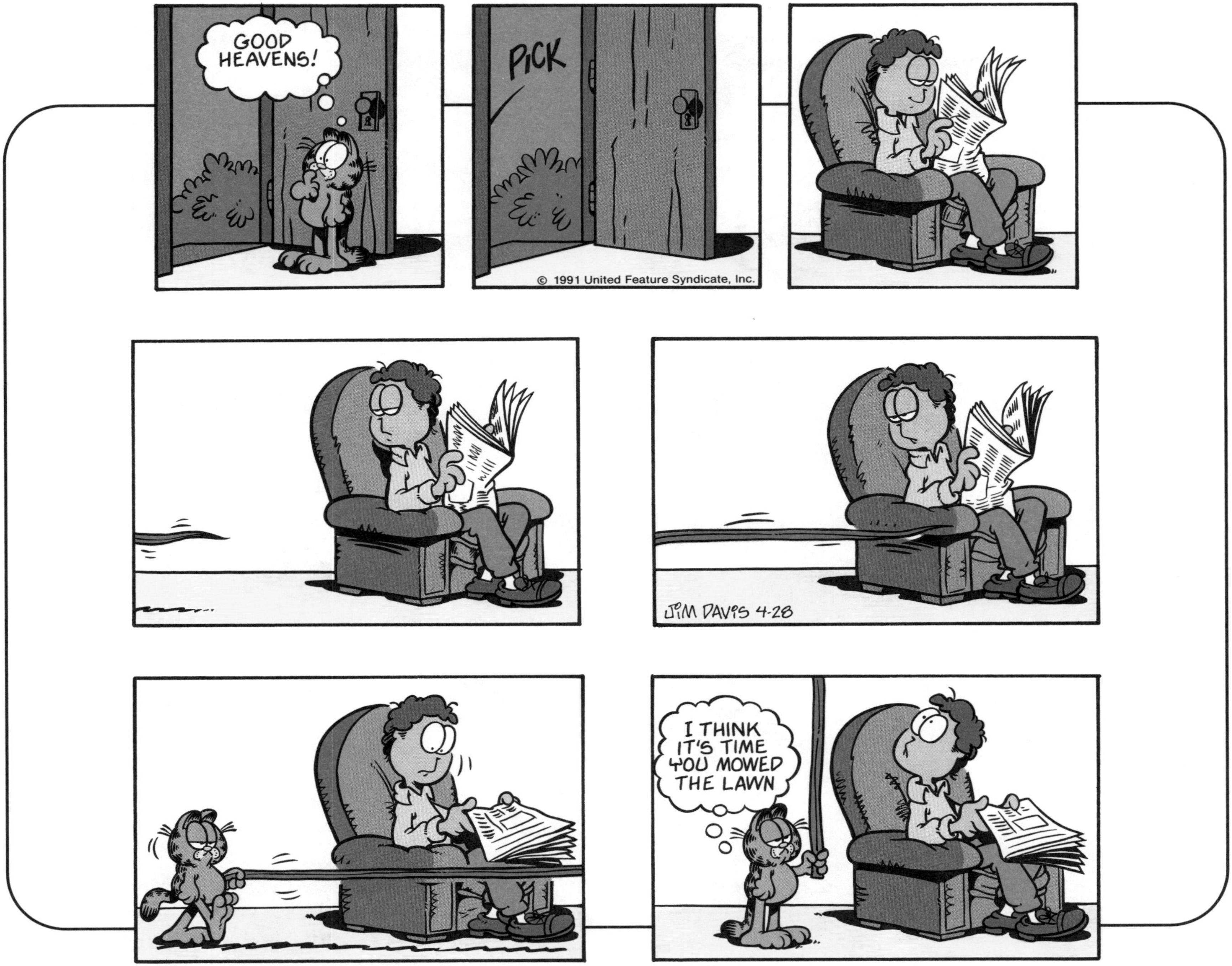

GOOD HEAVENS!
PICK
© 1991 United Feature Syndicate, Inc.
JIM DAVIS 4-28
I THINK IT'S TIME YOU MOWED THE LAWN

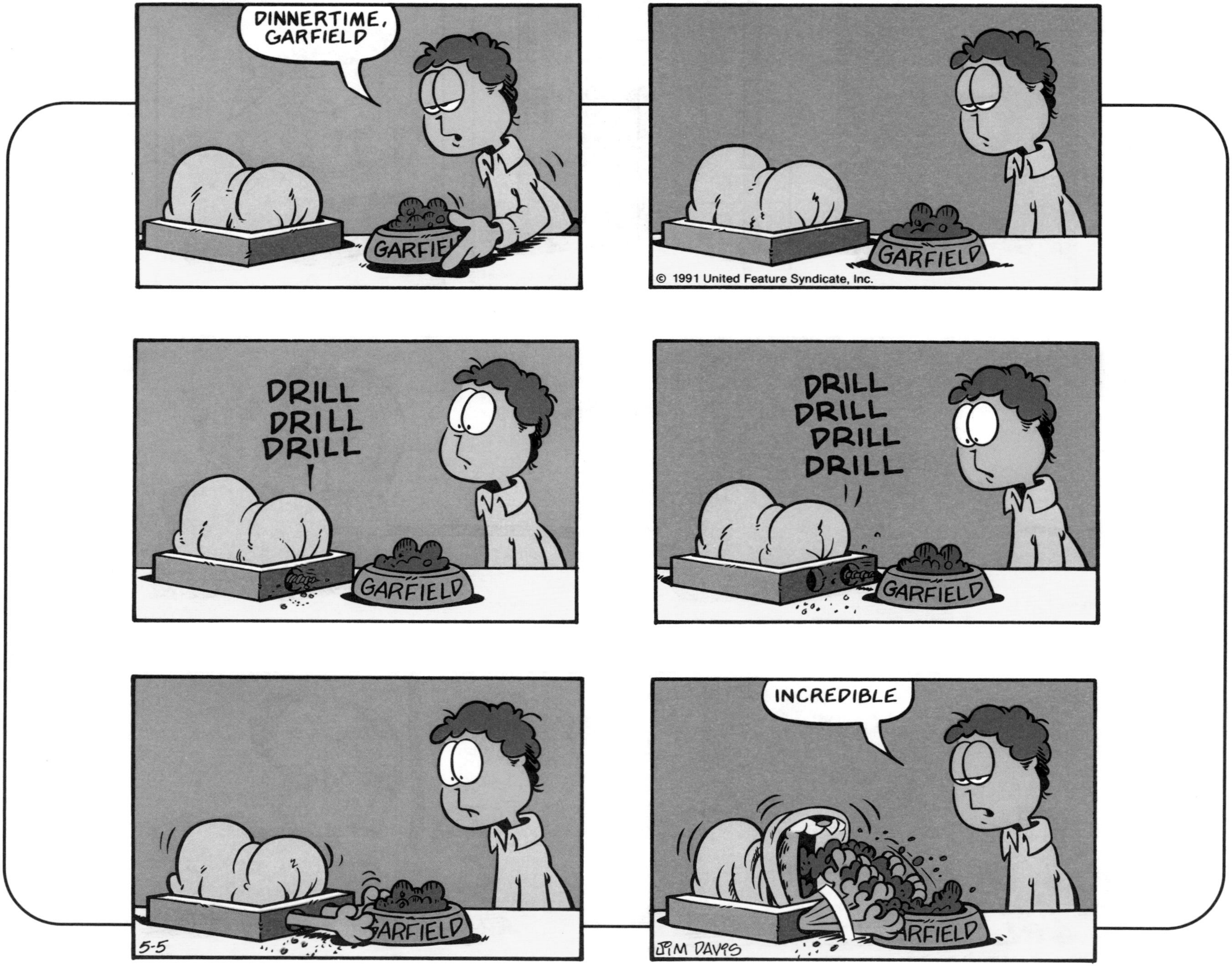
DINNERTIME, GARFIELD
GARFIELD
GARFIELD
© 1991 United Feature Syndicate, Inc.
DRILL DRILL DRILL
GARFIELD
DRILL DRILL DRILL DRILL
GARFIELD
ARFIELD
5-5
INCREDIBLE
ARFIELD
JIM DAVIS

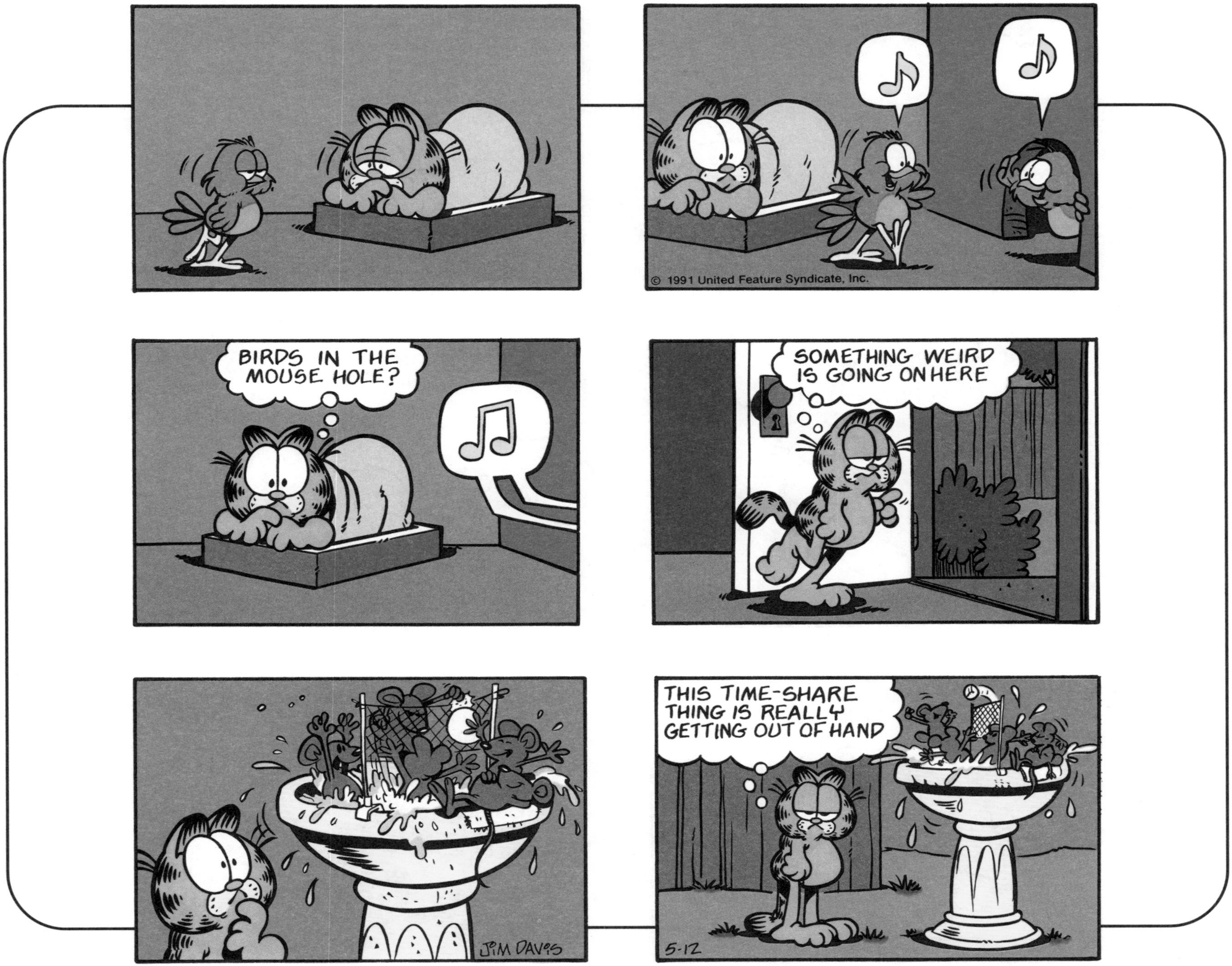
© 1991 United Feature Syndicate, Inc.
BIRDS IN THE MOUSE HOLE?
SOMETHING WEIRD IS GOING ON HERE
JIM DAVIS
THIS TIME-SHARE THING IS REALLY GETTING OUT OF HAND
5-12

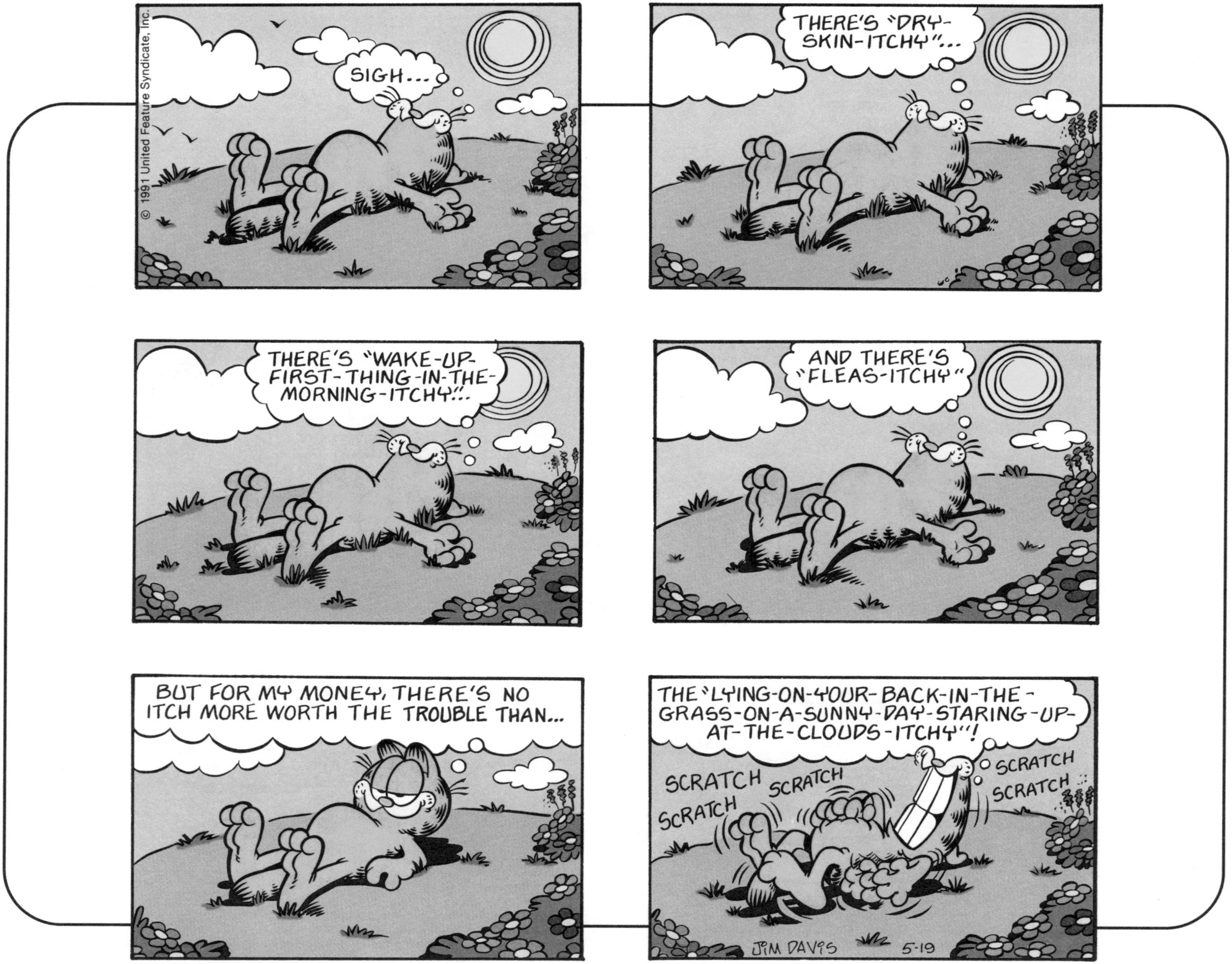
© 1991 United Feature Syndicate, Inc.
SIGH...
THERE'S "DRY-SKIN-ITCHY"...
THERE'S "WAKE-UP-FIRST-THING-IN-THE-MORNING-ITCHY"...
AND THERE'S "FLEAS-ITCHY"
BUT FOR MY MONEY, THERE'S NO ITCH MORE WORTH THE TROUBLE THAN...
THE "LYING-ON-YOUR-BACK-IN-THE-GRASS-ON-A-SUNNY-DAY-STARING-UP-AT-THE-CLOUDS-ITCHY"!
SCRATCH
SCRATCH
SCRATCH
SCRATCH
SCRATCH
JIM DAVIS 5-19

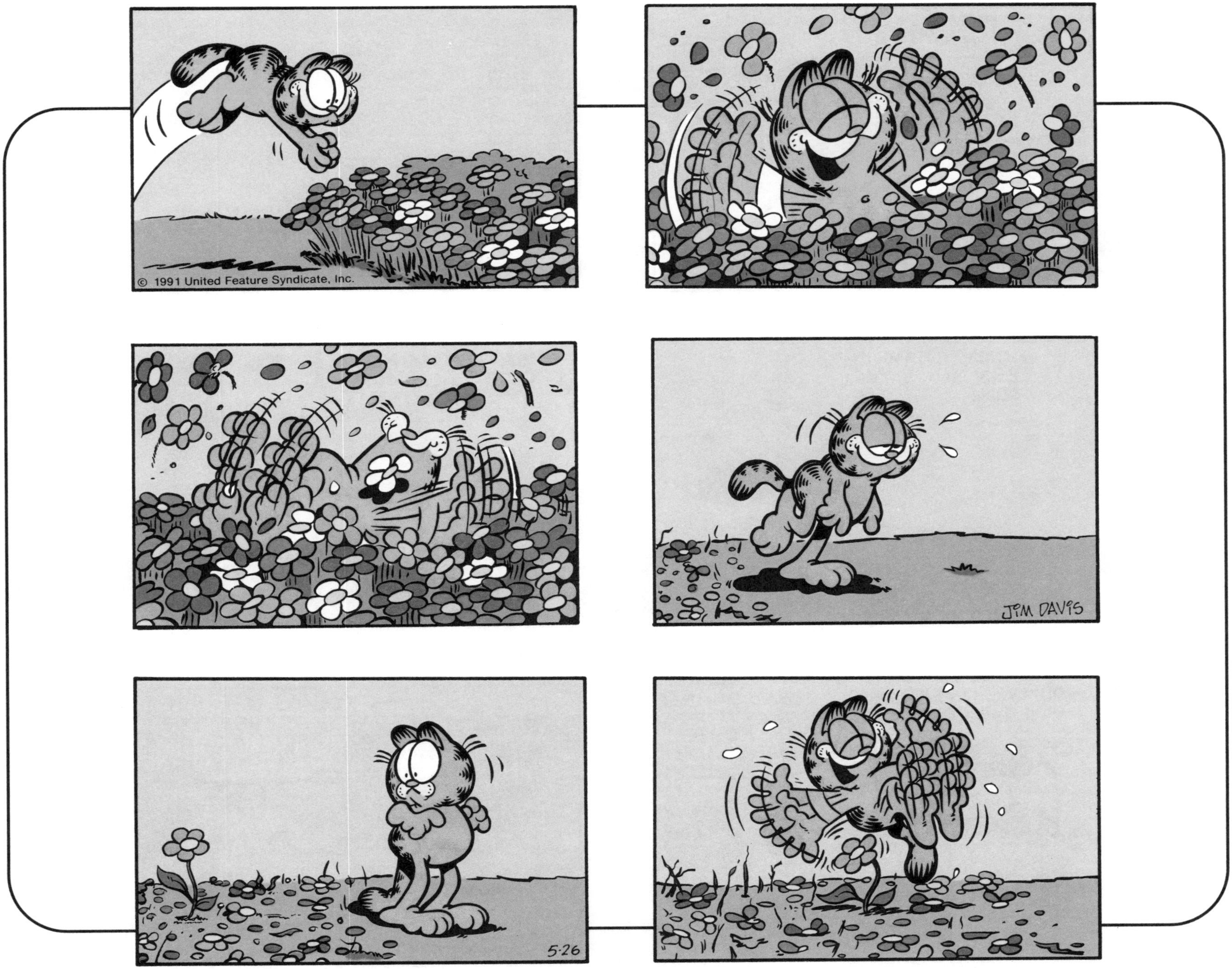
© 1991 United Feature Syndicate, Inc.
JIM DAVIS
5-26

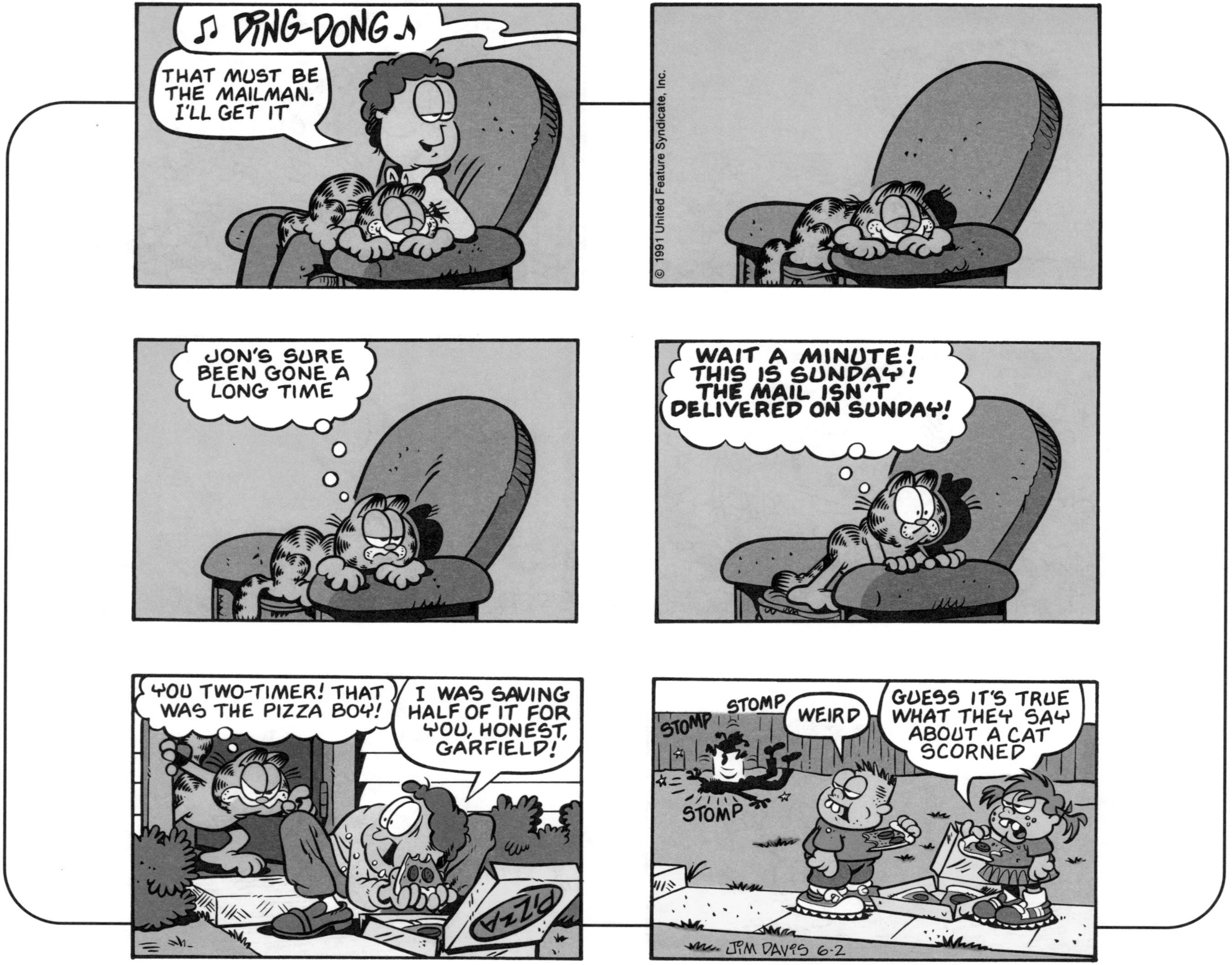

♫ DING-DONG ♪
THAT MUST BE THE MAILMAN. I'LL GET IT
© 1991 United Feature Syndicate, Inc.
JON'S SURE BEEN GONE A LONG TIME
WAIT A MINUTE! THIS IS SUNDAY! THE MAIL ISN'T DELIVERED ON SUNDAY!
YOU TWO-TIMER! THAT WAS THE PIZZA BOY!
I WAS SAVING HALF OF IT FOR YOU, HONEST, GARFIELD!
PIZZA
STOMP
STOMP
STOMP
WEIRD
GUESS IT'S TRUE WHAT THEY SAY ABOUT A CAT SCORNED
JIM DAVIS 6-2

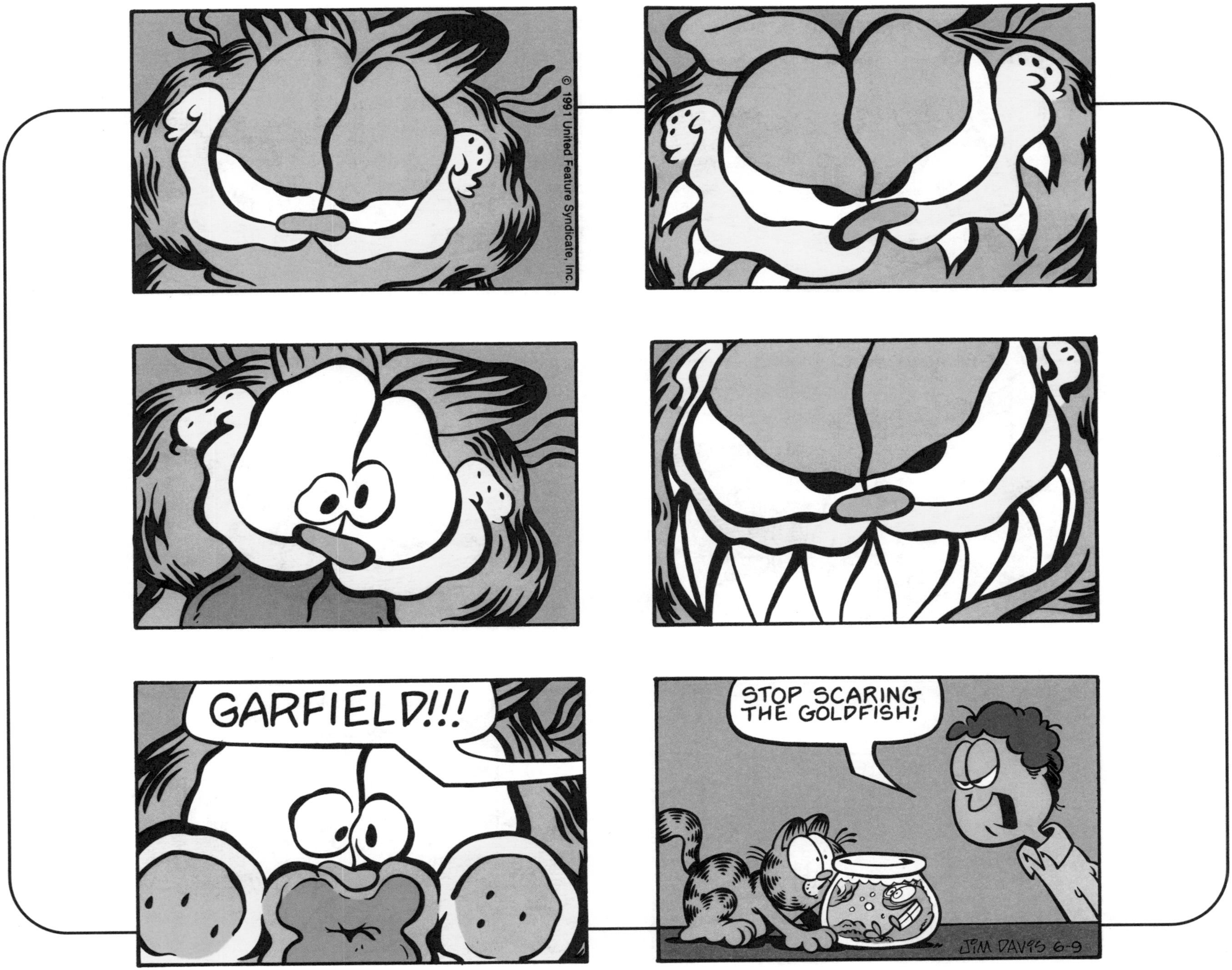
© 1991 United Feature Syndicate, Inc.
GARFIELD!!!
STOP SCARING THE GOLDFISH!
JIM DAVIS 6-9

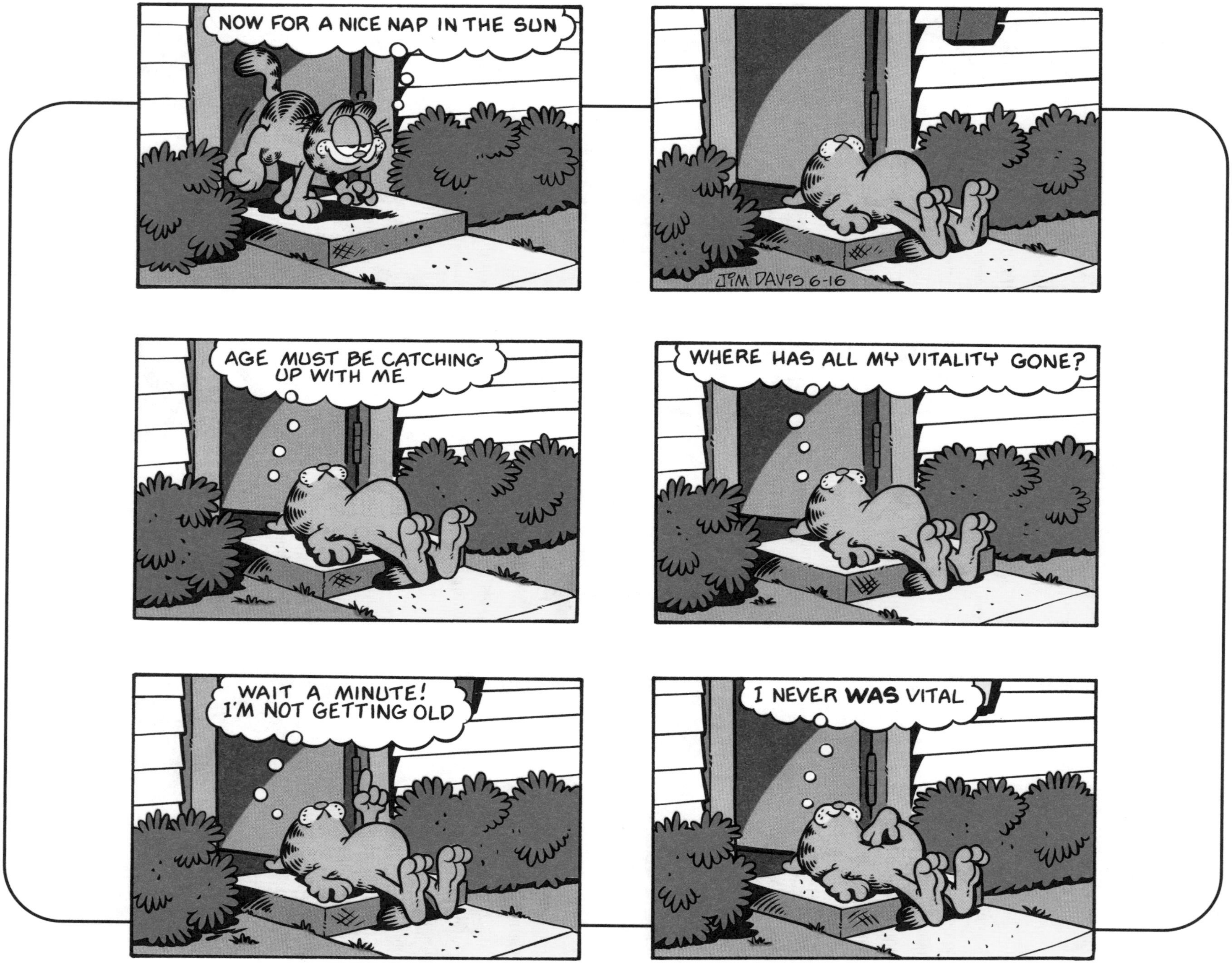
NOW FOR A NICE NAP IN THE SUN
JIM DAVIS 6-16
AGE MUST BE CATCHING UP WITH ME
WHERE HAS ALL MY VITALITY GONE?
WAIT A MINUTE! I'M NOT GETTING OLD
I NEVER **WAS** VITAL

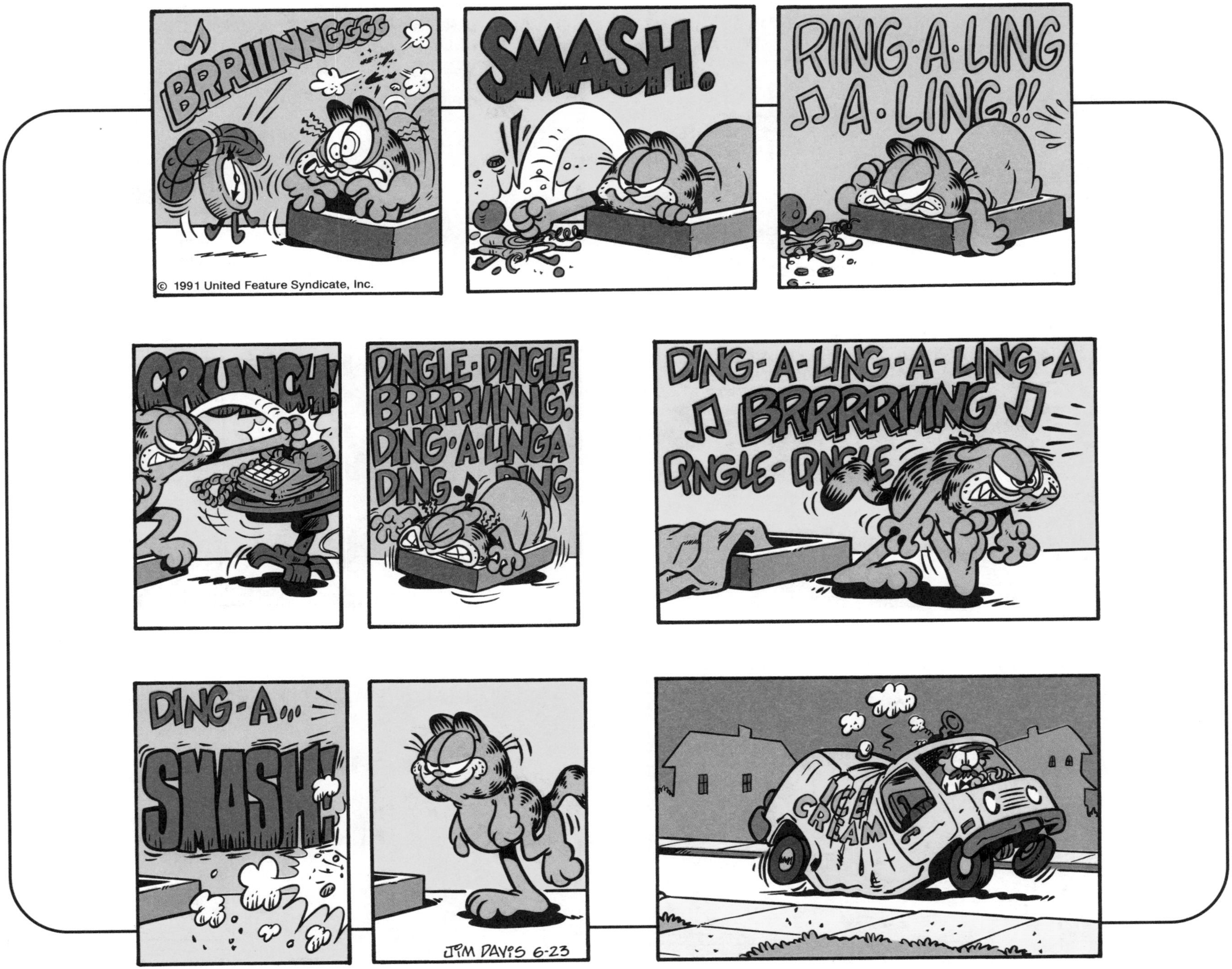
BRRIIINNGGGG
© 1991 United Feature Syndicate, Inc.
SMASH!
RING-A-LING A-LING!!
CRUNCH!
DINGLE-DINGLE
BRRRIIINNG!
DING-A-LINGA
DING
DING-A-LING-A-LING-A
BRRRRIIING
DINGLE-DINGLE
DING-A...
SMASH!
JIM DAVIS 6-23
ICE CREAM

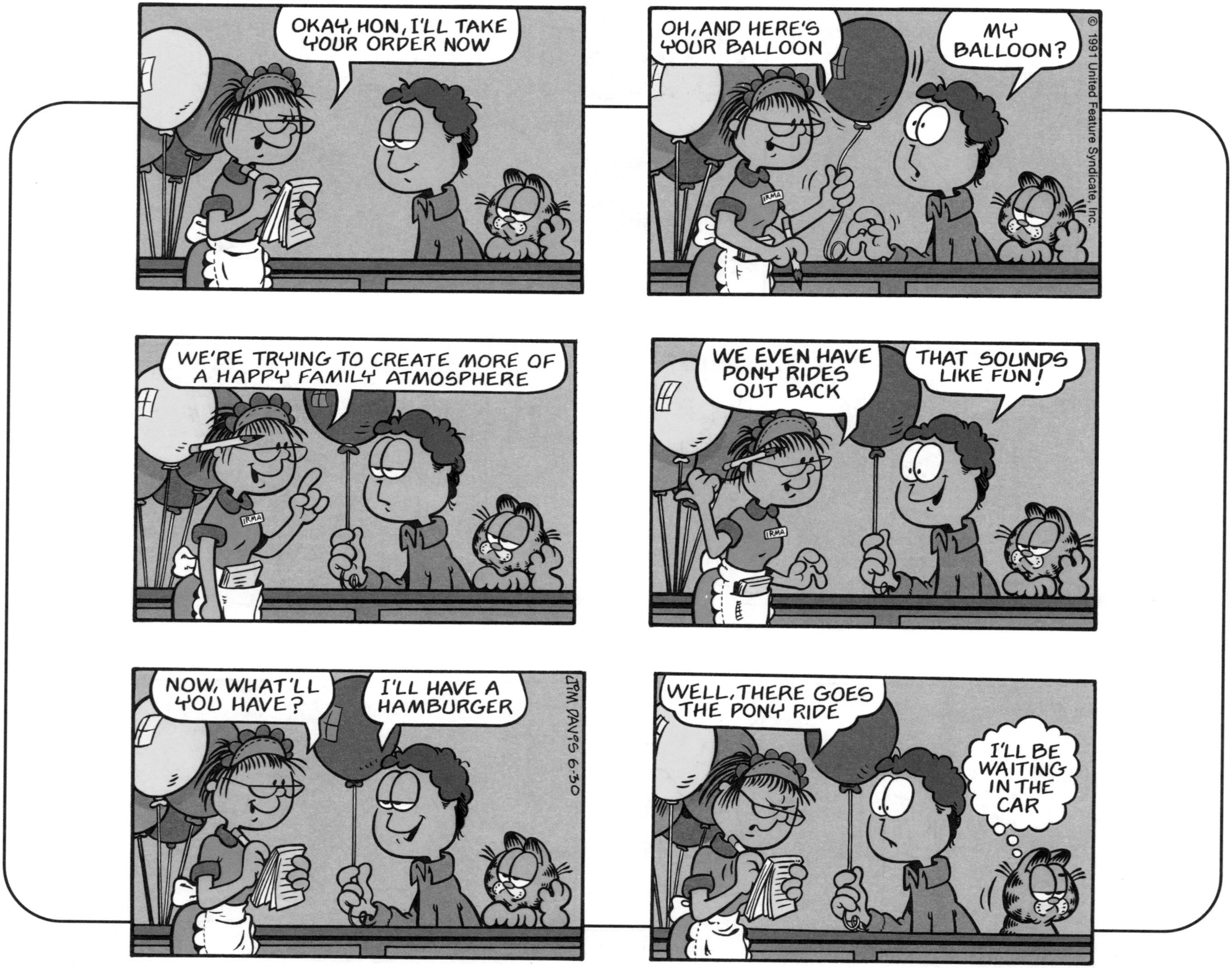
OKAY, HON, I'LL TAKE YOUR ORDER NOW
OH, AND HERE'S YOUR BALLOON
MY BALLOON?
© 1991 United Feature Syndicate, Inc.
WE'RE TRYING TO CREATE MORE OF A HAPPY FAMILY ATMOSPHERE
IRMA
WE EVEN HAVE PONY RIDES OUT BACK
THAT SOUNDS LIKE FUN!
NOW, WHAT'LL YOU HAVE?
I'LL HAVE A HAMBURGER
JIM DAVIS 6-30
WELL, THERE GOES THE PONY RIDE
I'LL BE WAITING IN THE CAR

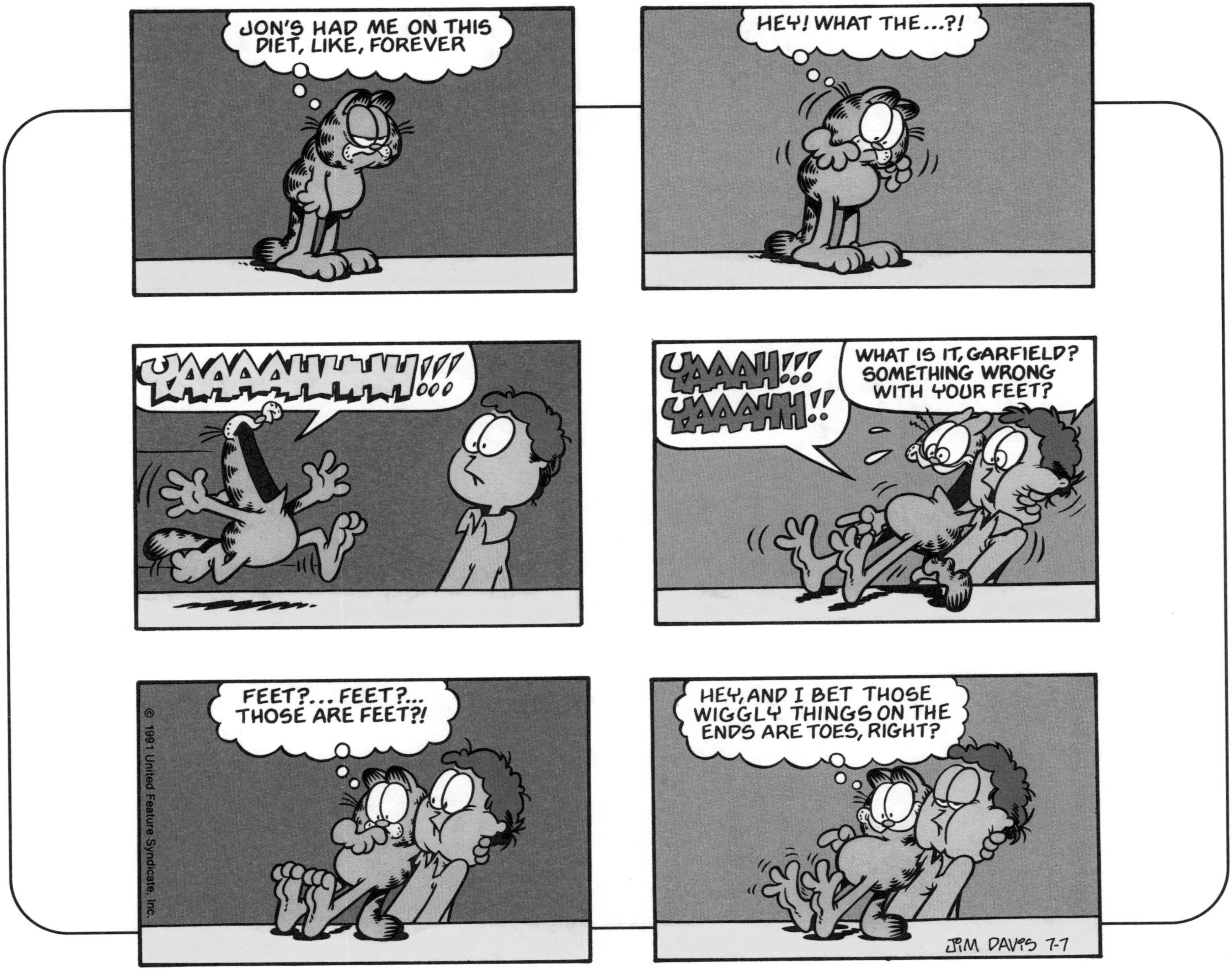

JON'S HAD ME ON THIS DIET, LIKE, FOREVER
HEY! WHAT THE...?!
YAAAAHHHH!!!
YAAAH!!! YAAAHH!!
WHAT IS IT, GARFIELD? SOMETHING WRONG WITH YOUR FEET?
FEET?... FEET?... THOSE ARE FEET?!
© 1991 United Feature Syndicate, Inc.
HEY, AND I BET THOSE WIGGLY THINGS ON THE ENDS ARE TOES, RIGHT?
JIM DAVIS 7-7

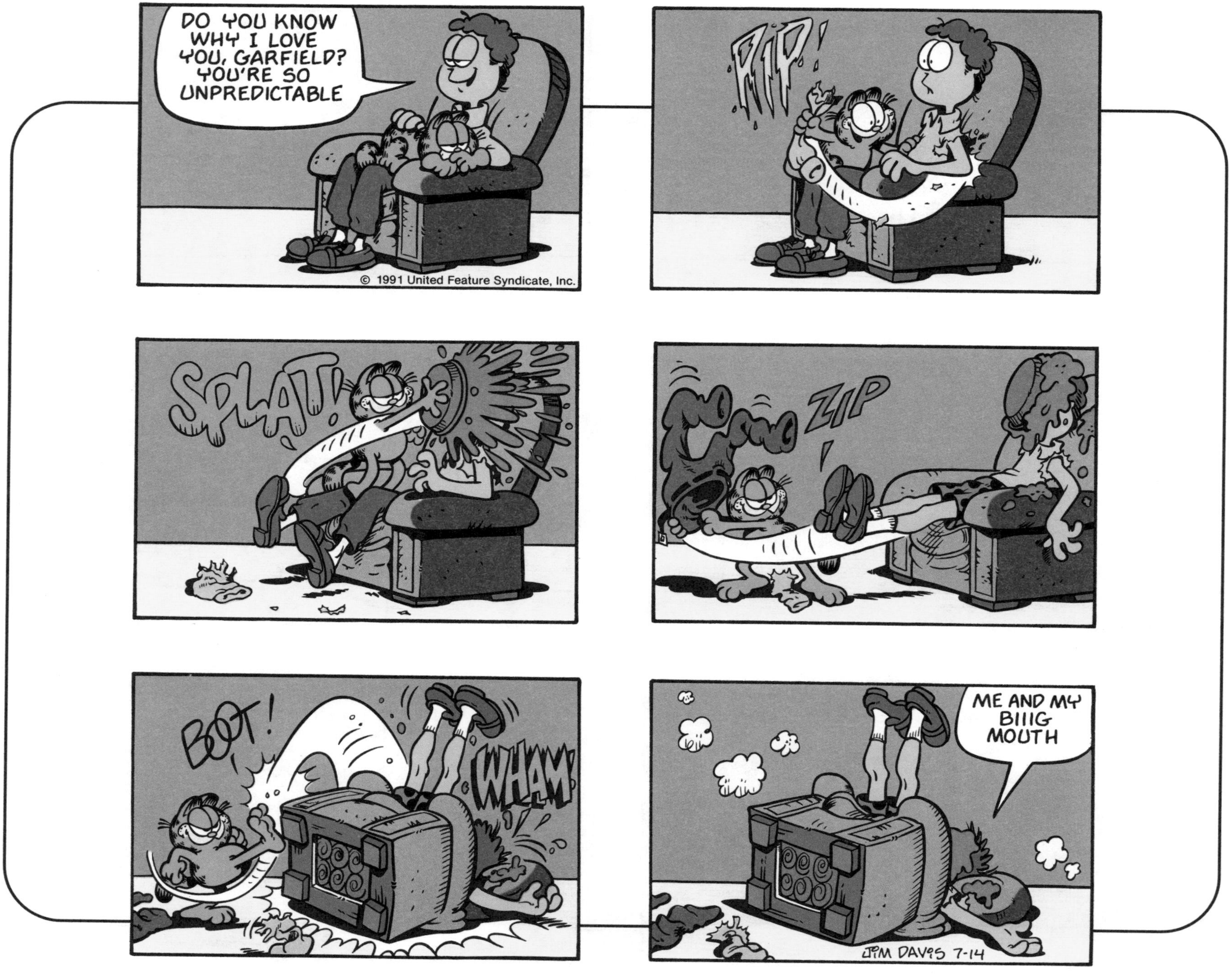
DO YOU KNOW WHY I LOVE YOU, GARFIELD? YOU'RE SO UNPREDICTABLE
© 1991 United Feature Syndicate, Inc.
RIP!
SPLAT!
ZIP
BOOT!
WHAM!
ME AND MY BIIIG MOUTH
JIM DAVIS 7-14

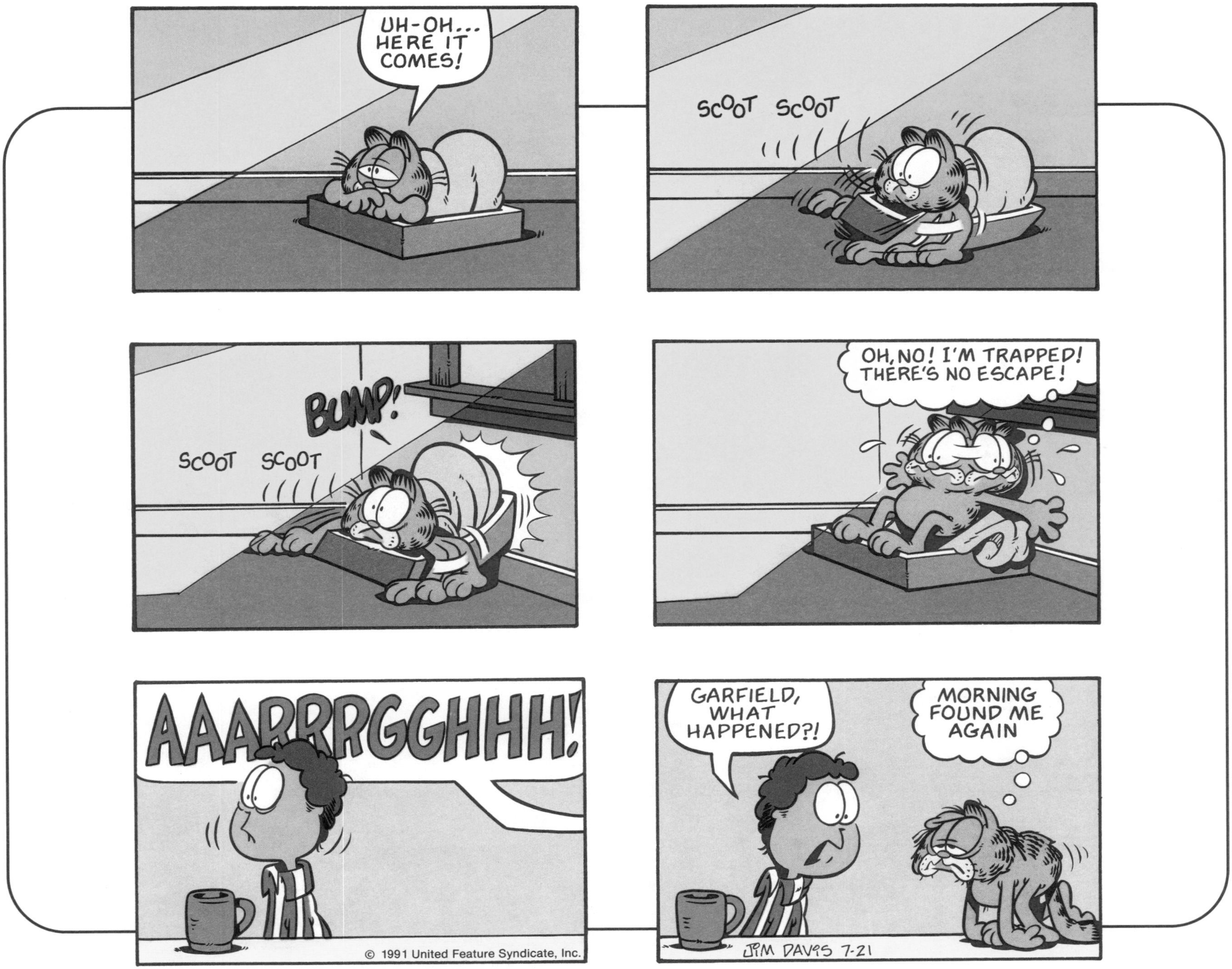
UH-OH... HERE IT COMES!
SCOOT SCOOT
SCOOT SCOOT
BUMP!
OH, NO! I'M TRAPPED! THERE'S NO ESCAPE!
AAARRRGGHHH!
© 1991 United Feature Syndicate, Inc.
GARFIELD, WHAT HAPPENED?!
MORNING FOUND ME AGAIN
JIM DAVIS 7-21

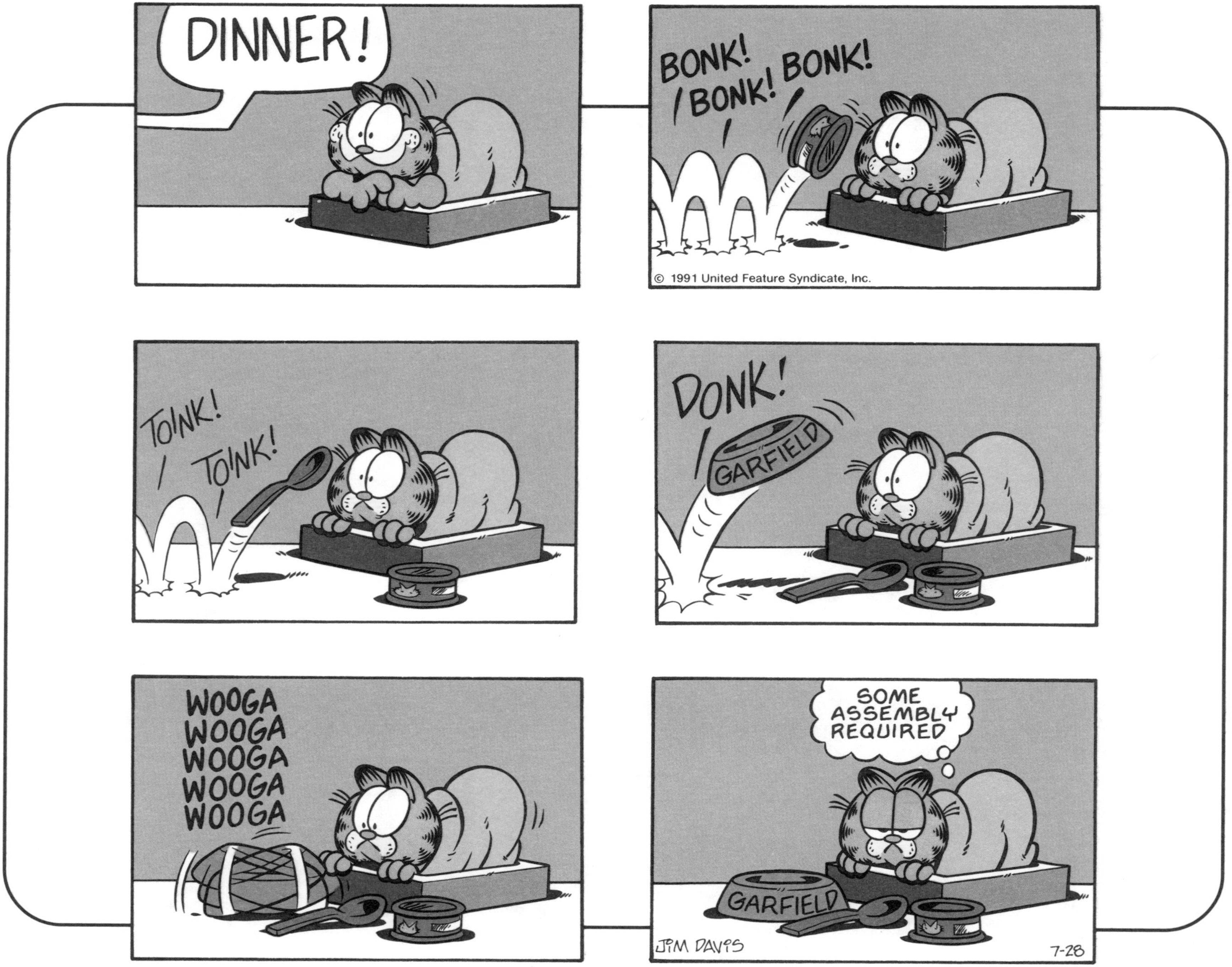
DINNER!
BONK! BONK! BONK!
© 1991 United Feature Syndicate, Inc.
TOINK! TOINK!
DONK!
GARFIELD
WOOGA WOOGA WOOGA WOOGA WOOGA
SOME ASSEMBLY REQUIRED
GARFIELD
JIM DAVIS
7-28

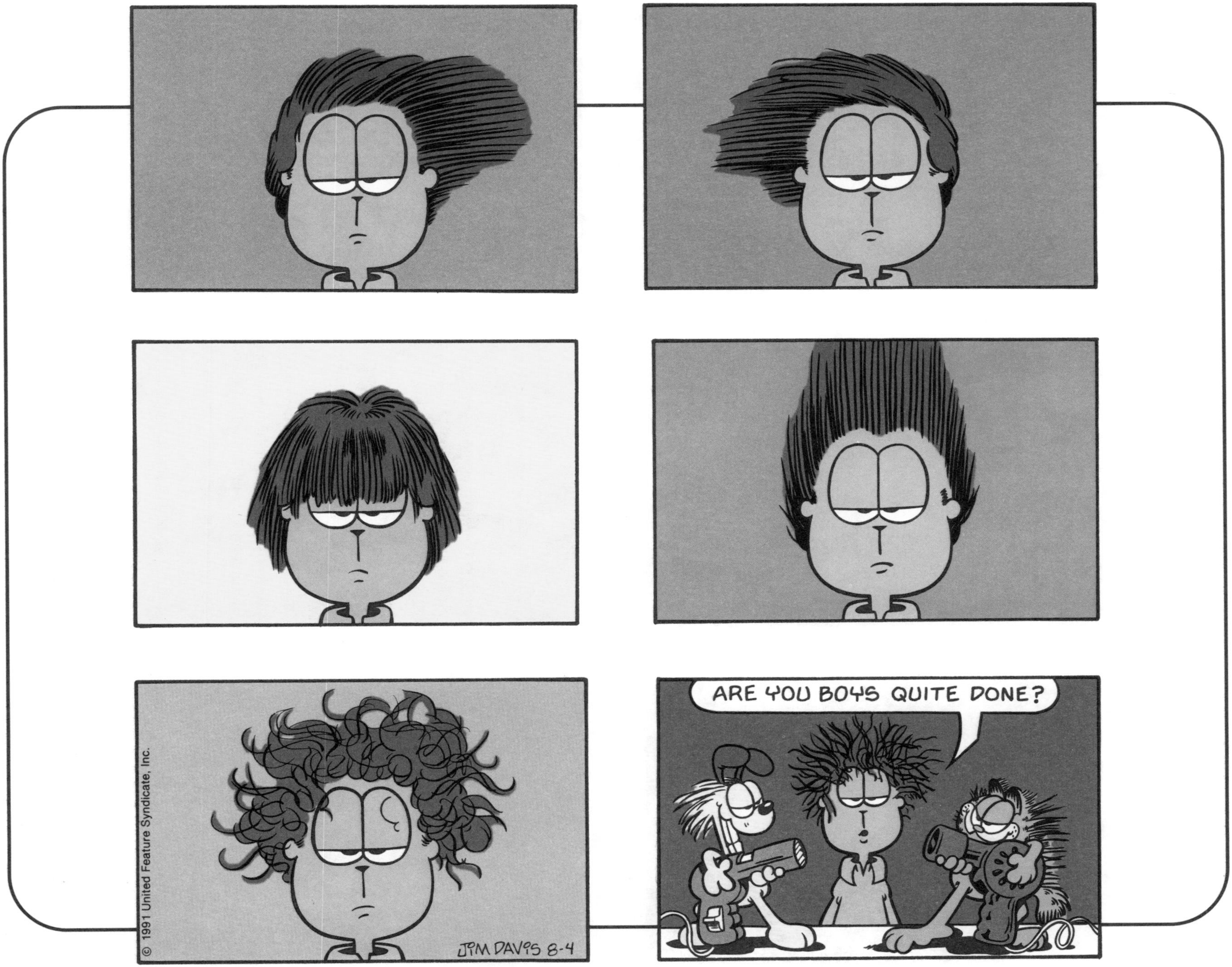
ARE YOU BOYS QUITE DONE?
© 1991 United Feature Syndicate, Inc.
JIM DAVIS 8-4

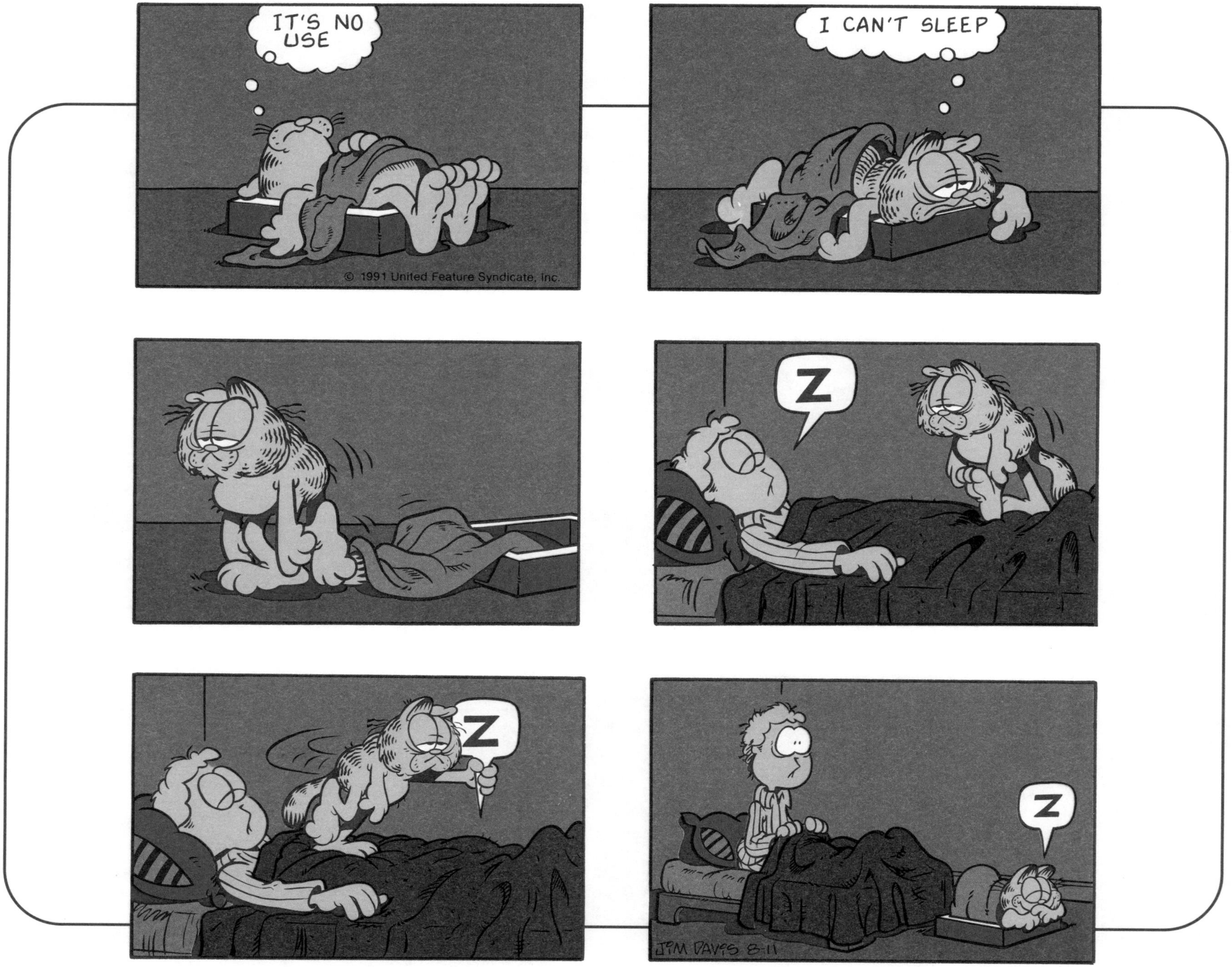
IT'S NO USE
© 1991 United Feature Syndicate, Inc.
I CAN'T SLEEP
Z
Z
Z
JIM DAVIS 8-11

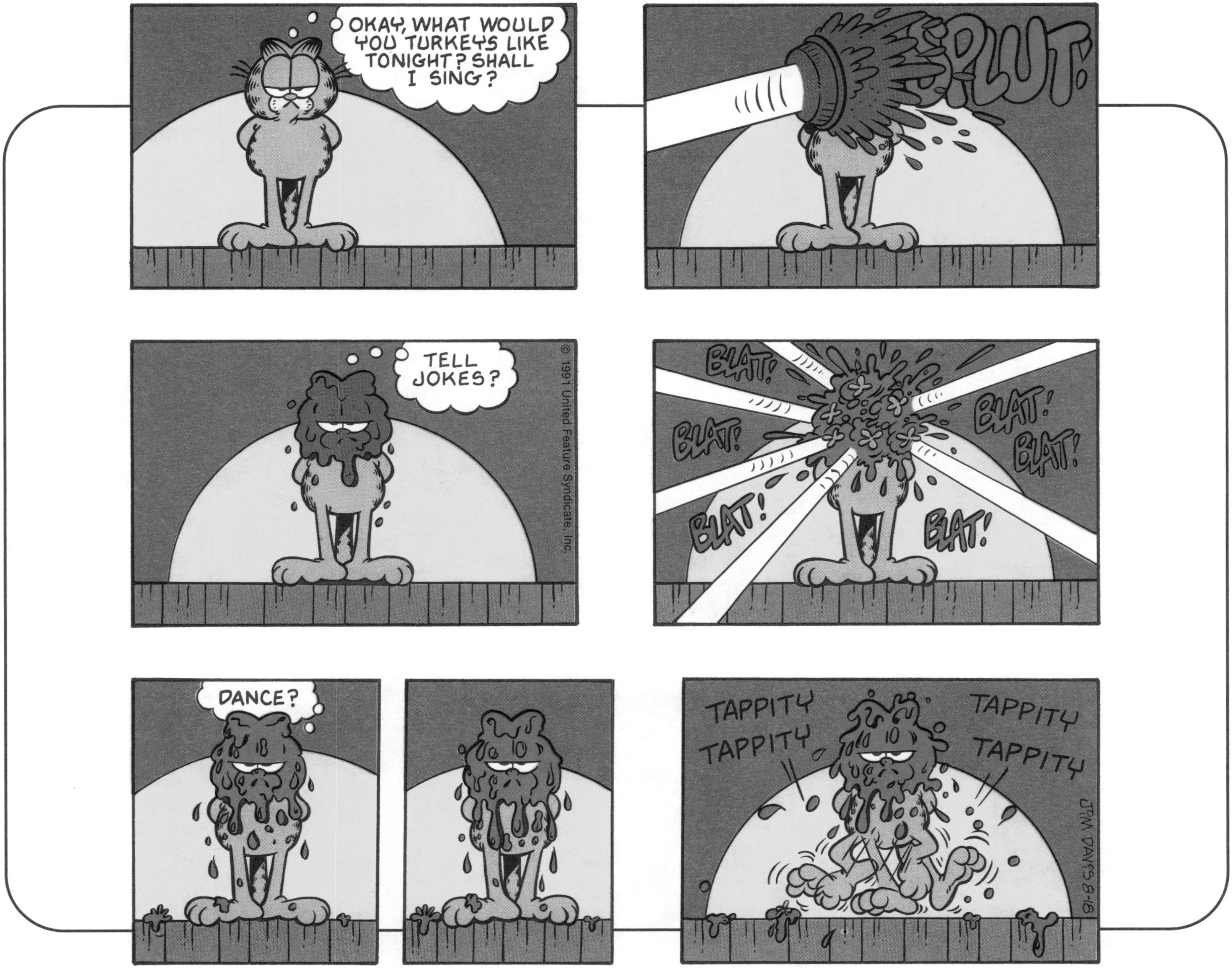
OKAY, WHAT WOULD YOU TURKEYS LIKE TONIGHT? SHALL I SING?
SPLUT!
TELL JOKES?
BLAT!
BLAT!
BLAT!
BLAT!
BLAT!
BLAT!
DANCE?
TAPPITY TAPPITY
TAPPITY TAPPITY
JIM DAVIS 8-18

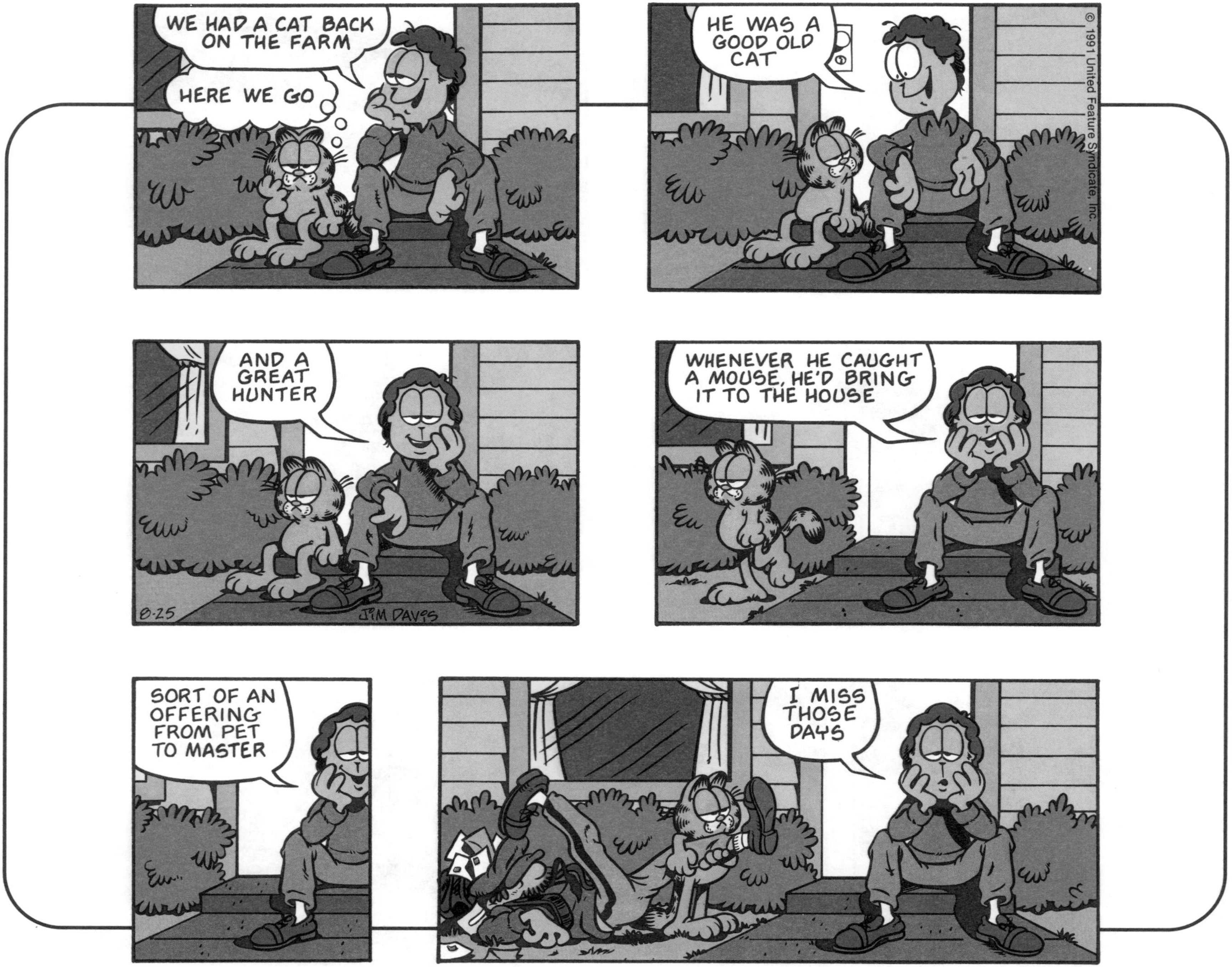

WE HAD A CAT BACK ON THE FARM
HERE WE GO
HE WAS A GOOD OLD CAT
© 1991 United Feature Syndicate, Inc.
AND A GREAT HUNTER
8-25
JIM DAVIS
WHENEVER HE CAUGHT A MOUSE, HE'D BRING IT TO THE HOUSE
SORT OF AN OFFERING FROM PET TO MASTER
I MISS THOSE DAYS

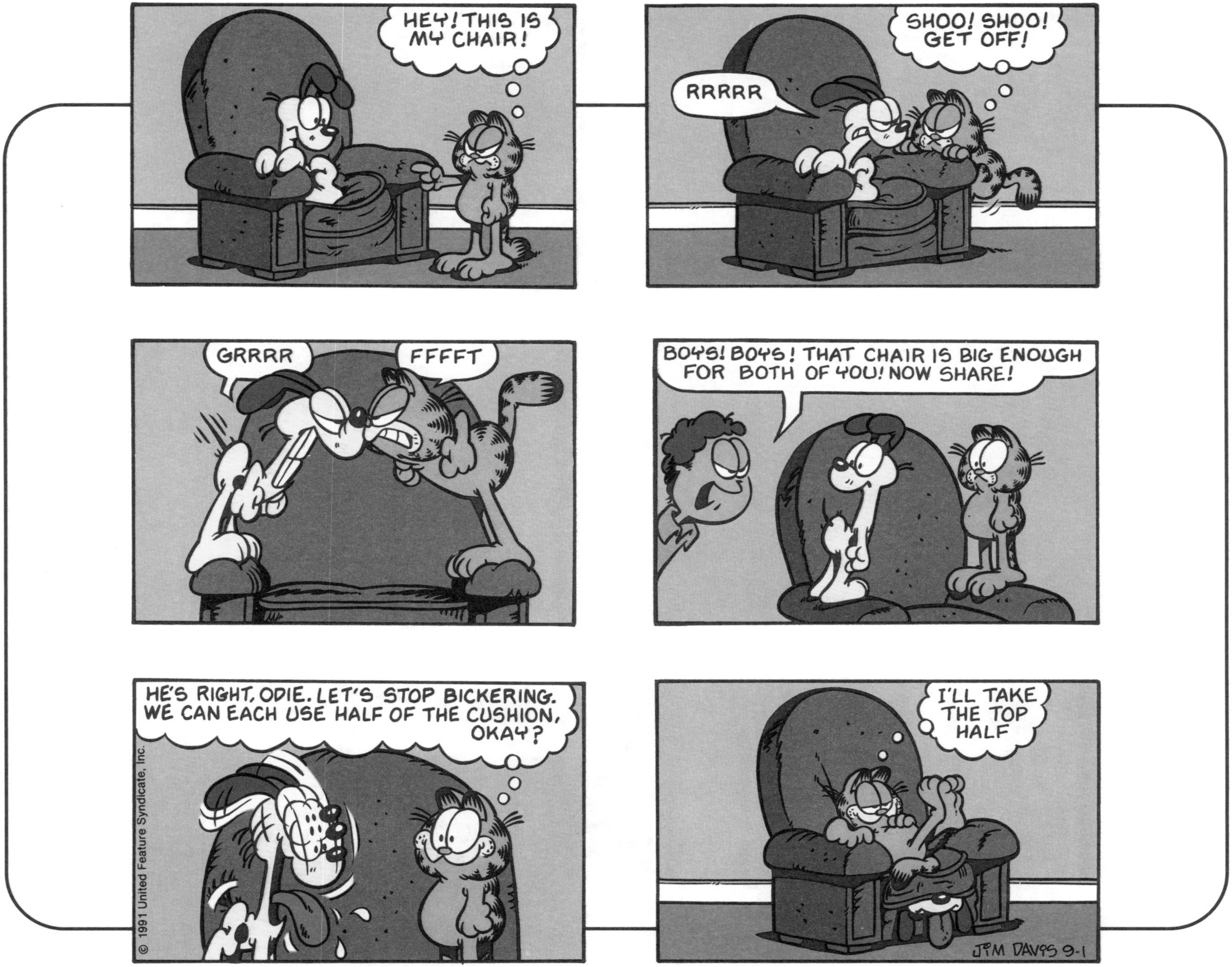
HEY! THIS IS MY CHAIR!
RRRRR
SHOO! SHOO! GET OFF!
GRRRR
FFFFT
BOYS! BOYS! THAT CHAIR IS BIG ENOUGH FOR BOTH OF YOU! NOW SHARE!
HE'S RIGHT, ODIE. LET'S STOP BICKERING. WE CAN EACH USE HALF OF THE CUSHION, OKAY?
I'LL TAKE THE TOP HALF
JIM DAVIS 9-1

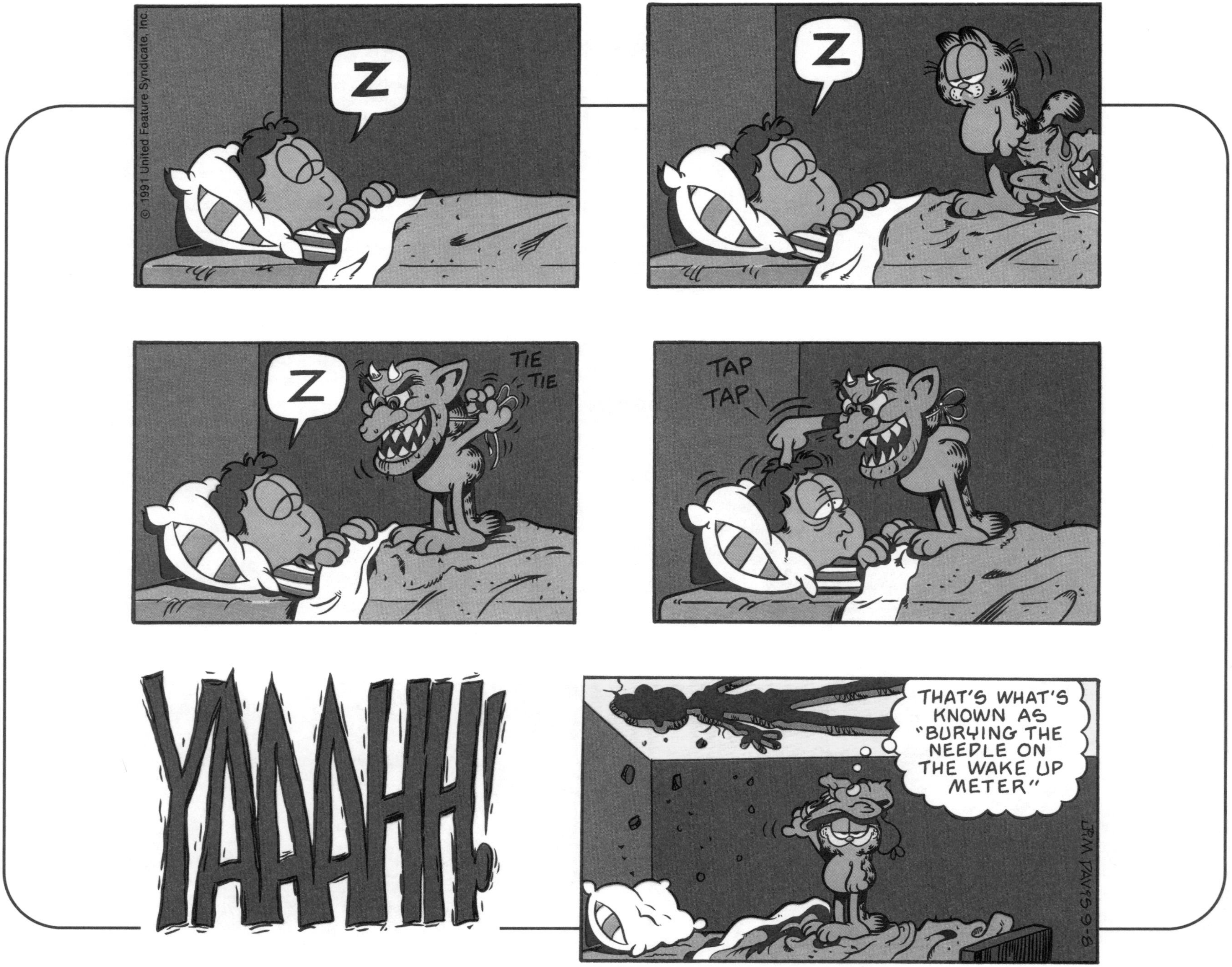

© 1991 United Feature Syndicate, Inc.
Z
Z
Z
TIE TIE
TAP TAP
YAAAHH!
THAT'S WHAT'S KNOWN AS "BURYING THE NEEDLE ON THE WAKE UP METER"
JIM DAVIS 9-8

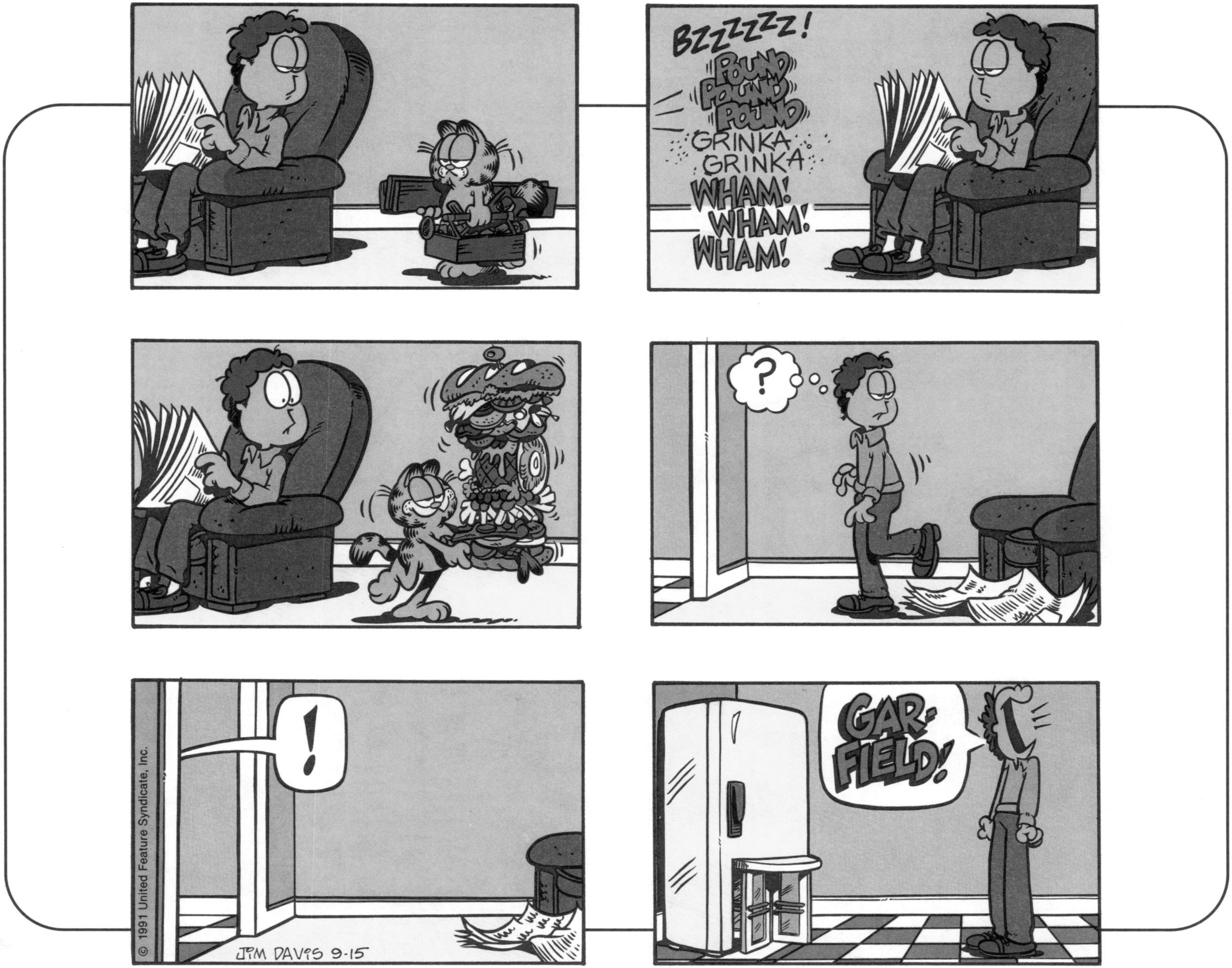
BZZZZZZ!
POUND
POUND
POUND
GRINKA
GRINKA
WHAM!
WHAM!
WHAM!
?
!
GAR-FIELD!
© 1991 United Feature Syndicate, Inc.
JIM DAVIS 9-15

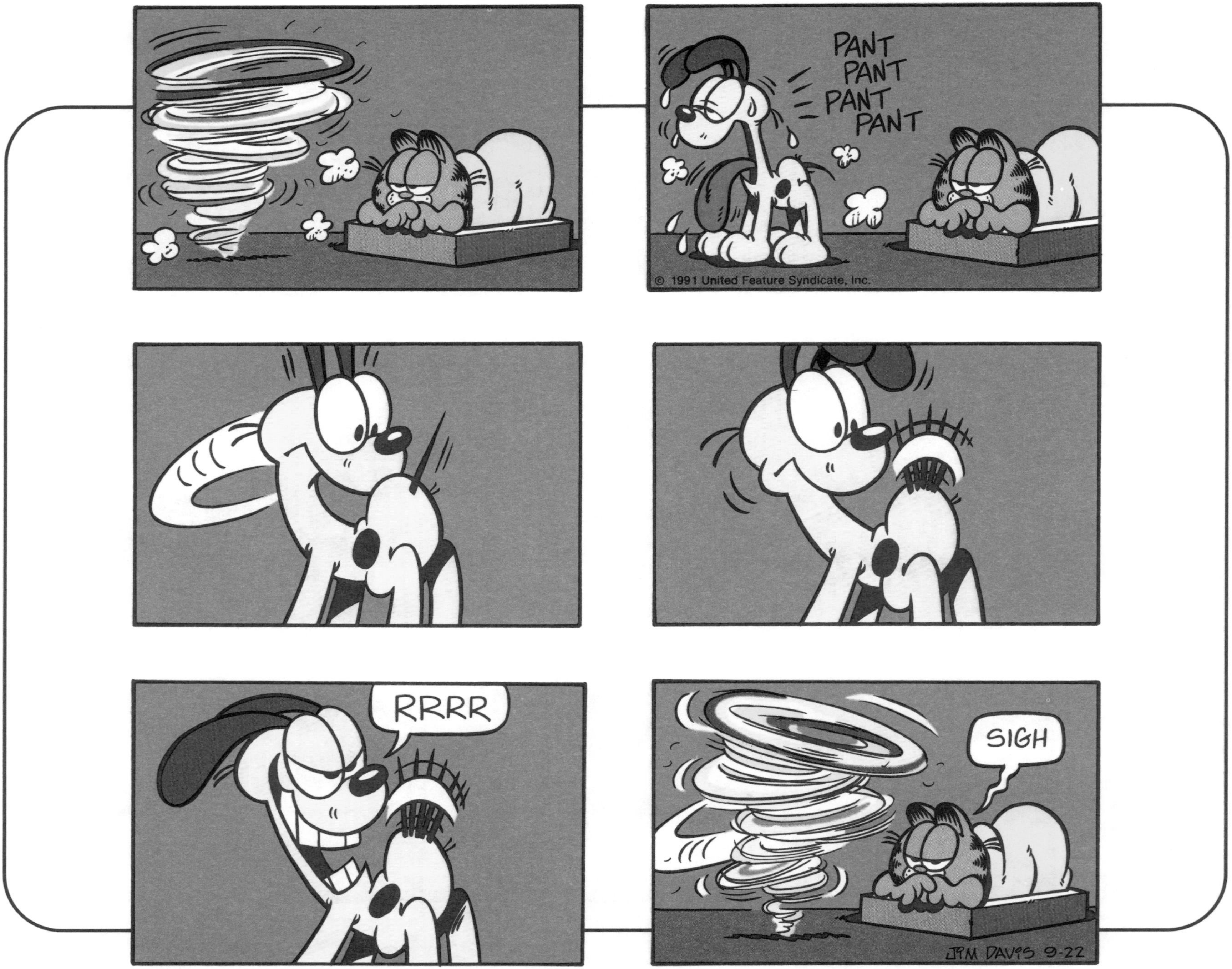
PANT PANT PANT PANT
© 1991 United Feature Syndicate, Inc.
RRRR
SIGH
JIM DAVIS 9-22

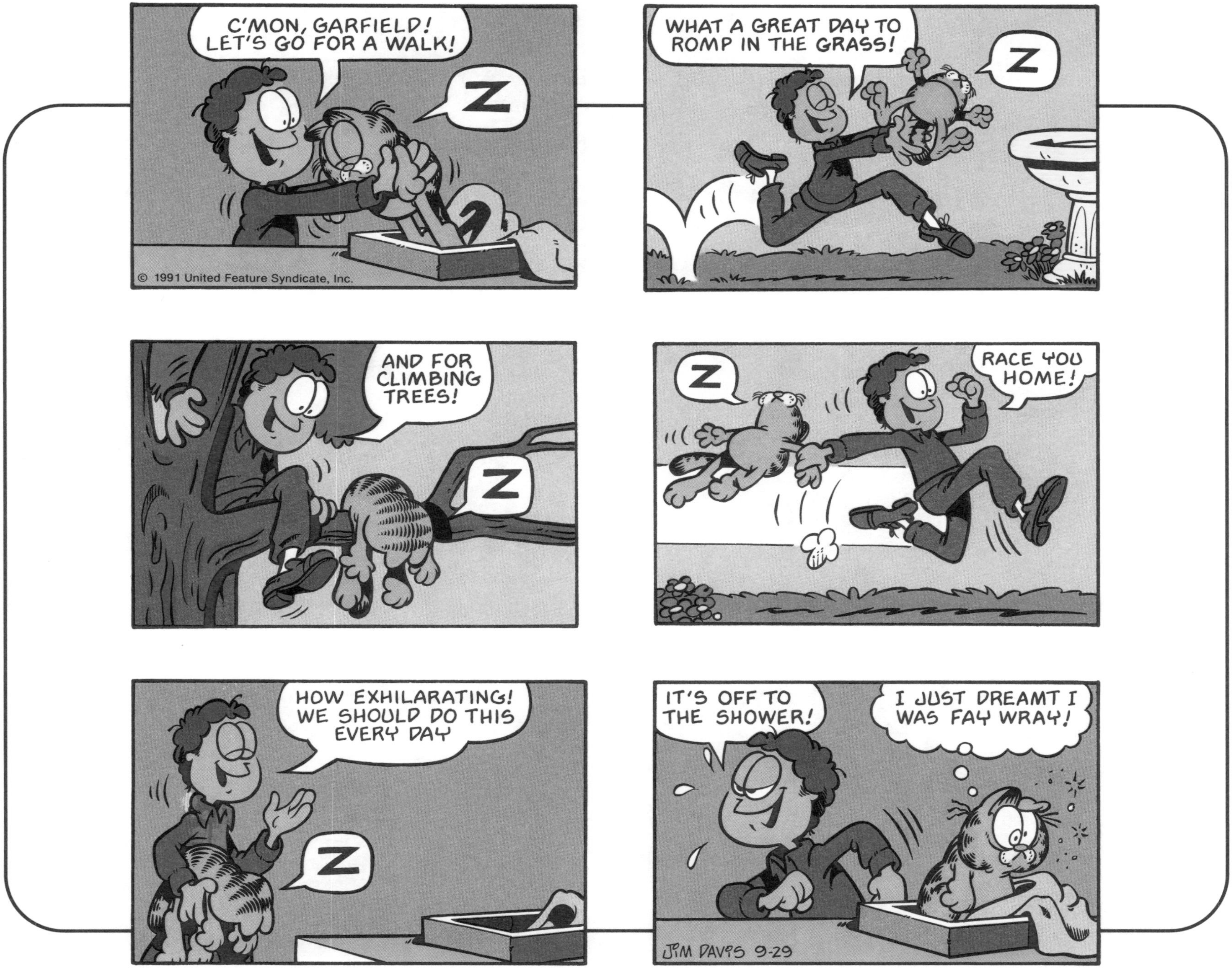
C'MON, GARFIELD! LET'S GO FOR A WALK!
Z
© 1991 United Feature Syndicate, Inc.
WHAT A GREAT DAY TO ROMP IN THE GRASS!
Z
AND FOR CLIMBING TREES!
Z
Z
RACE YOU HOME!
HOW EXHILARATING! WE SHOULD DO THIS EVERY DAY
Z
IT'S OFF TO THE SHOWER!
I JUST DREAMT I WAS FAY WRAY!
JIM DAVIS 9-29

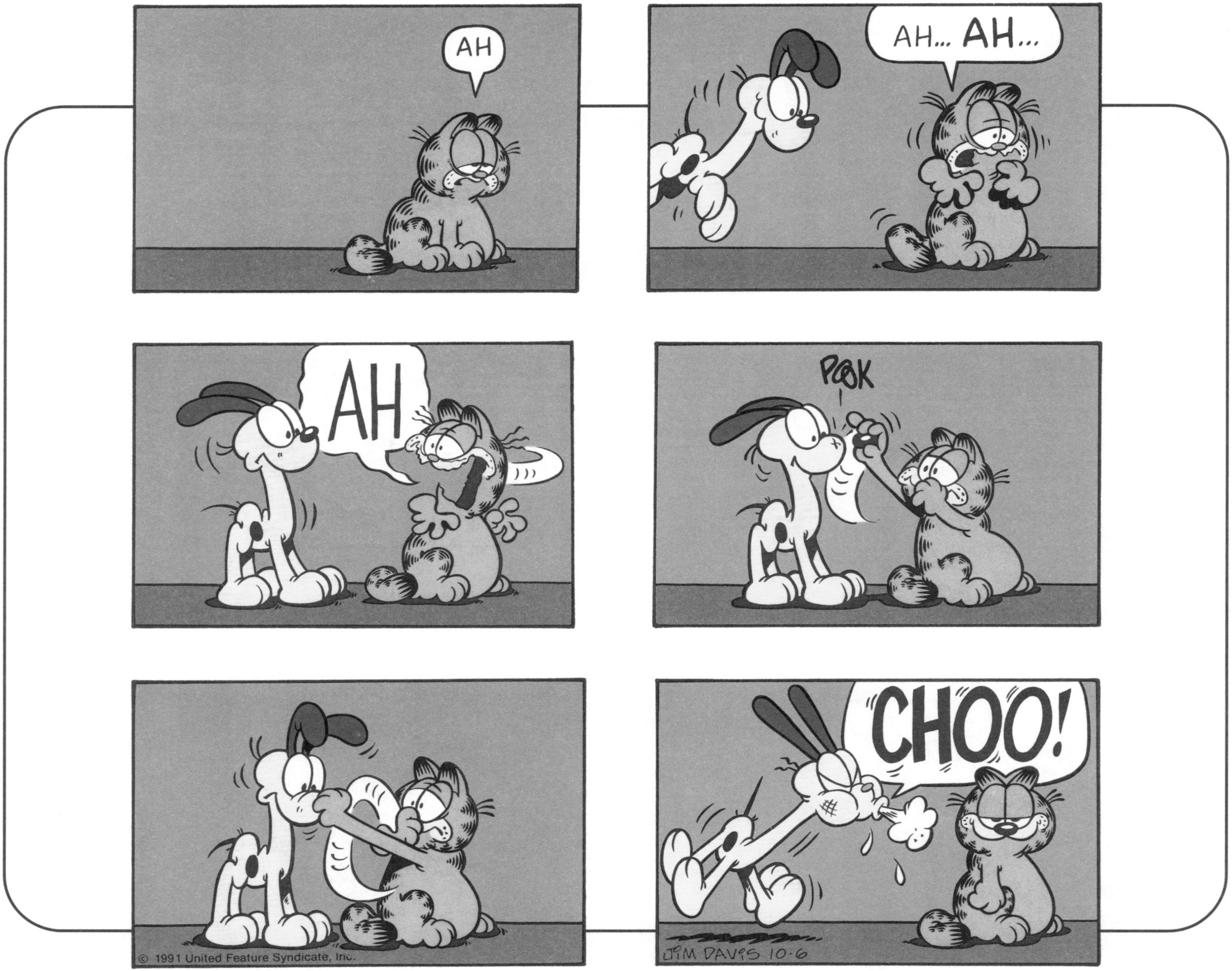
AH
AH... AH...
AH
POOK
CHOO!
JIM DAVIS 10-6

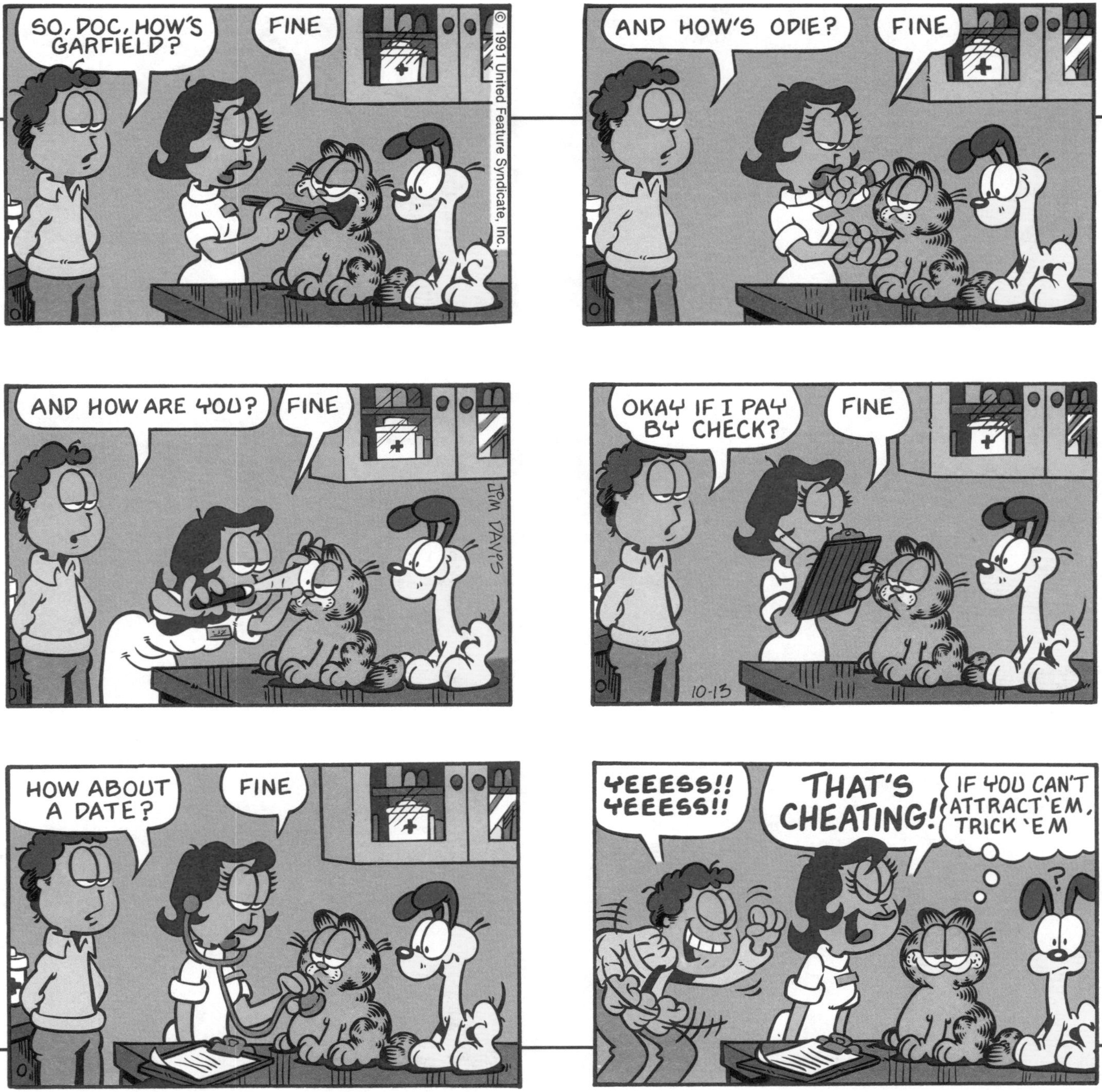
SO, DOC, HOW'S GARFIELD?
FINE
© 1991 United Feature Syndicate, Inc.
AND HOW'S ODIE?
FINE
AND HOW ARE YOU?
FINE
JIM DAVIS
OKAY IF I PAY BY CHECK?
FINE
10-13
HOW ABOUT A DATE?
FINE
YEEESS!! YEEESS!!
THAT'S CHEATING!
IF YOU CAN'T ATTRACT 'EM, TRICK 'EM
?

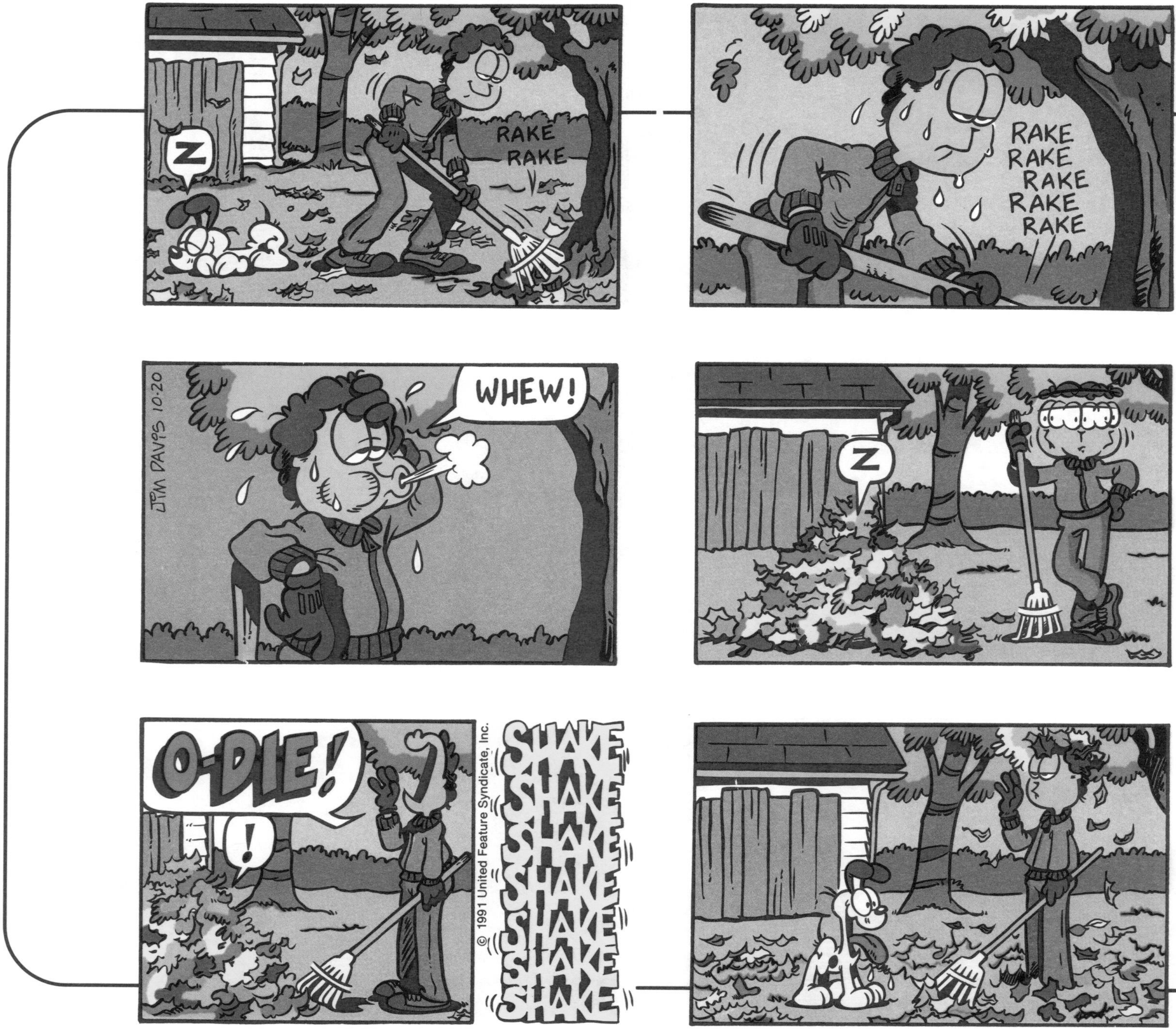
Z
RAKE
RAKE
RAKE
RAKE
RAKE
RAKE
RAKE
JIM DAVIS 10-20
WHEW!
Z
O-DIE!
!
© 1991 United Feature Syndicate, Inc.
SHAKE
SHAKE
SHAKE
SHAKE
SHAKE
SHAKE
SHAKE
SHAKE

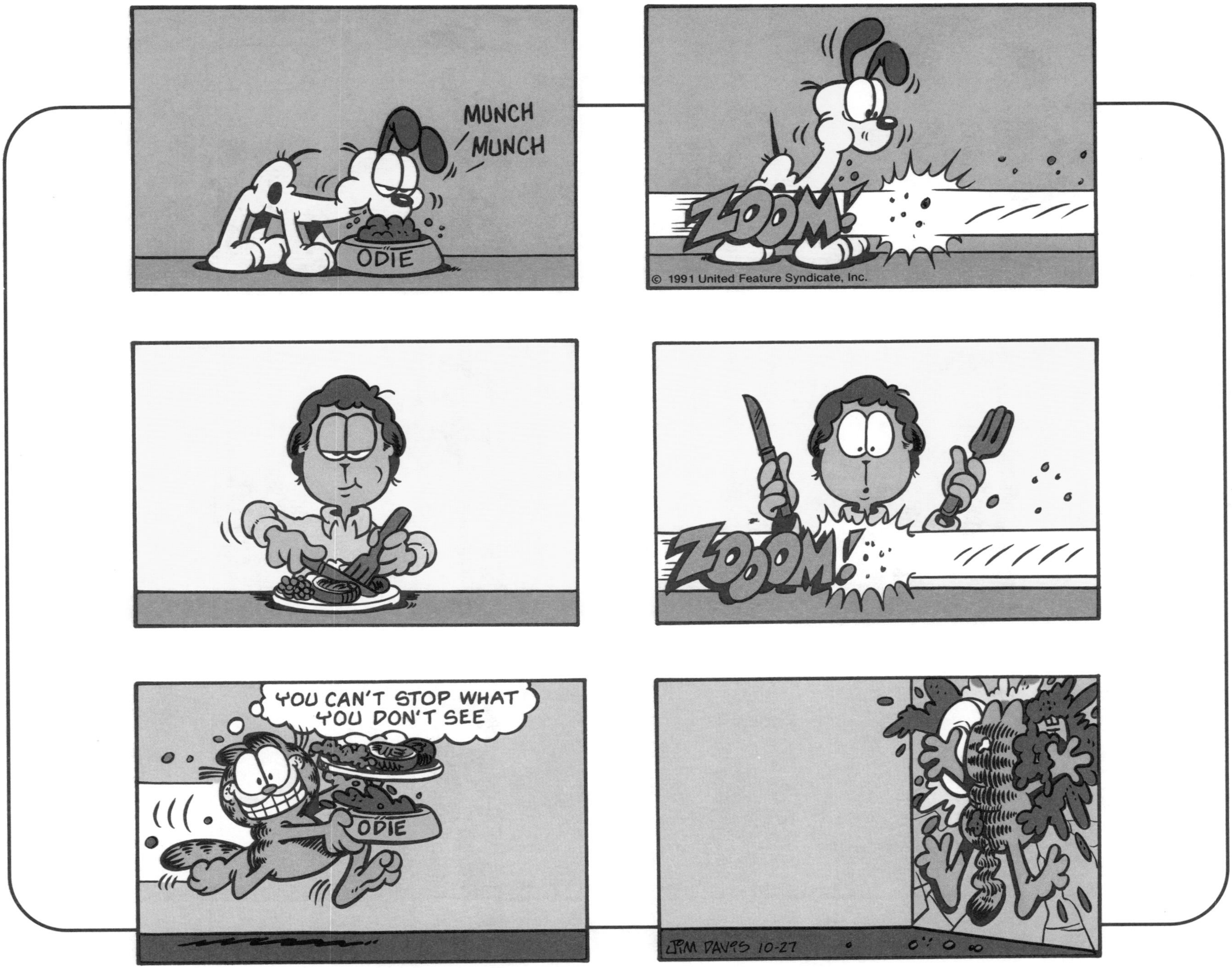
MUNCH MUNCH
ODIE
ZOOM!
© 1991 United Feature Syndicate, Inc.
ZOOOM!
YOU CAN'T STOP WHAT YOU DON'T SEE
ODIE
JIM DAVIS 10-27

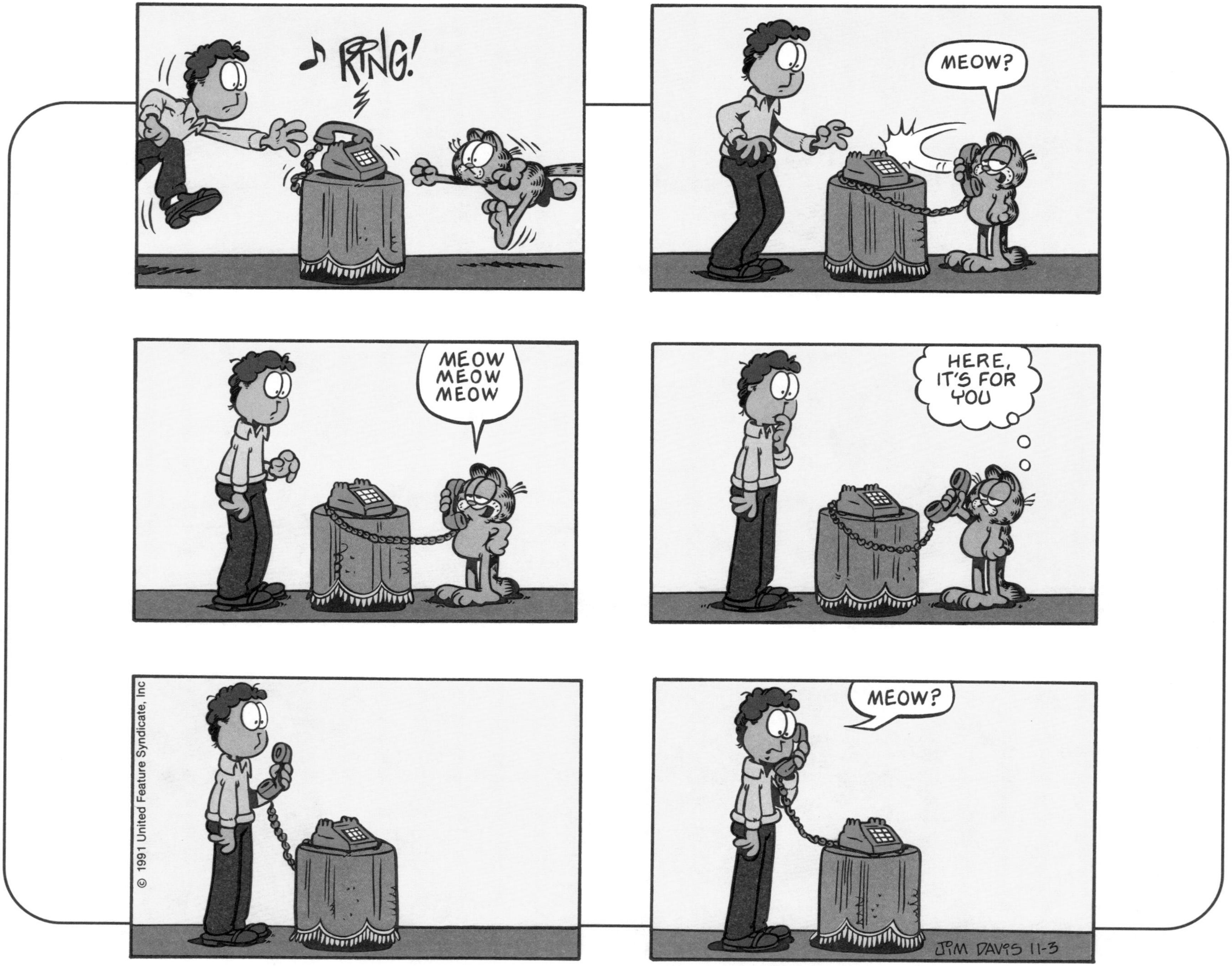
♪ RING!
MEOW?
MEOW MEOW MEOW
HERE, IT'S FOR YOU
MEOW?
JIM DAVIS 11-3

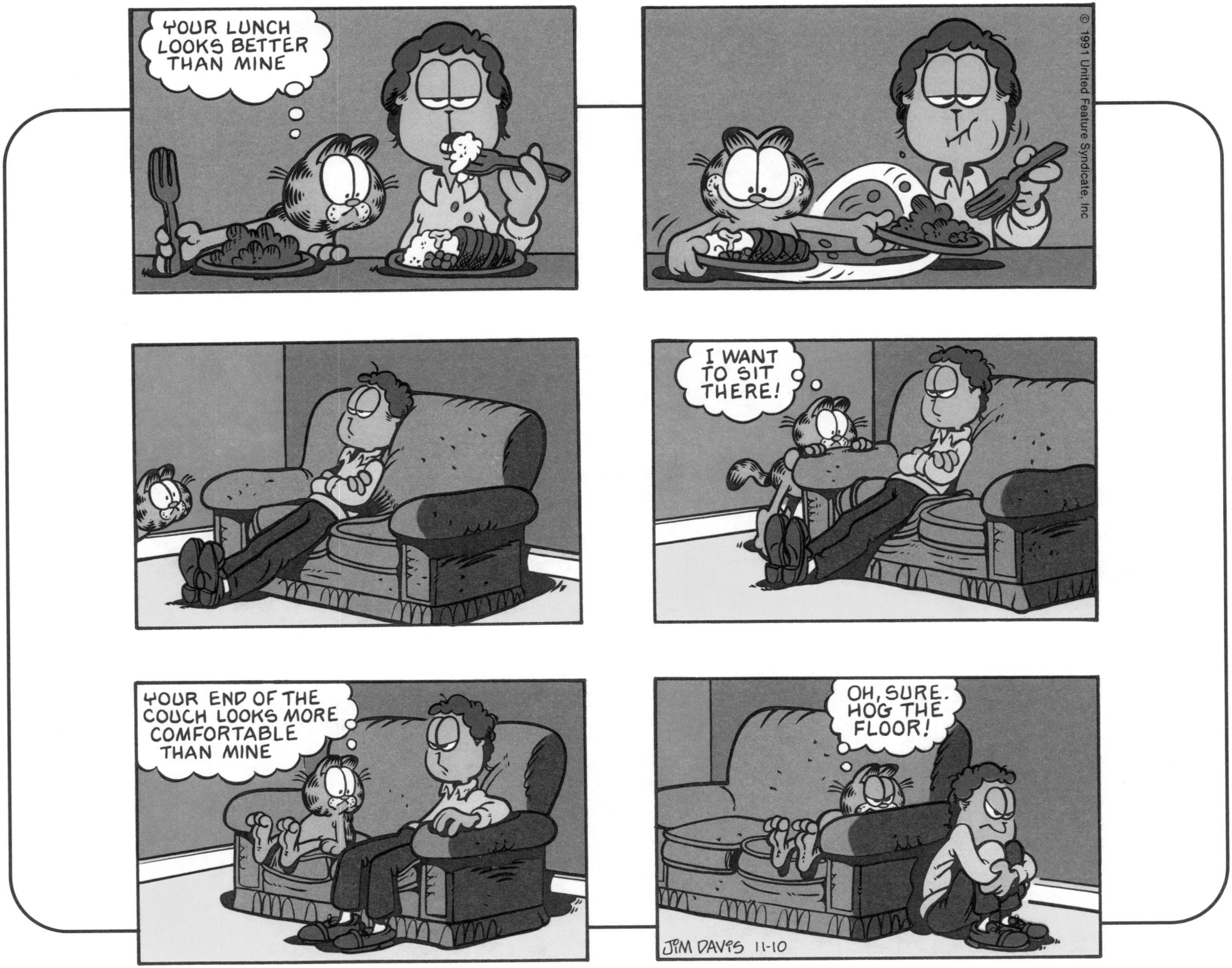
YOUR LUNCH LOOKS BETTER THAN MINE
© 1991 United Feature Syndicate, Inc
I WANT TO SIT THERE!
YOUR END OF THE COUCH LOOKS MORE COMFORTABLE THAN MINE
OH, SURE. HOG THE FLOOR!
JIM DAVIS 11-10

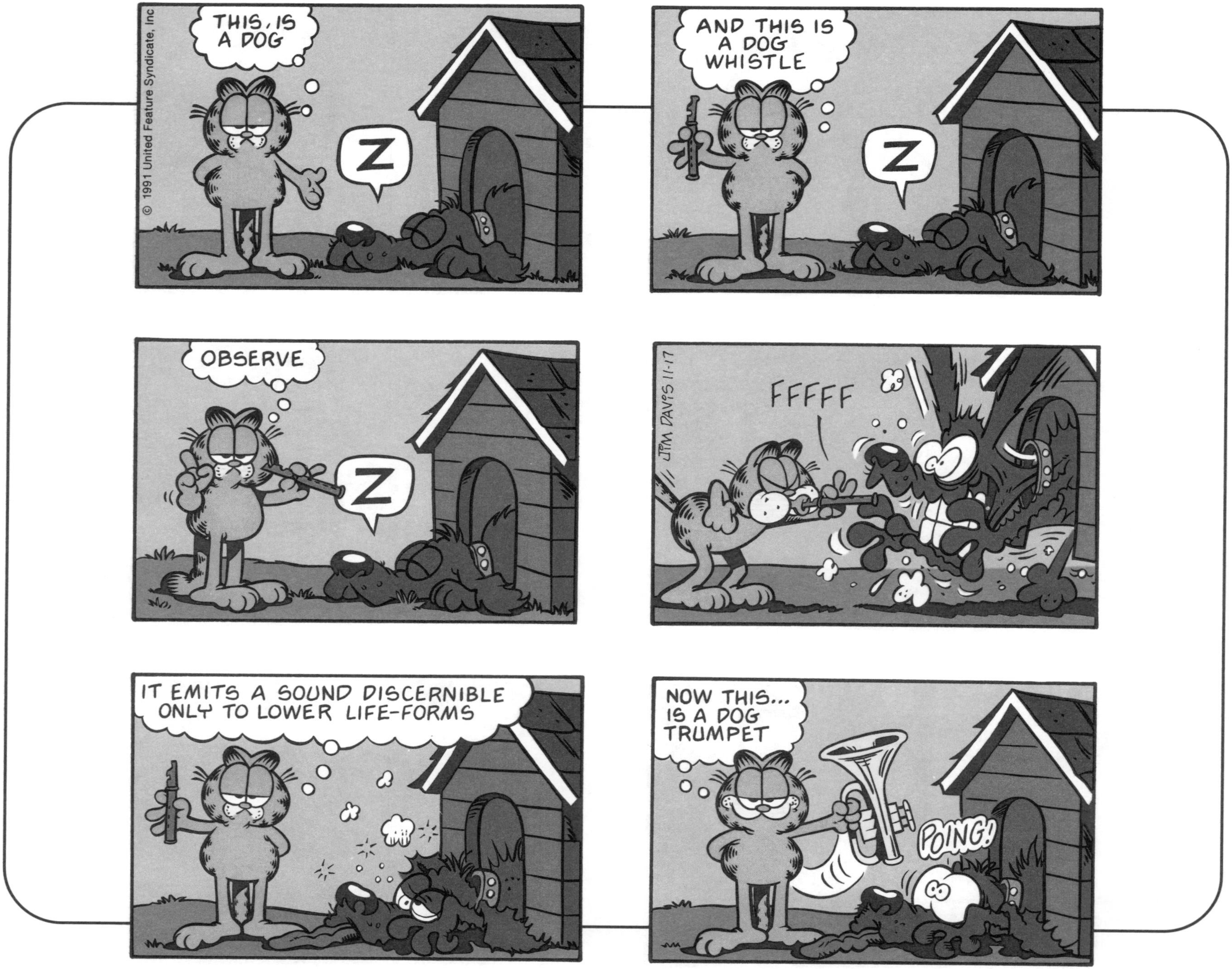
© 1991 United Feature Syndicate, Inc
THIS, IS A DOG
Z
AND THIS IS A DOG WHISTLE
Z
OBSERVE
Z
JPM DAVPS 11-17
FFFFF
IT EMITS A SOUND DISCERNIBLE ONLY TO LOWER LIFE-FORMS
NOW THIS... IS A DOG TRUMPET
POING!

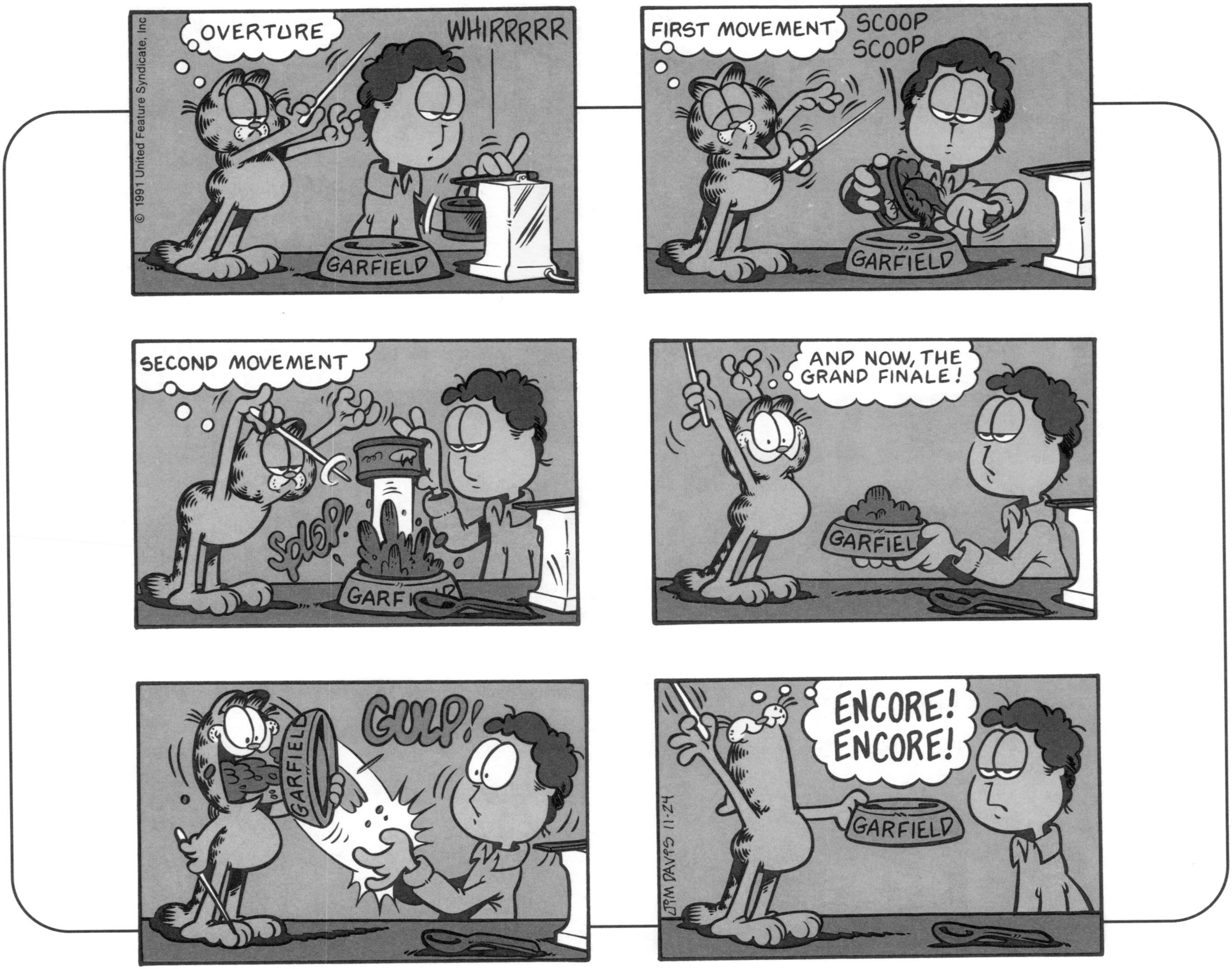

© 1991 United Feature Syndicate, Inc
OVERTURE
WHIRRRRR
GARFIELD
FIRST MOVEMENT
SCOOP
SCOOP
GARFIELD
SECOND MOVEMENT
SPLOP!
GARFIELD
AND NOW, THE GRAND FINALE!
GARFIELD
GULP!
GARFIELD
ENCORE! ENCORE!
GARFIELD
JIM DAVIS 11-24

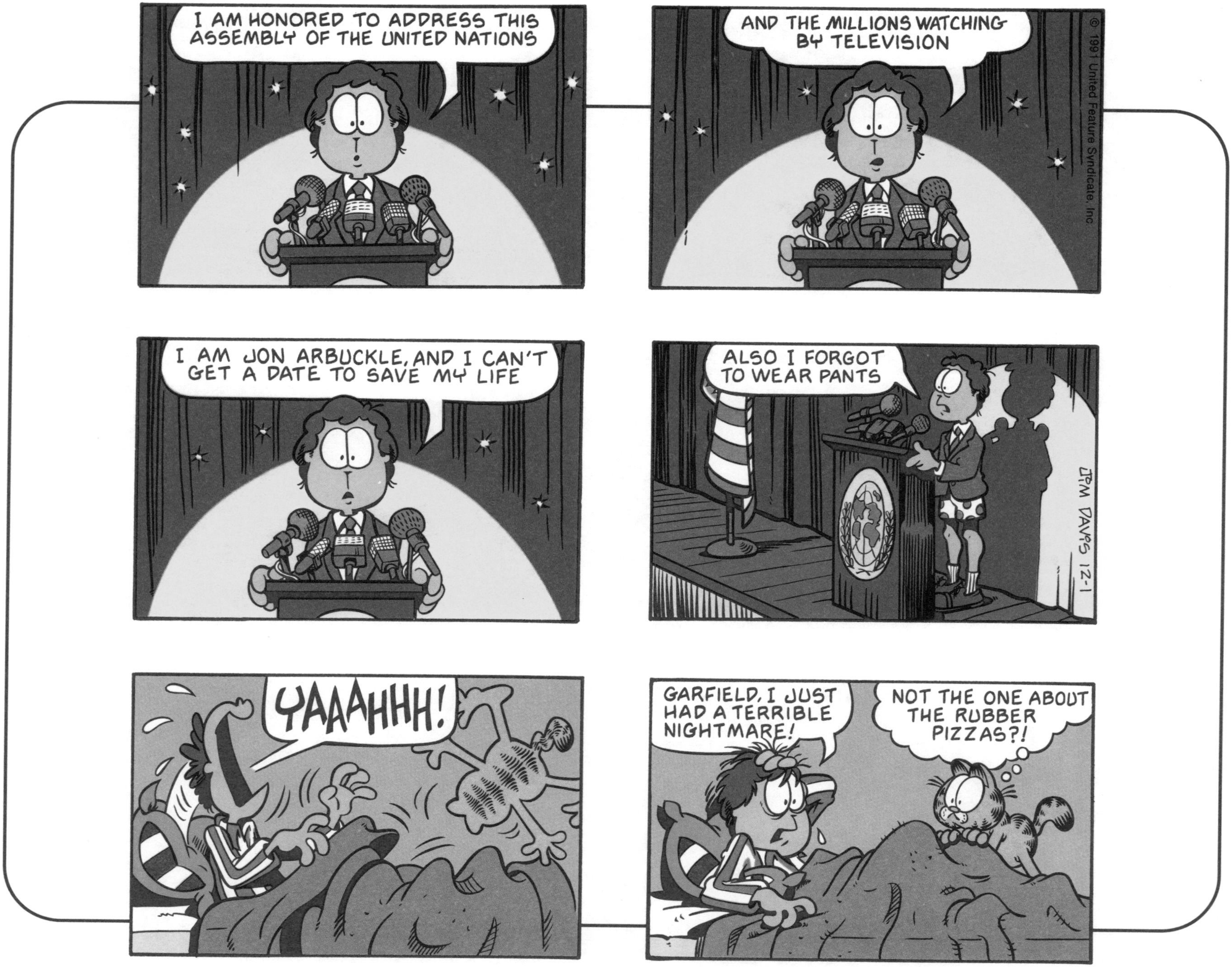
I AM HONORED TO ADDRESS THIS ASSEMBLY OF THE UNITED NATIONS
AND THE MILLIONS WATCHING BY TELEVISION
© 1991 United Feature Syndicate, Inc.
I AM JON ARBUCKLE, AND I CAN'T GET A DATE TO SAVE MY LIFE
ALSO I FORGOT TO WEAR PANTS
JPM DAVPS 12-1
YAAAHHH!
GARFIELD, I JUST HAD A TERRIBLE NIGHTMARE!
NOT THE ONE ABOUT THE RUBBER PIZZAS?!

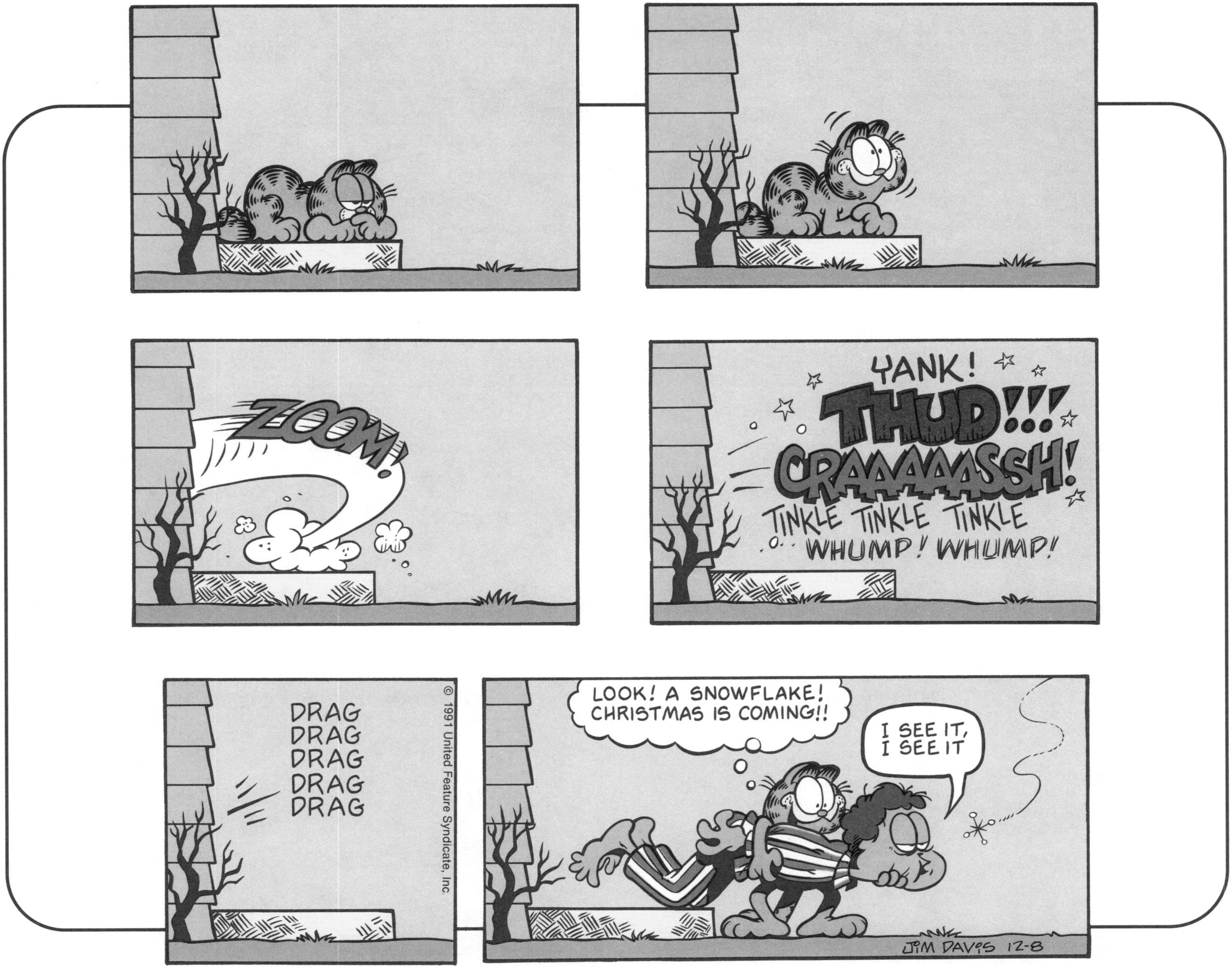
ZOOM!
YANK!
THUD!!!
CRAAAAASSH!
TINKLE TINKLE TINKLE
WHUMP! WHUMP!
DRAG
DRAG
DRAG
DRAG
DRAG
© 1991 United Feature Syndicate, Inc.
LOOK! A SNOWFLAKE! CHRISTMAS IS COMING!!
I SEE IT, I SEE IT
JIM DAVIS 12-8

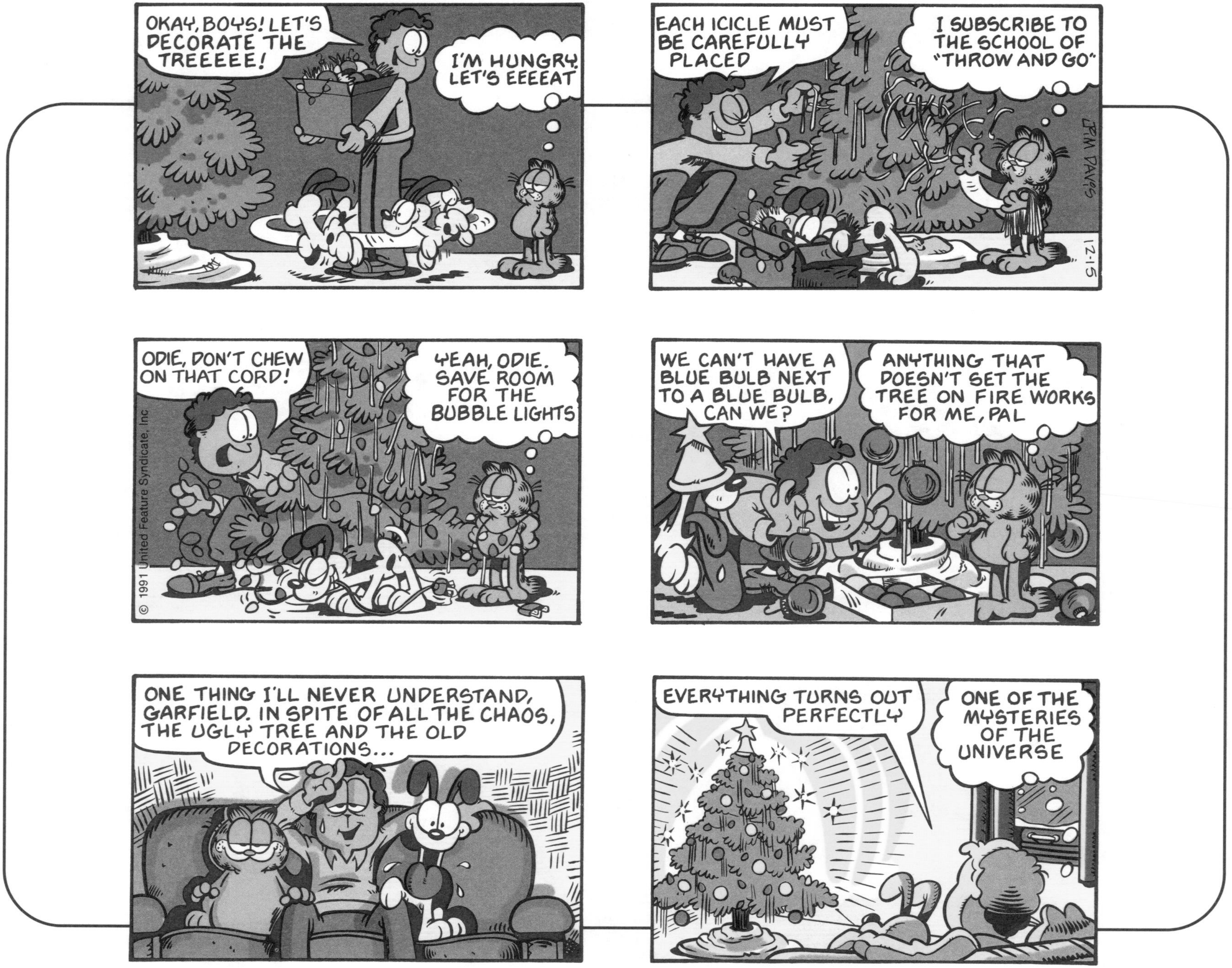

OKAY, BOYS! LET'S DECORATE THE TREEEEE!
I'M HUNGRY. LET'S EEEEAT
EACH ICICLE MUST BE CAREFULLY PLACED
I SUBSCRIBE TO THE SCHOOL OF "THROW AND GO"
JIM DAVIS
12-15
ODIE, DON'T CHEW ON THAT CORD!
YEAH, ODIE. SAVE ROOM FOR THE BUBBLE LIGHTS
© 1991 United Feature Syndicate, Inc
WE CAN'T HAVE A BLUE BULB NEXT TO A BLUE BULB, CAN WE?
ANYTHING THAT DOESN'T SET THE TREE ON FIRE WORKS FOR ME, PAL
ONE THING I'LL NEVER UNDERSTAND, GARFIELD. IN SPITE OF ALL THE CHAOS, THE UGLY TREE AND THE OLD DECORATIONS...
EVERYTHING TURNS OUT PERFECTLY
ONE OF THE MYSTERIES OF THE UNIVERSE

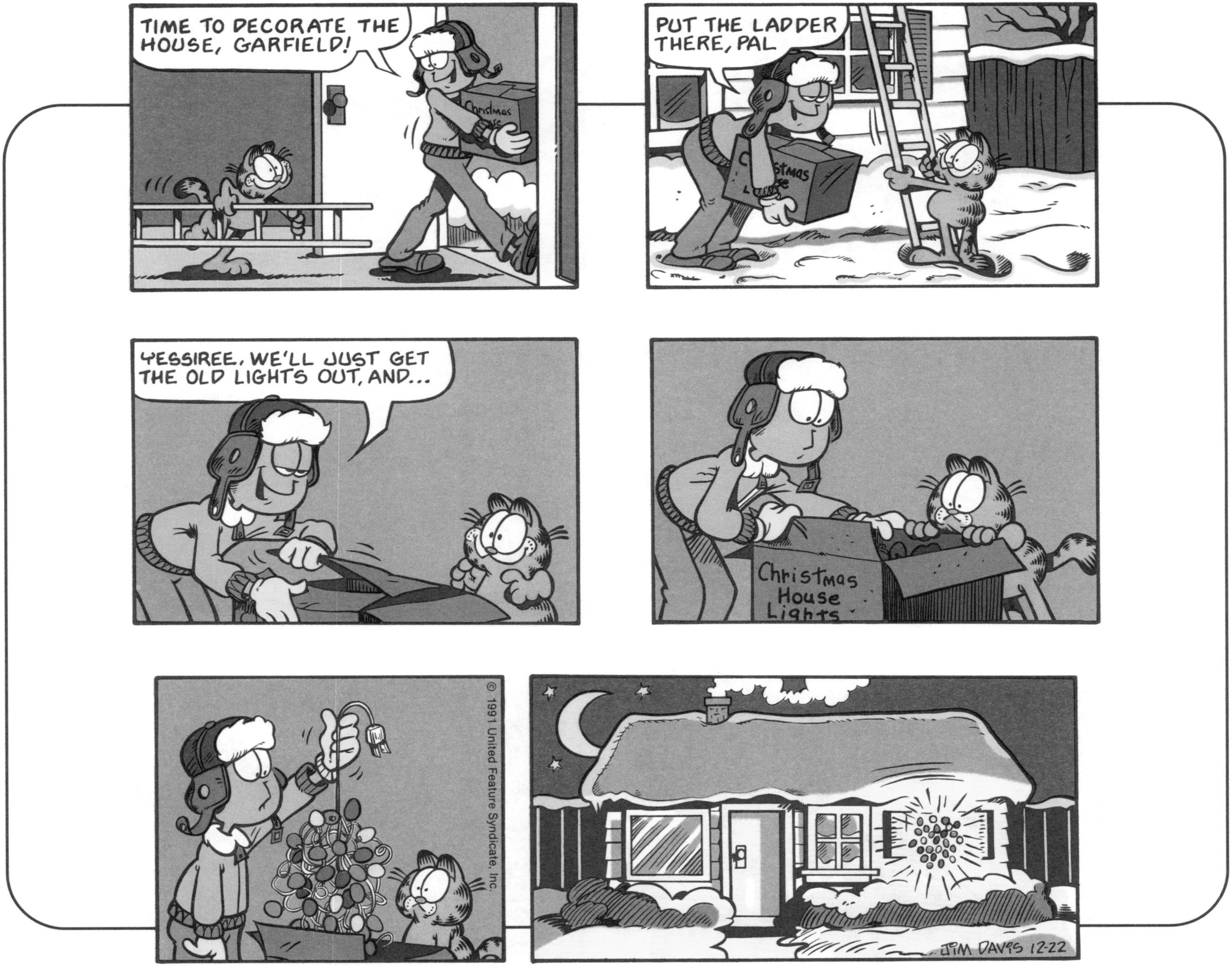
TIME TO DECORATE THE HOUSE, GARFIELD!
Christmas House
PUT THE LADDER THERE, PAL
YESSIREE. WE'LL JUST GET THE OLD LIGHTS OUT, AND...
Christmas House Lights
JIM DAVIS 12-22

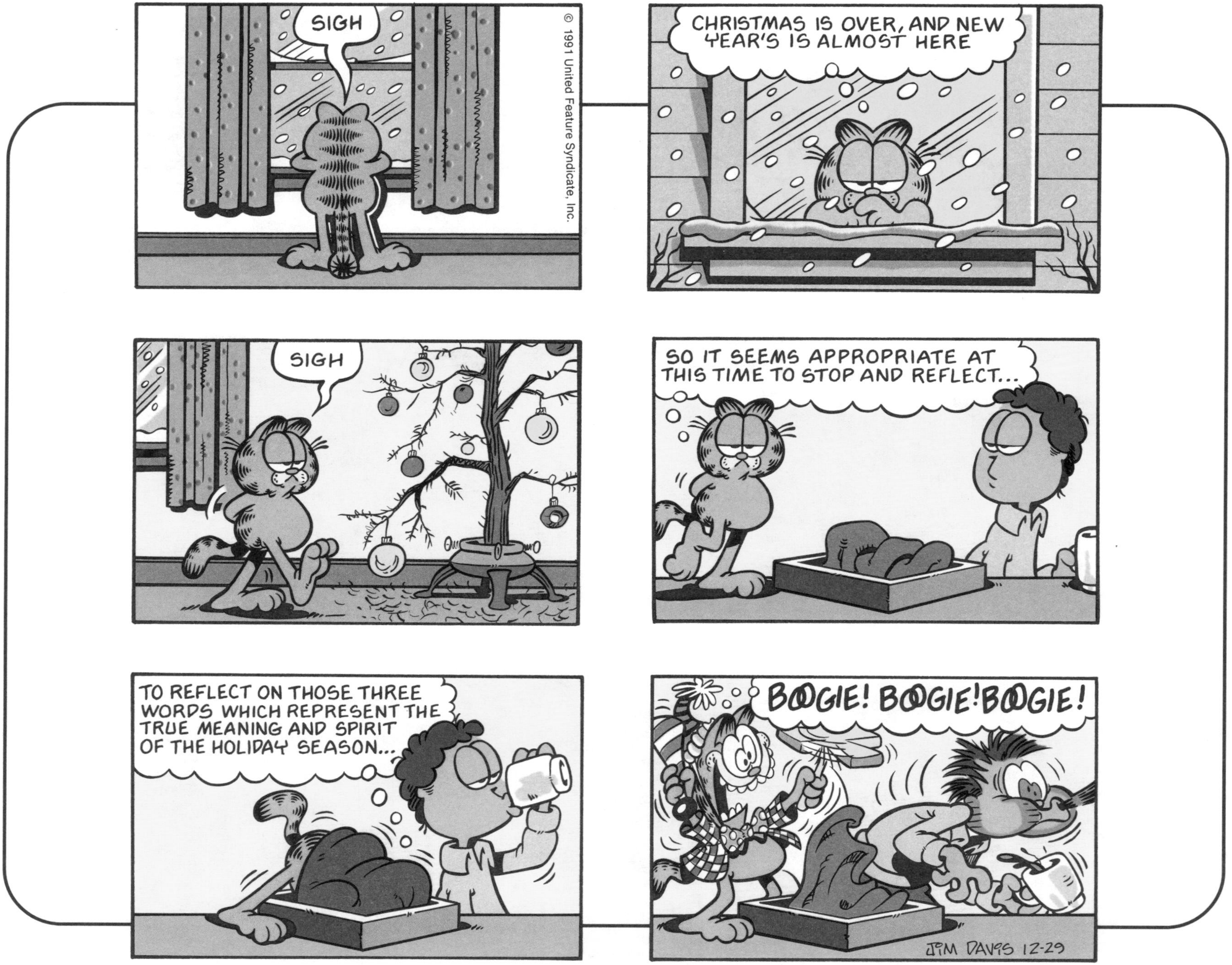
SIGH
© 1991 United Feature Syndicate, Inc.
CHRISTMAS IS OVER, AND NEW YEAR'S IS ALMOST HERE
SIGH
SO IT SEEMS APPROPRIATE AT THIS TIME TO STOP AND REFLECT...
TO REFLECT ON THOSE THREE WORDS WHICH REPRESENT THE TRUE MEANING AND SPIRIT OF THE HOLIDAY SEASON...
BOOGIE! BOOGIE! BOOGIE!
JIM DAVIS 12-29

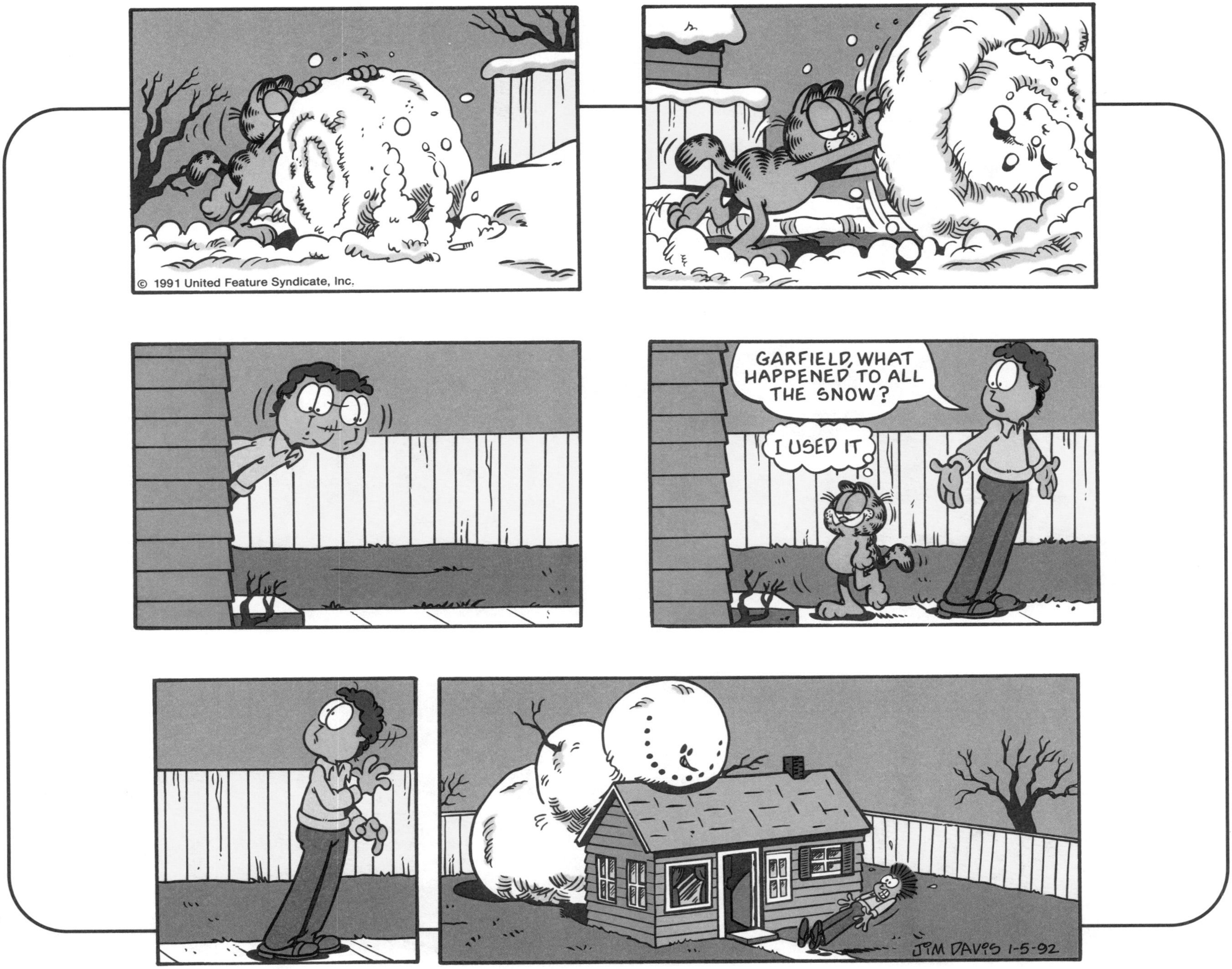
© 1991 United Feature Syndicate, Inc.
GARFIELD, WHAT HAPPENED TO ALL THE SNOW?
I USED IT
JIM DAVIS 1-5-92

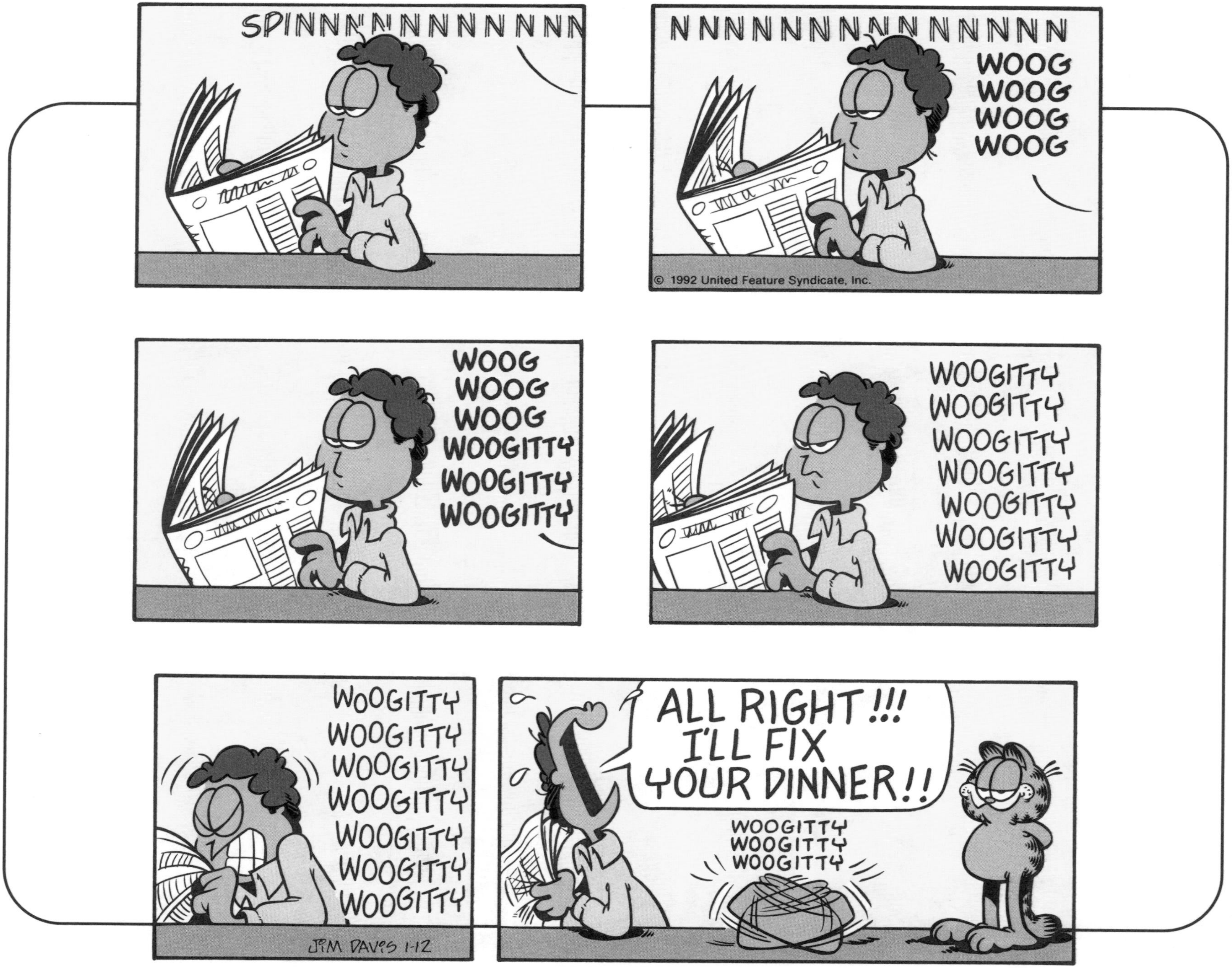
SPINNNNNNNNNNNNN
NNNNNNNNNNNNNNN
WOOG WOOG WOOG WOOG
© 1992 United Feature Syndicate, Inc.
WOOG WOOG WOOG WOOGITTY WOOGITTY WOOGITTY
WOOGITTY WOOGITTY WOOGITTY WOOGITTY WOOGITTY WOOGITTY WOOGITTY
WOOGITTY WOOGITTY WOOGITTY WOOGITTY WOOGITTY WOOGITTY WOOGITTY
JIM DAVIS 1-12
ALL RIGHT!!! I'LL FIX YOUR DINNER!!
WOOGITTY WOOGITTY WOOGITTY

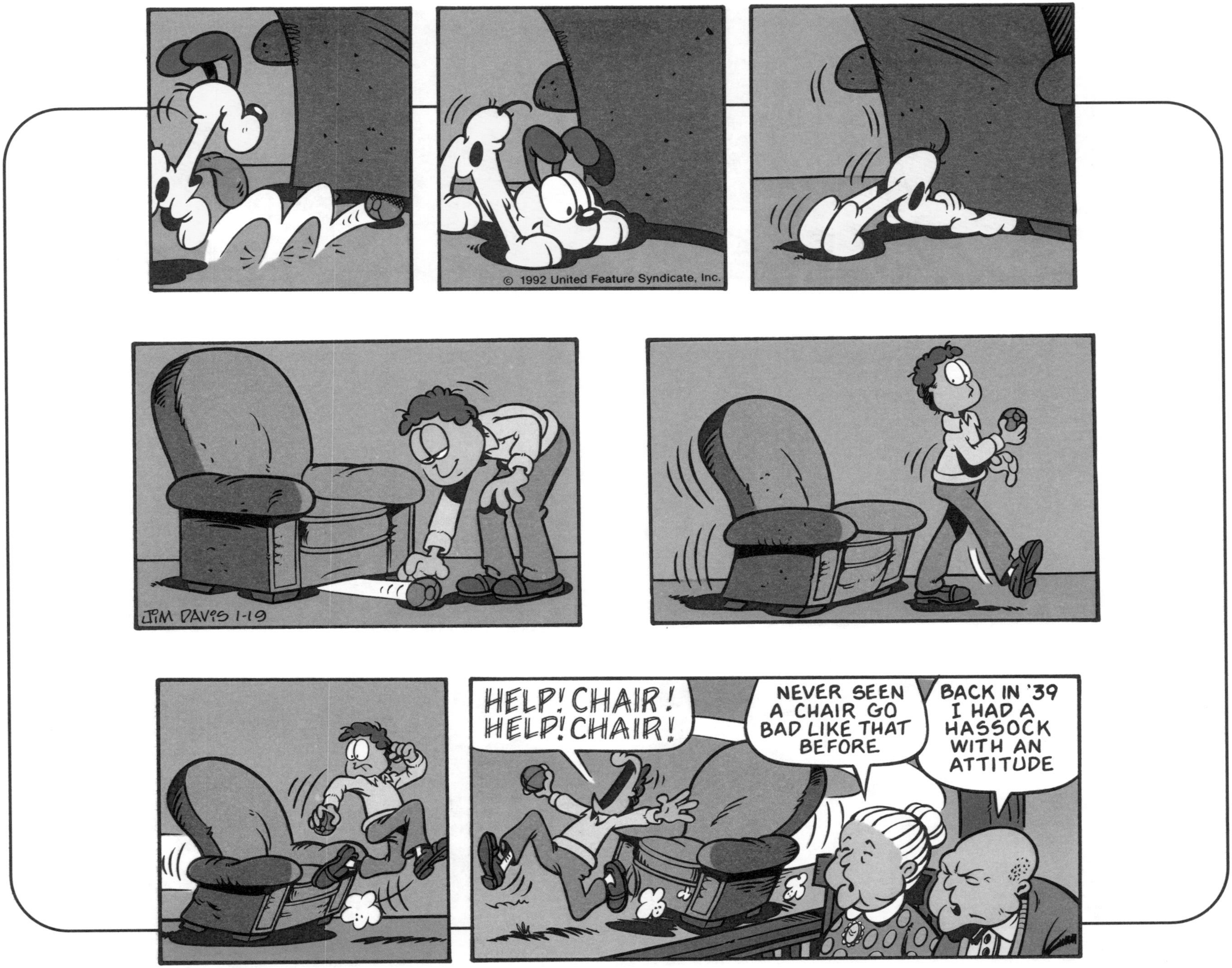
© 1992 United Feature Syndicate, Inc.
JIM DAVIS 1-19
HELP! CHAIR! HELP! CHAIR!
NEVER SEEN A CHAIR GO BAD LIKE THAT BEFORE
BACK IN '39 I HAD A HASSOCK WITH AN ATTITUDE

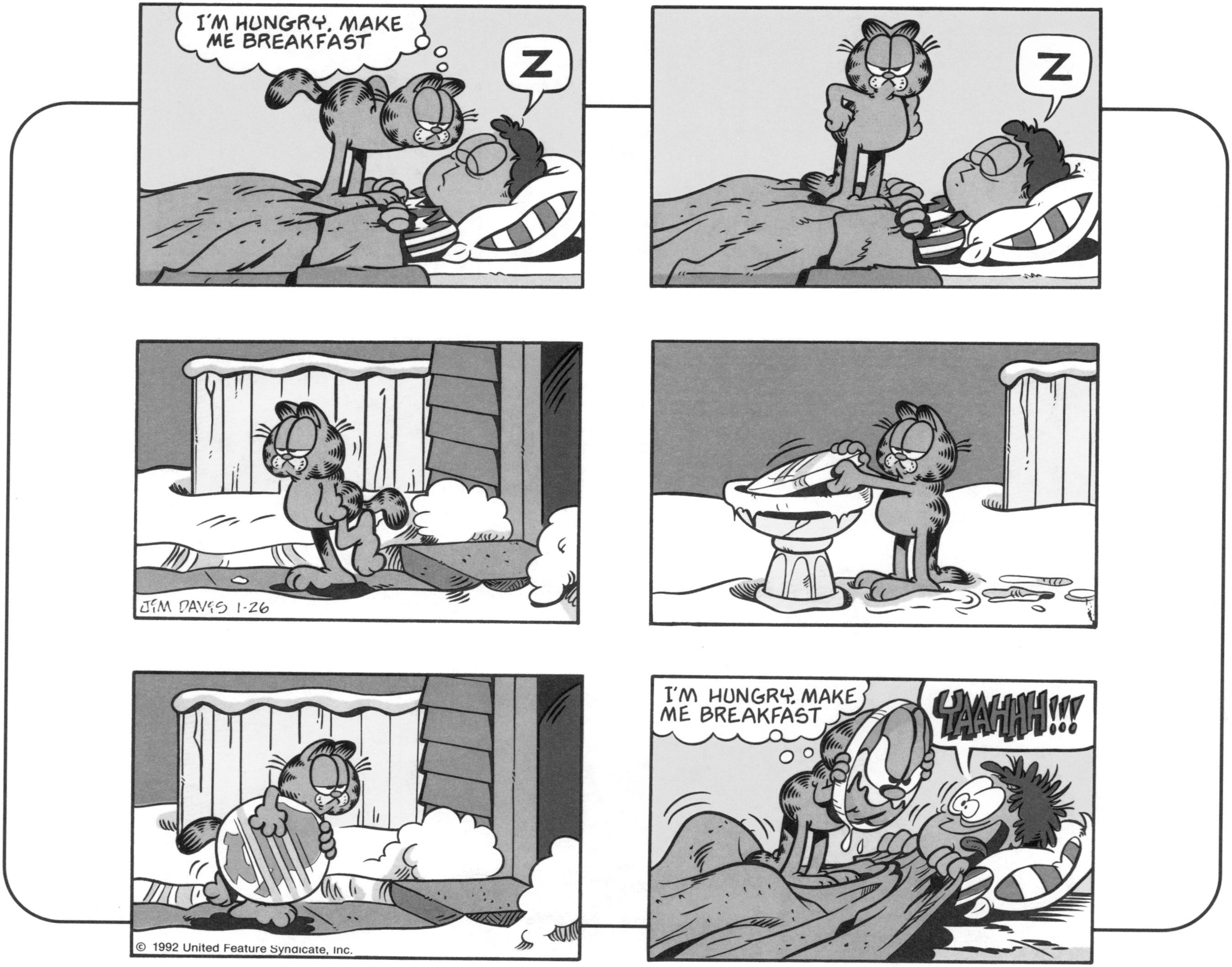
I'M HUNGRY. MAKE ME BREAKFAST
Z
Z
JIM DAVIS 1-26
I'M HUNGRY. MAKE ME BREAKFAST
YAAHHH!!!

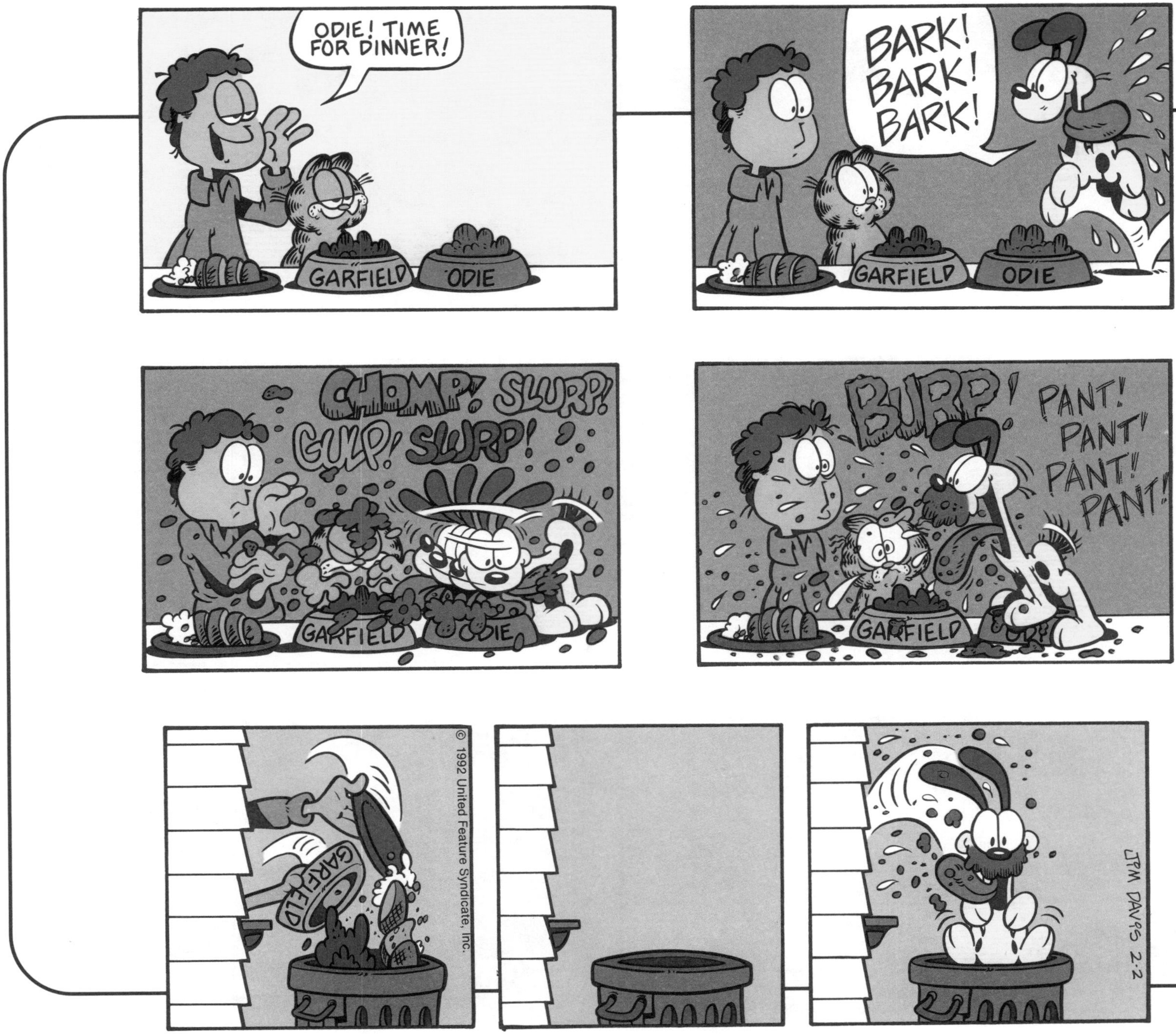
ODIE! TIME FOR DINNER!
GARFIELD
ODIE
BARK! BARK! BARK!
GARFIELD
ODIE
CHOMP! SLURP!
GULP! SLURP!
GARFIELD
ODIE
BURP!
PANT! PANT! PANT! PANT!
GARFIELD
GARFIELD
© 1992 United Feature Syndicate, Inc.
JPM DAVIS 2-2

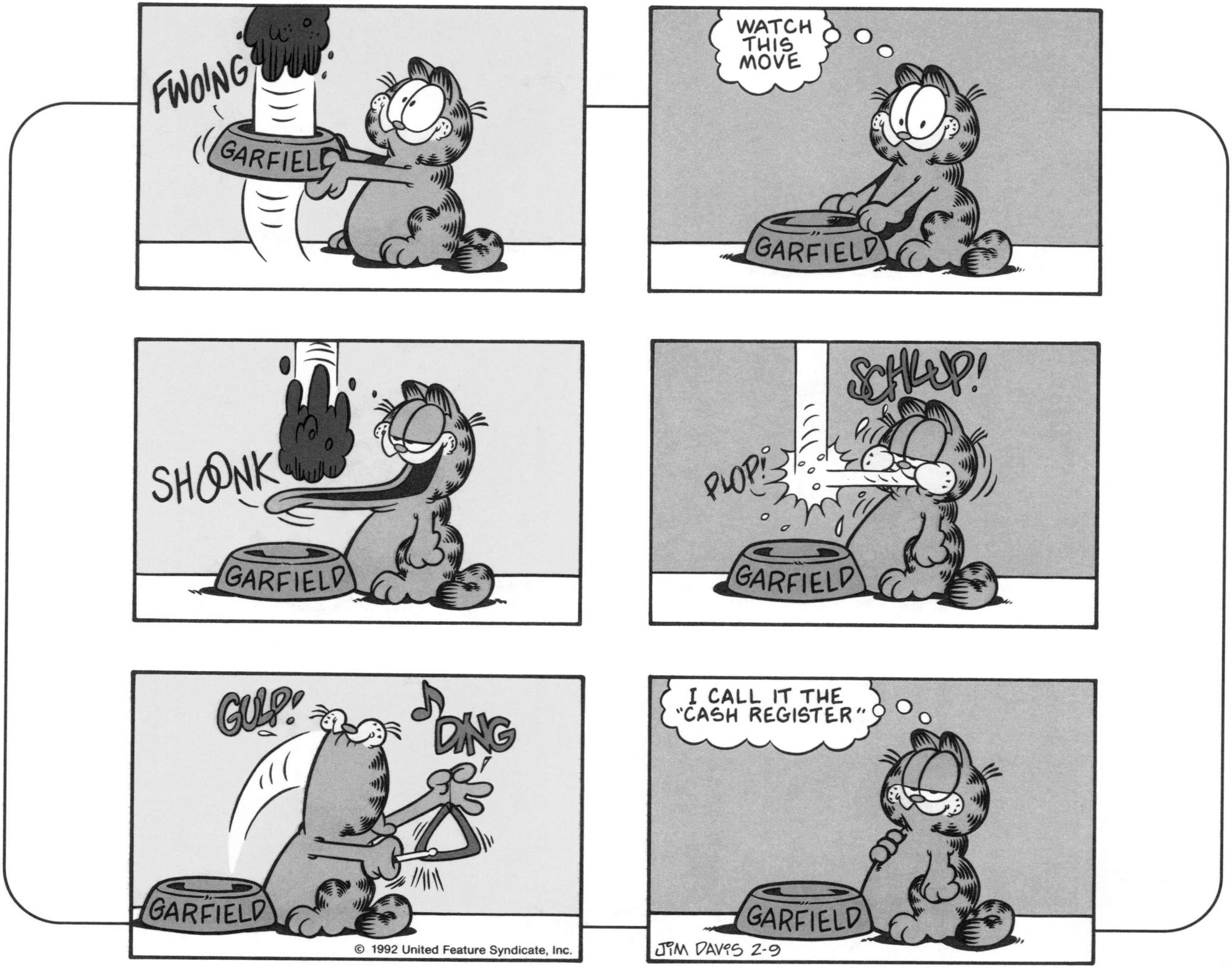
FWOING
GARFIELD
WATCH THIS MOVE
GARFIELD
SHOONK
GARFIELD
SCHLUP!
PLOP!
GARFIELD
GULP!
DING
GARFIELD
I CALL IT THE "CASH REGISTER"
GARFIELD
JIM DAVIS 2-9

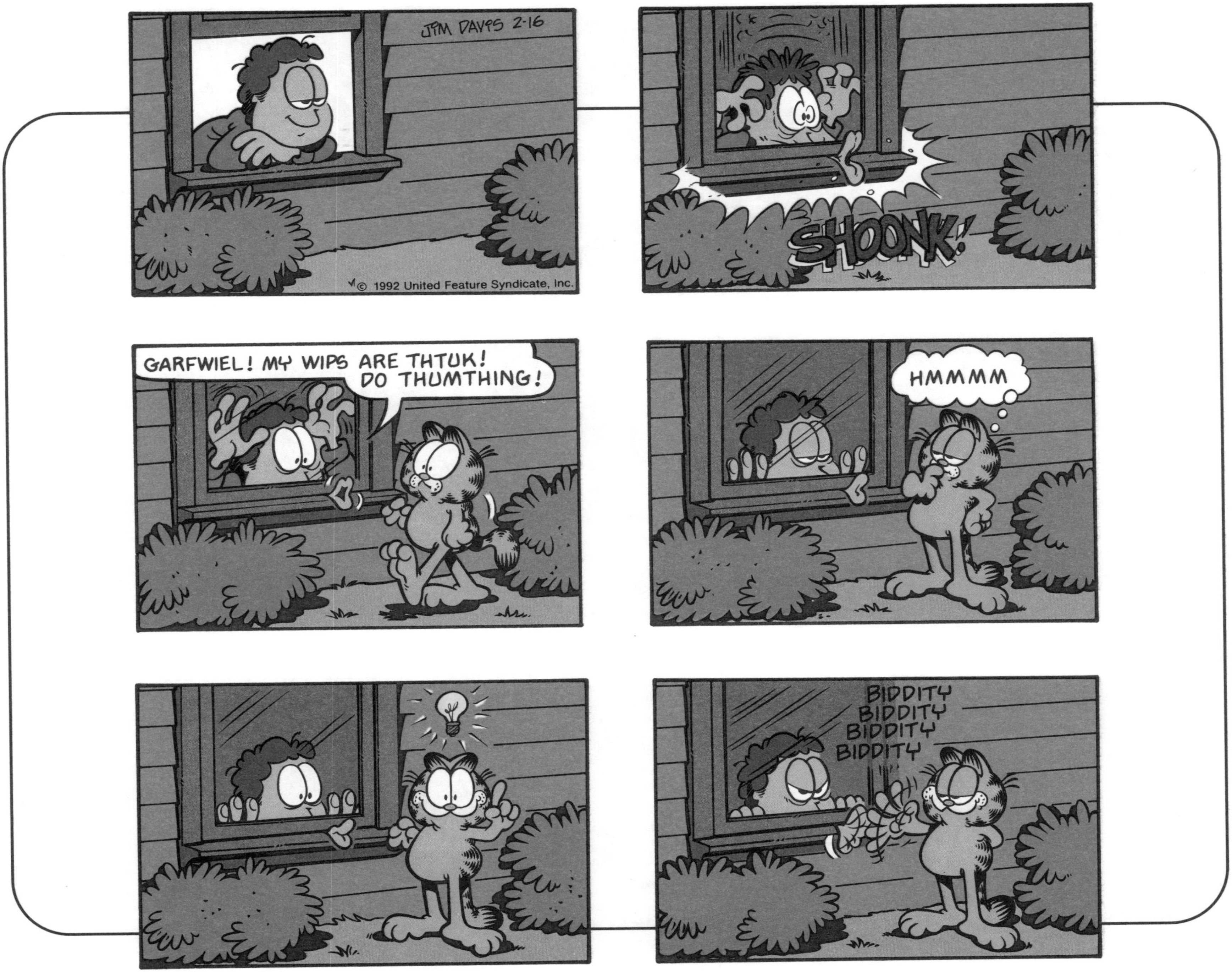
JIM DAVIS 2-16
© 1992 United Feature Syndicate, Inc.
SHOONK!
GARFWIEL! MY WIPS ARE THTUK! DO THUMTHING!
HMMMM
BIDDITY
BIDDITY
BIDDITY
BIDDITY

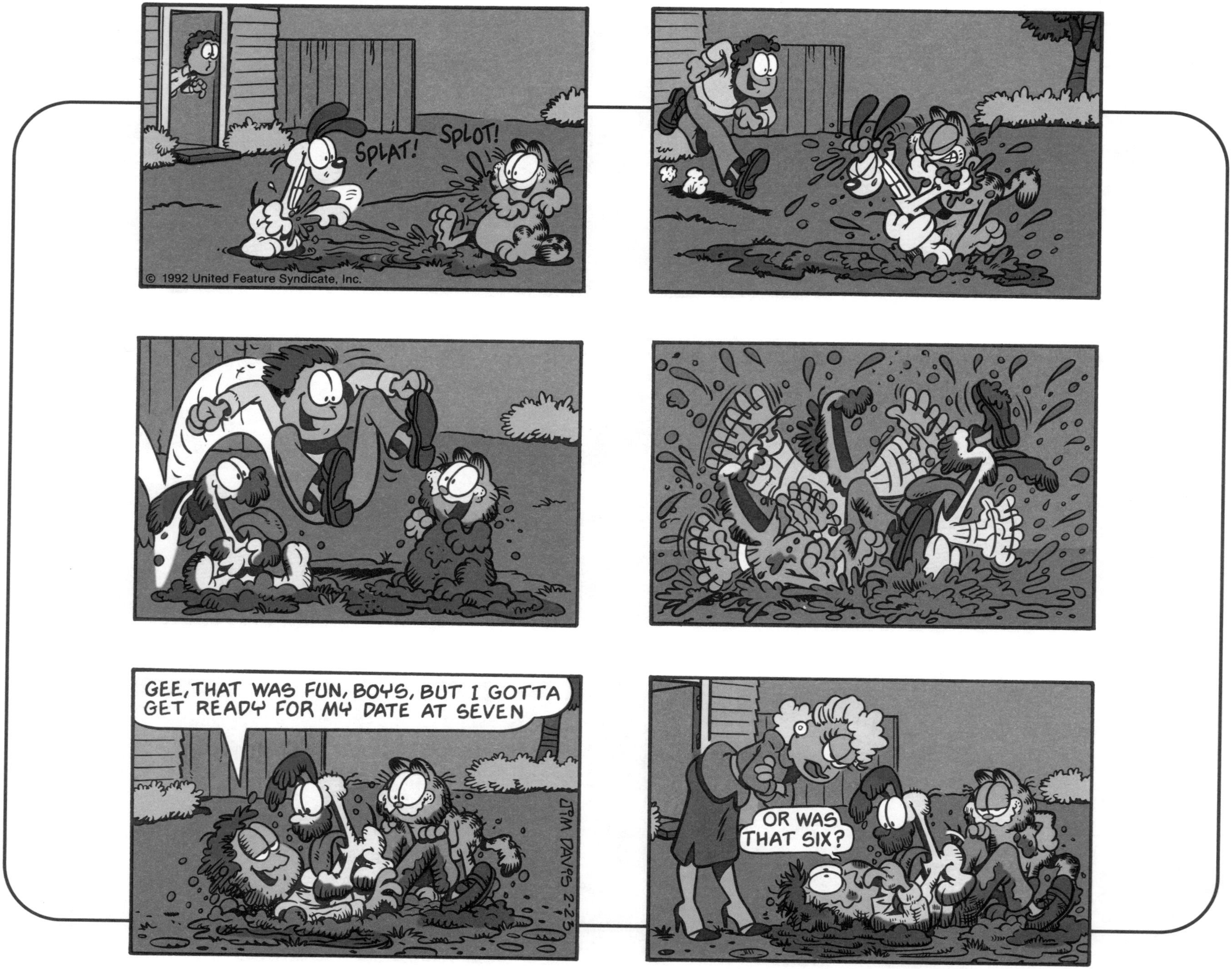
SPLAT!
SPLOT!
© 1992 United Feature Syndicate, Inc.
GEE, THAT WAS FUN, BOYS, BUT I GOTTA GET READY FOR MY DATE AT SEVEN
JIM DAVIS 2-23
OR WAS THAT SIX?

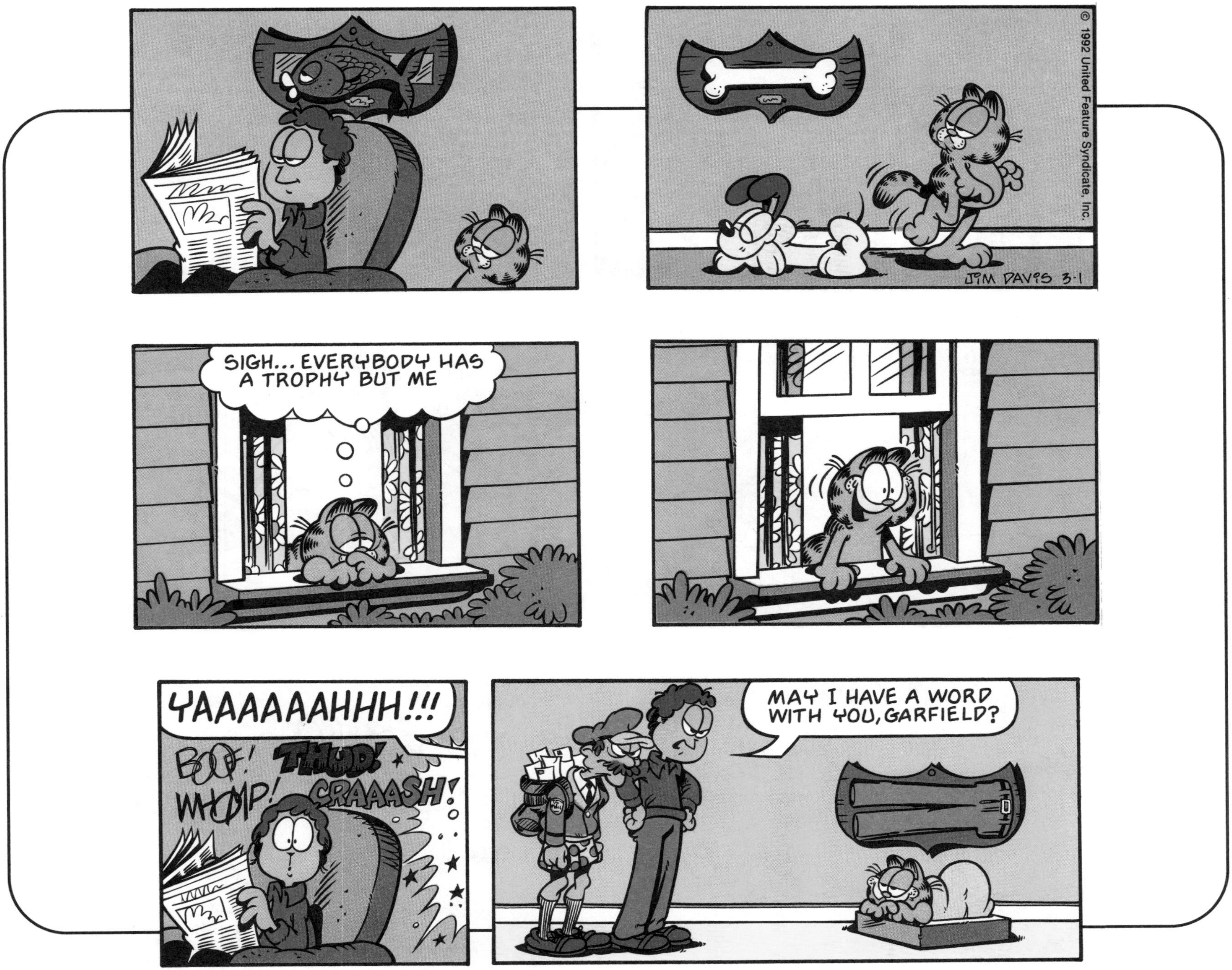
© 1992 United Feature Syndicate, Inc.
JIM DAVIS 3-1
SIGH... EVERYBODY HAS A TROPHY BUT ME
YAAAAAAHHH!!!
BOOF! THUD! WHOMP! CRAAASH!
MAY I HAVE A WORD WITH YOU, GARFIELD?

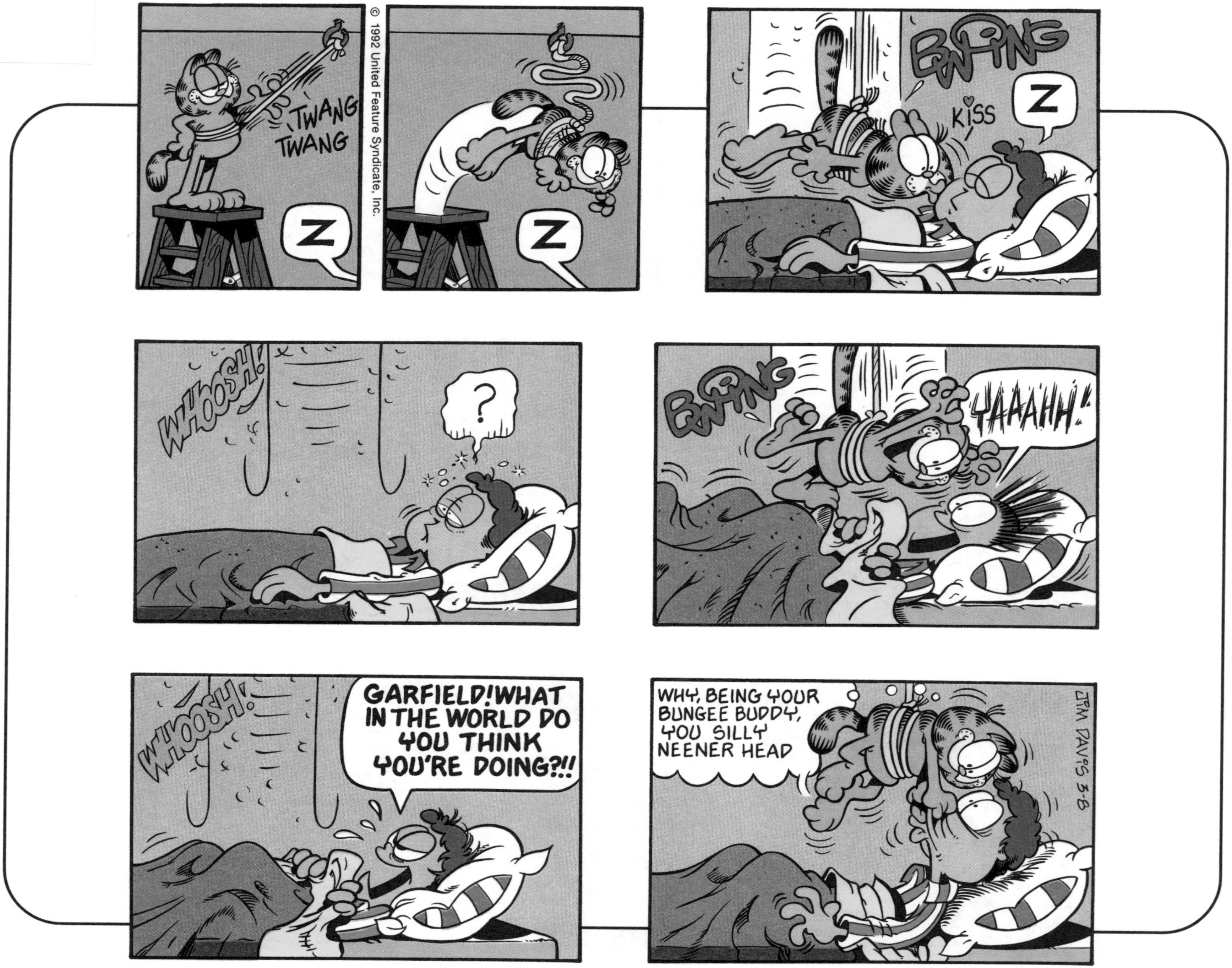
TWANG
TWANG
Z
© 1992 United Feature Syndicate, Inc.
Z
BWING
KISS
Z
WHOOSH!
?
BWING
YAAAHH!
WHOOSH!
GARFIELD! WHAT IN THE WORLD DO YOU THINK YOU'RE DOING?!!
WHY, BEING YOUR BUNGEE BUDDY, YOU SILLY NEENER HEAD
JIM DAVIS 3-8

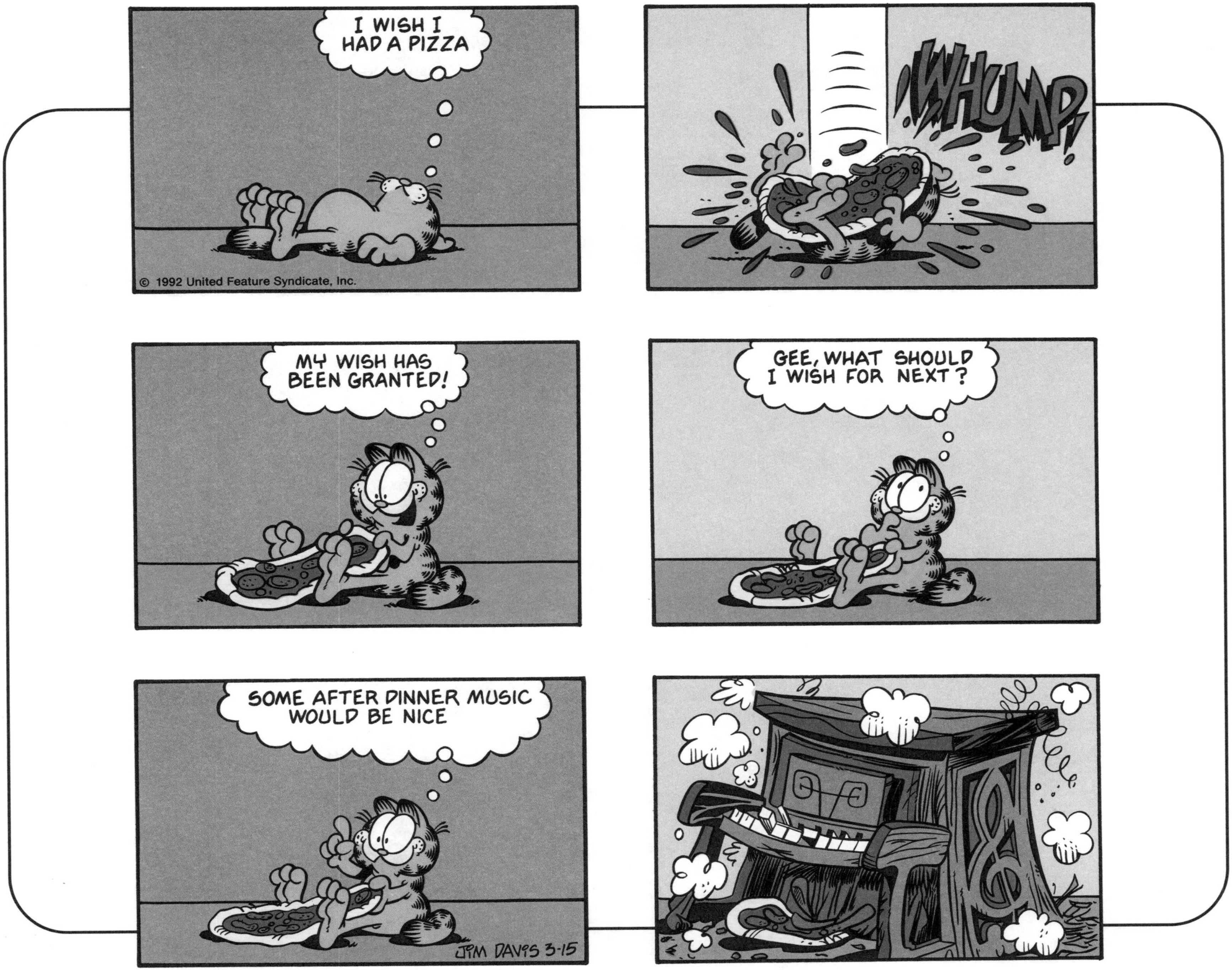
I WISH I HAD A PIZZA
© 1992 United Feature Syndicate, Inc.
WHUMP!
MY WISH HAS BEEN GRANTED!
GEE, WHAT SHOULD I WISH FOR NEXT?
SOME AFTER DINNER MUSIC WOULD BE NICE
JIM DAVIS 3-15

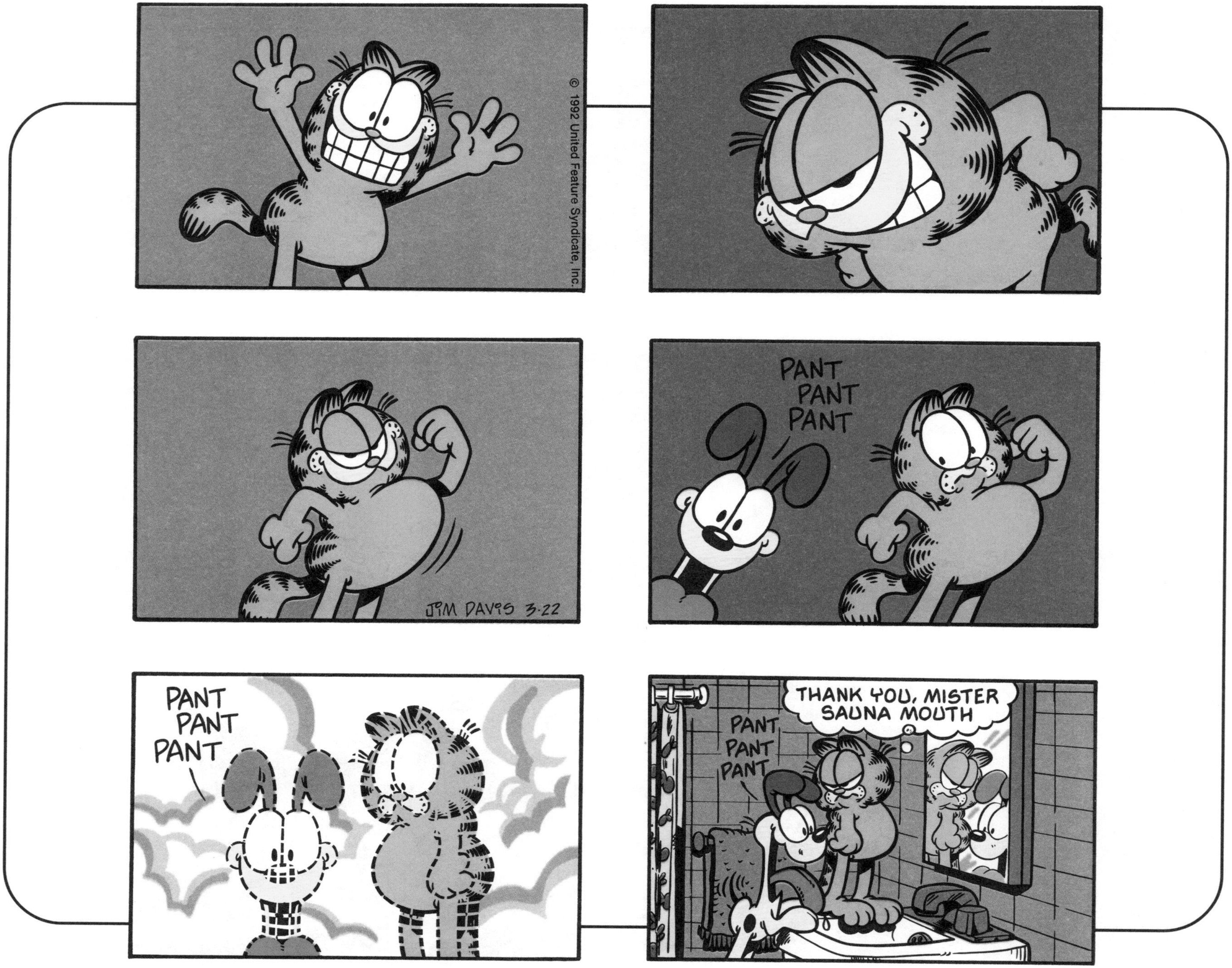
© 1992 United Feature Syndicate, Inc.
JIM DAVIS 3-22
PANT PANT PANT
PANT PANT PANT
PANT PANT PANT
THANK YOU, MISTER SAUNA MOUTH

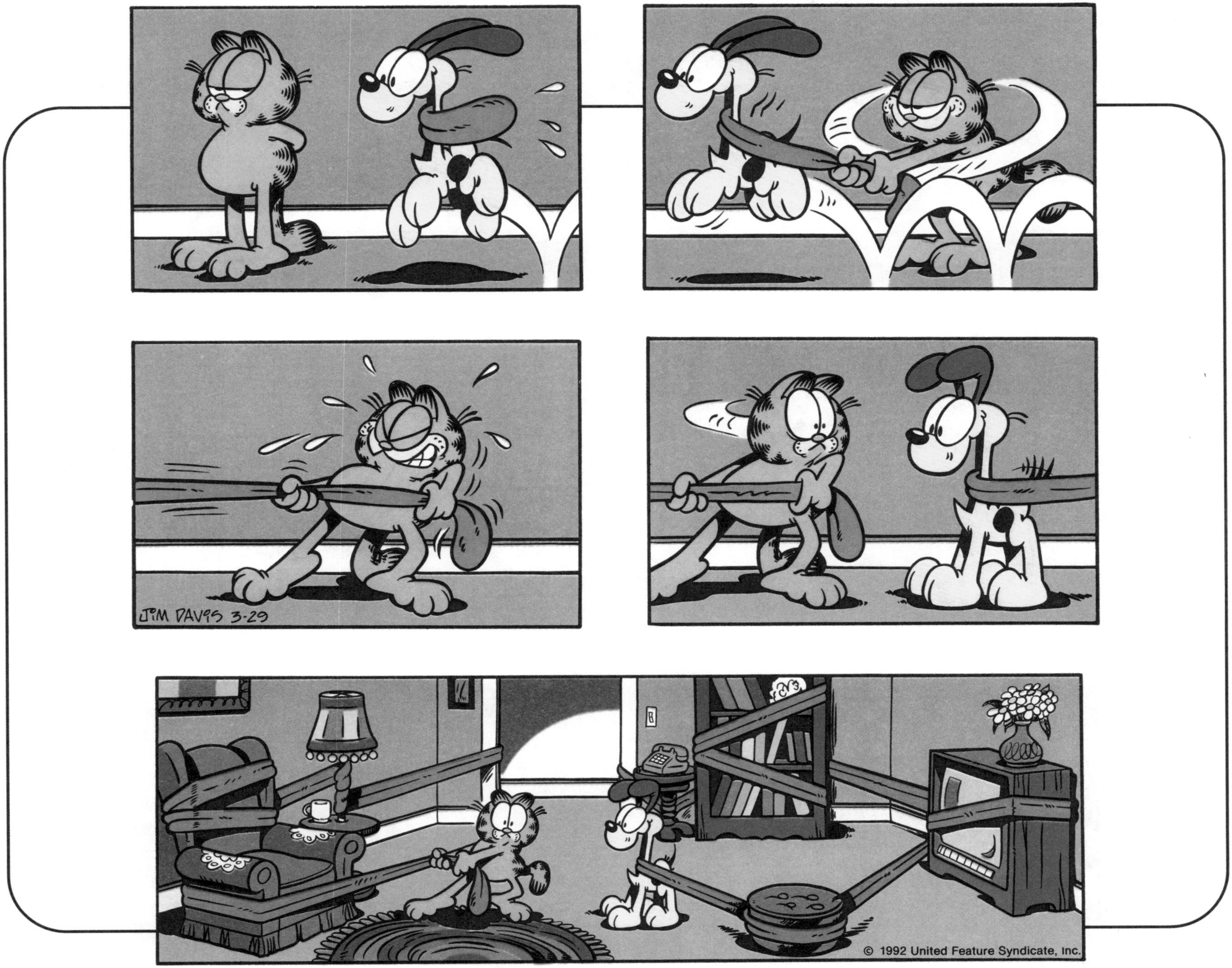
JIM DAVIS 3-29
© 1992 United Feature Syndicate, Inc.

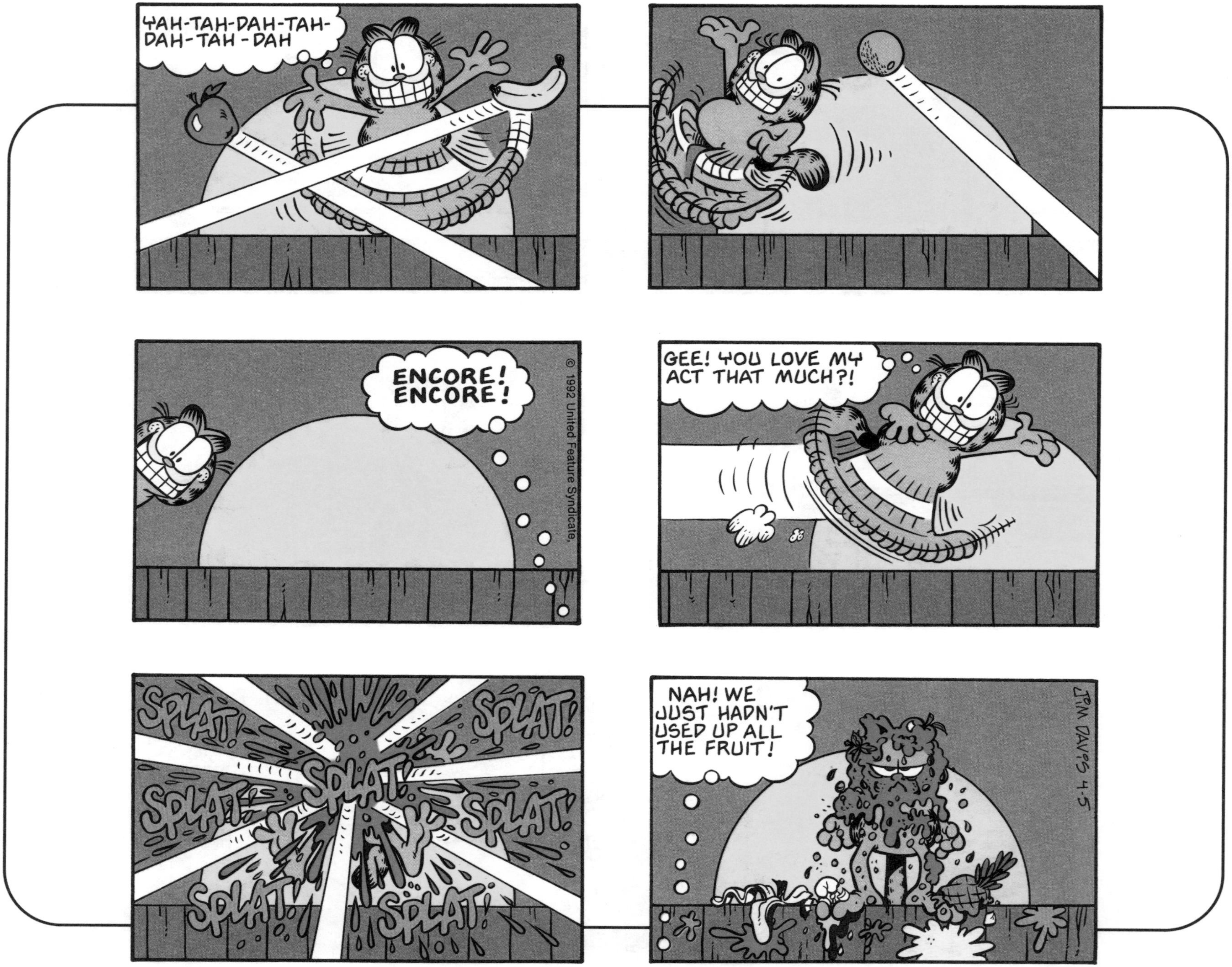
YAH-TAH-DAH-TAH-DAH-TAH-DAH
ENCORE! ENCORE!
© 1992 United Feature Syndicate,
GEE! YOU LOVE MY ACT THAT MUCH?!
SPLAT! SPLAT! SPLAT! SPLAT! SPLAT! SPLAT! SPLAT!
NAH! WE JUST HADN'T USED UP ALL THE FRUIT!
JIM DAVIS 4-5

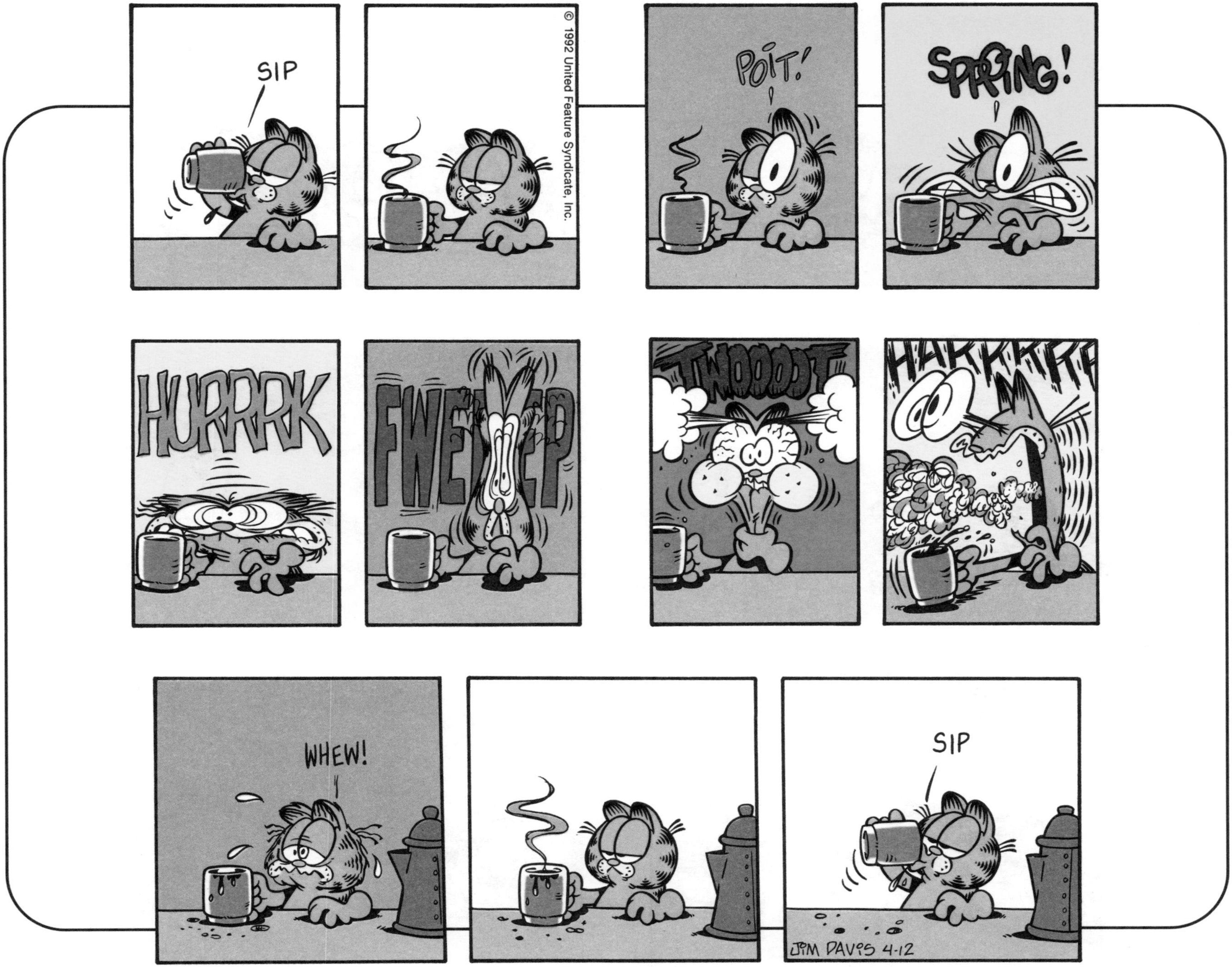
SIP
© 1992 United Feature Syndicate, Inc.
POIT!
SPROING!
HURRRK
TWOOOOT
WHEW!
SIP
JIM DAVIS 4-12

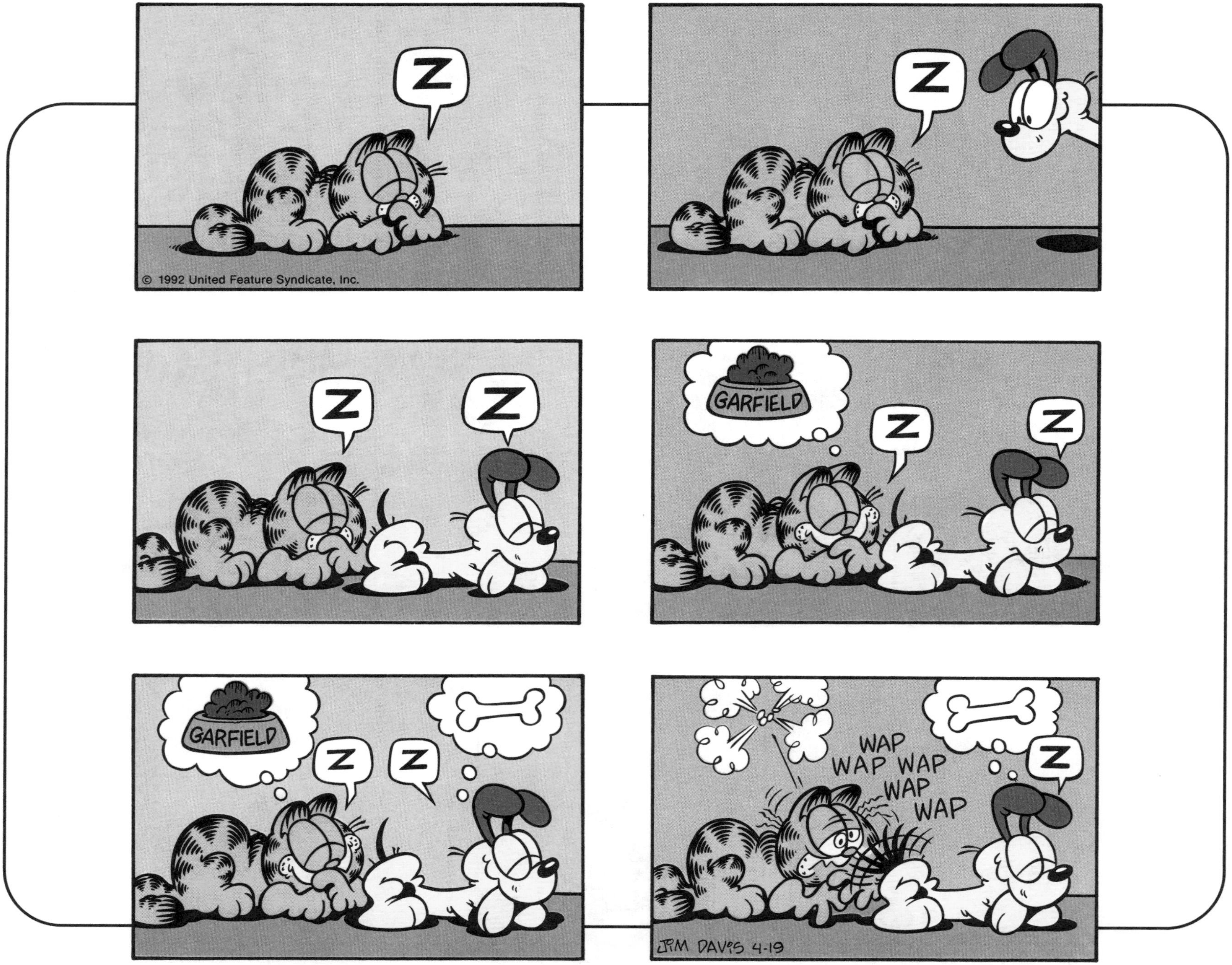
Z
© 1992 United Feature Syndicate, Inc.
Z
Z
Z
GARFIELD
Z
Z
GARFIELD
Z
Z
WAP
WAP WAP WAP
WAP
WAP
Z
JIM DAVIS 4-19

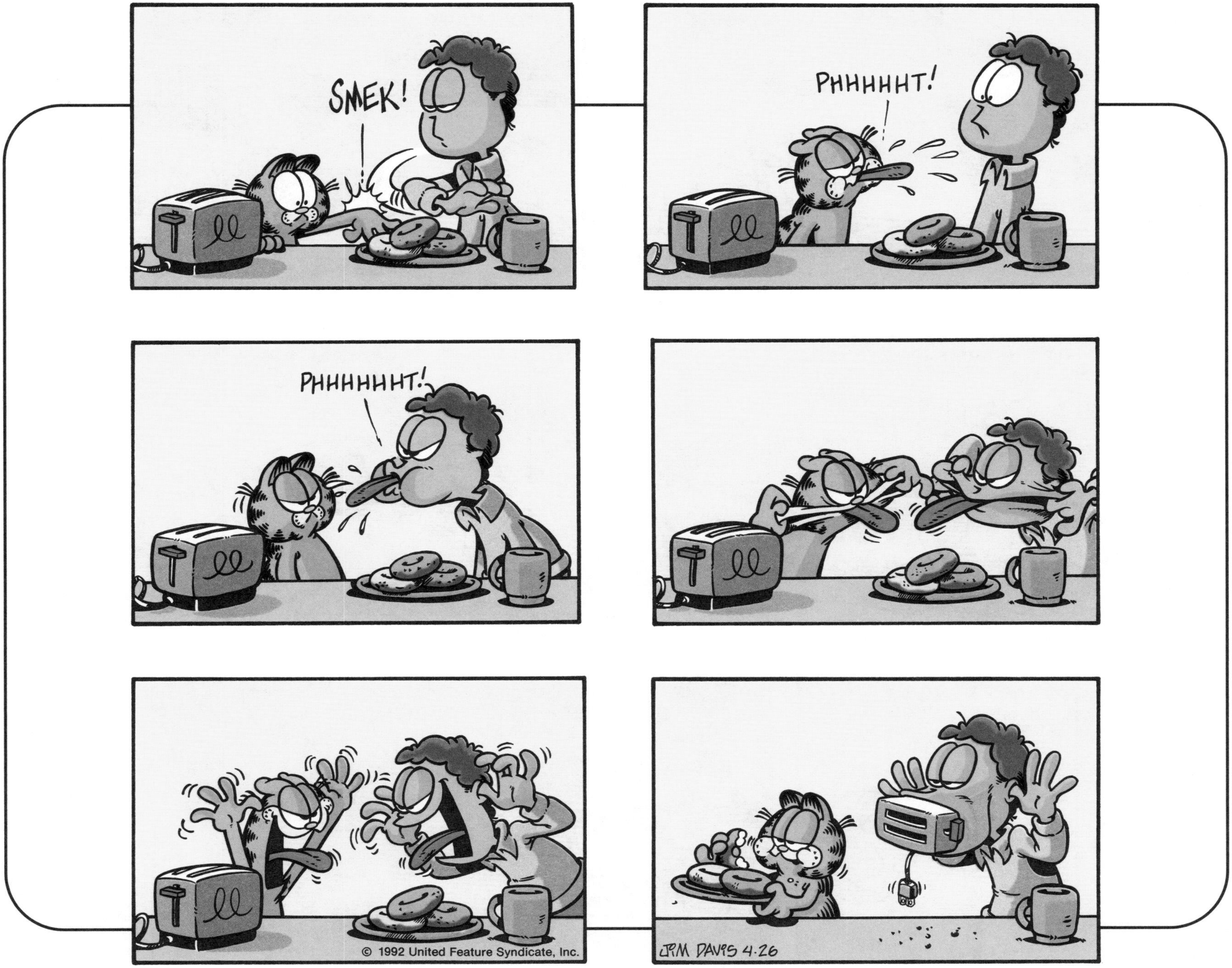
SMEK!
PHHHHHT!
PHHHHHHT!
© 1992 United Feature Syndicate, Inc.
JIM DAVIS 4·26

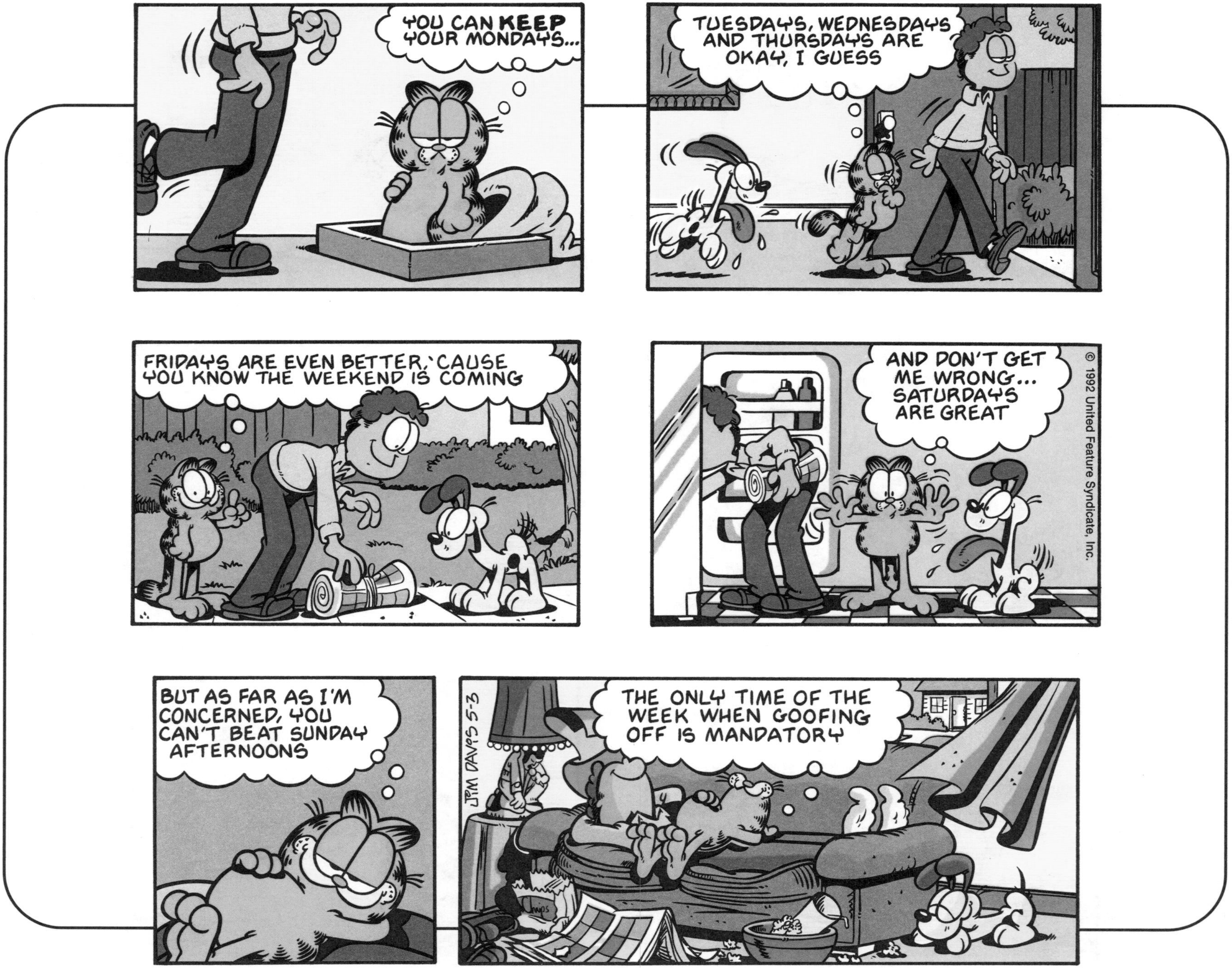
YOU CAN KEEP YOUR MONDAYS...
TUESDAYS, WEDNESDAYS AND THURSDAYS ARE OKAY, I GUESS
FRIDAYS ARE EVEN BETTER, 'CAUSE YOU KNOW THE WEEKEND IS COMING
AND DON'T GET ME WRONG... SATURDAYS ARE GREAT
© 1992 United Feature Syndicate, Inc.
BUT AS FAR AS I'M CONCERNED, YOU CAN'T BEAT SUNDAY AFTERNOONS
JPM DAVPS 5-3
THE ONLY TIME OF THE WEEK WHEN GOOFING OFF IS MANDATORY

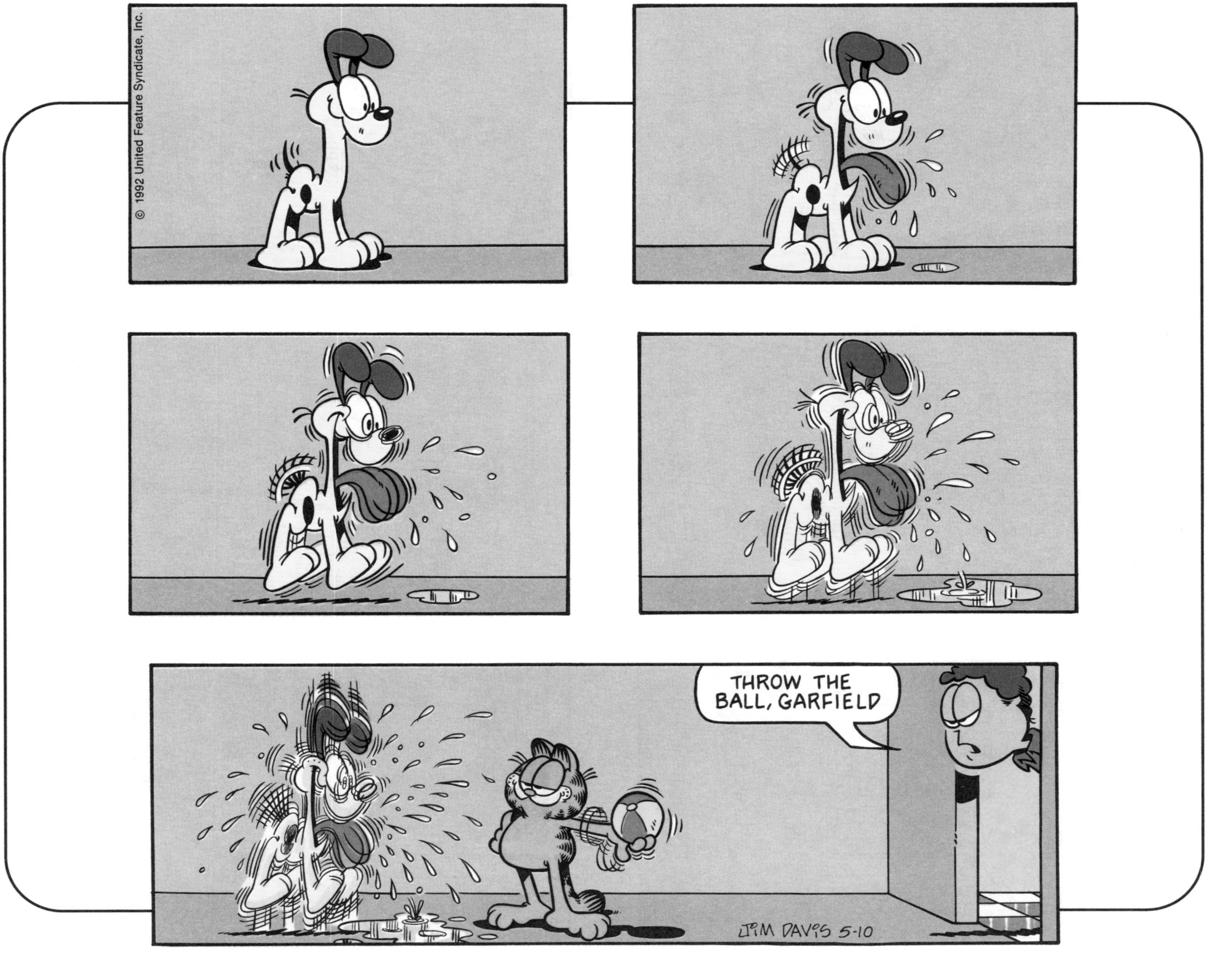
© 1992 United Feature Syndicate, Inc.
THROW THE BALL, GARFIELD
JIM DAVIS 5-10

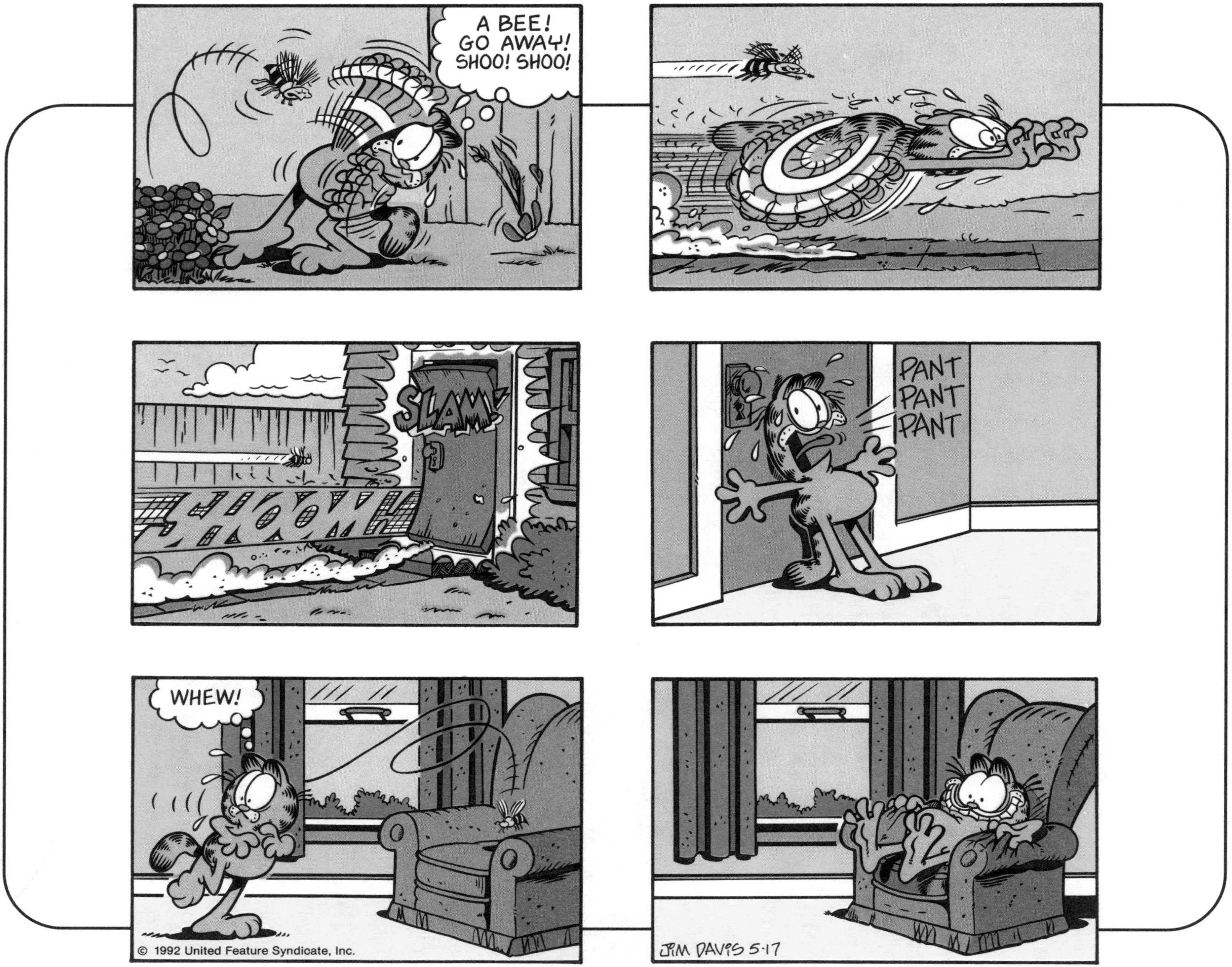
A BEE! GO AWAY! SHOO! SHOO!
SLAM!
SHOOM!
PANT PANT PANT
WHEW!
© 1992 United Feature Syndicate, Inc.
JIM DAVIS 5-17

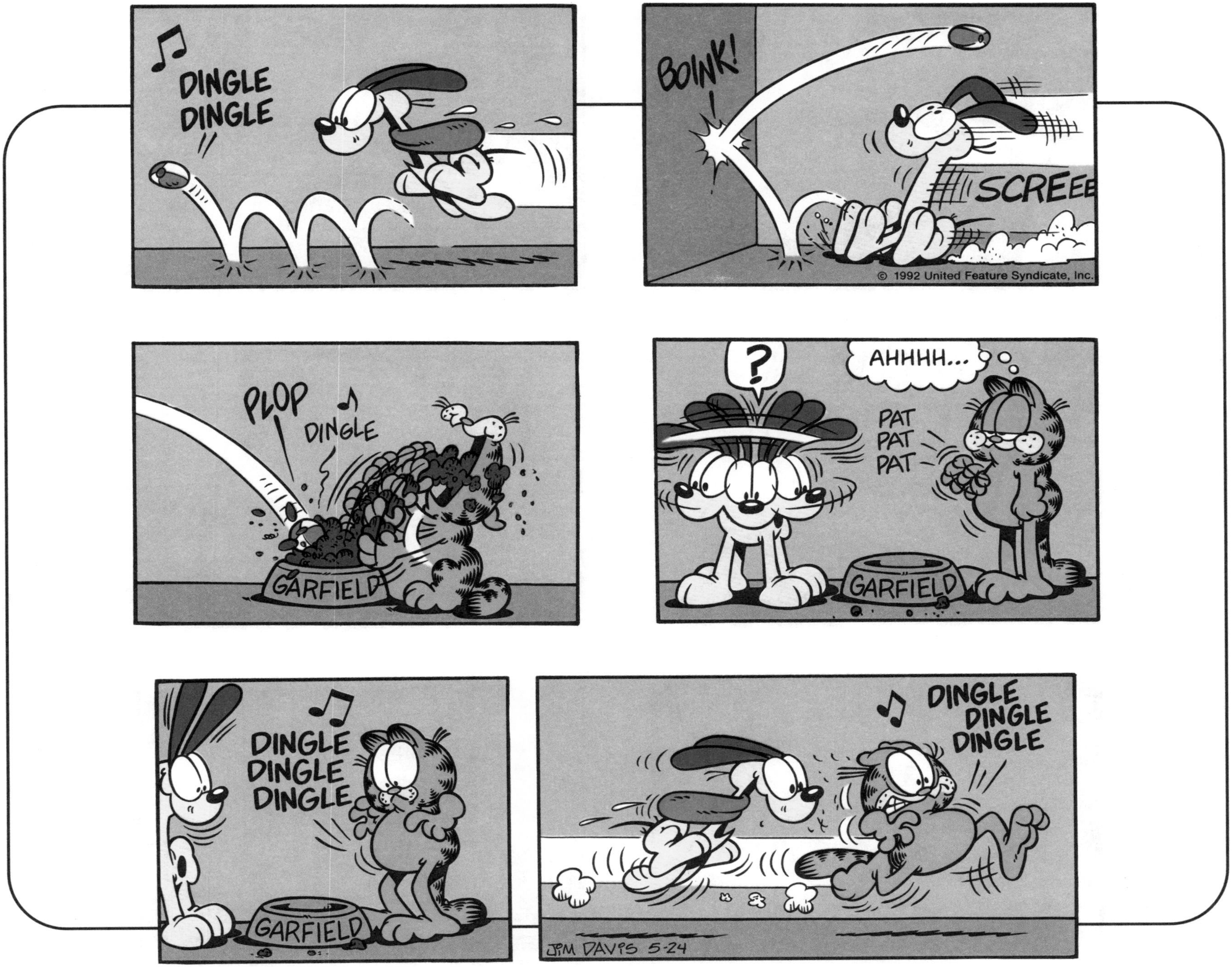

DINGLE DINGLE
BOINK!
SCREEE
© 1992 United Feature Syndicate, Inc.
PLOP
DINGLE
GARFIELD
?
AHHHH...
PAT PAT PAT
GARFIELD
DINGLE DINGLE DINGLE
GARFIELD
DINGLE DINGLE DINGLE
JIM DAVIS 5-24

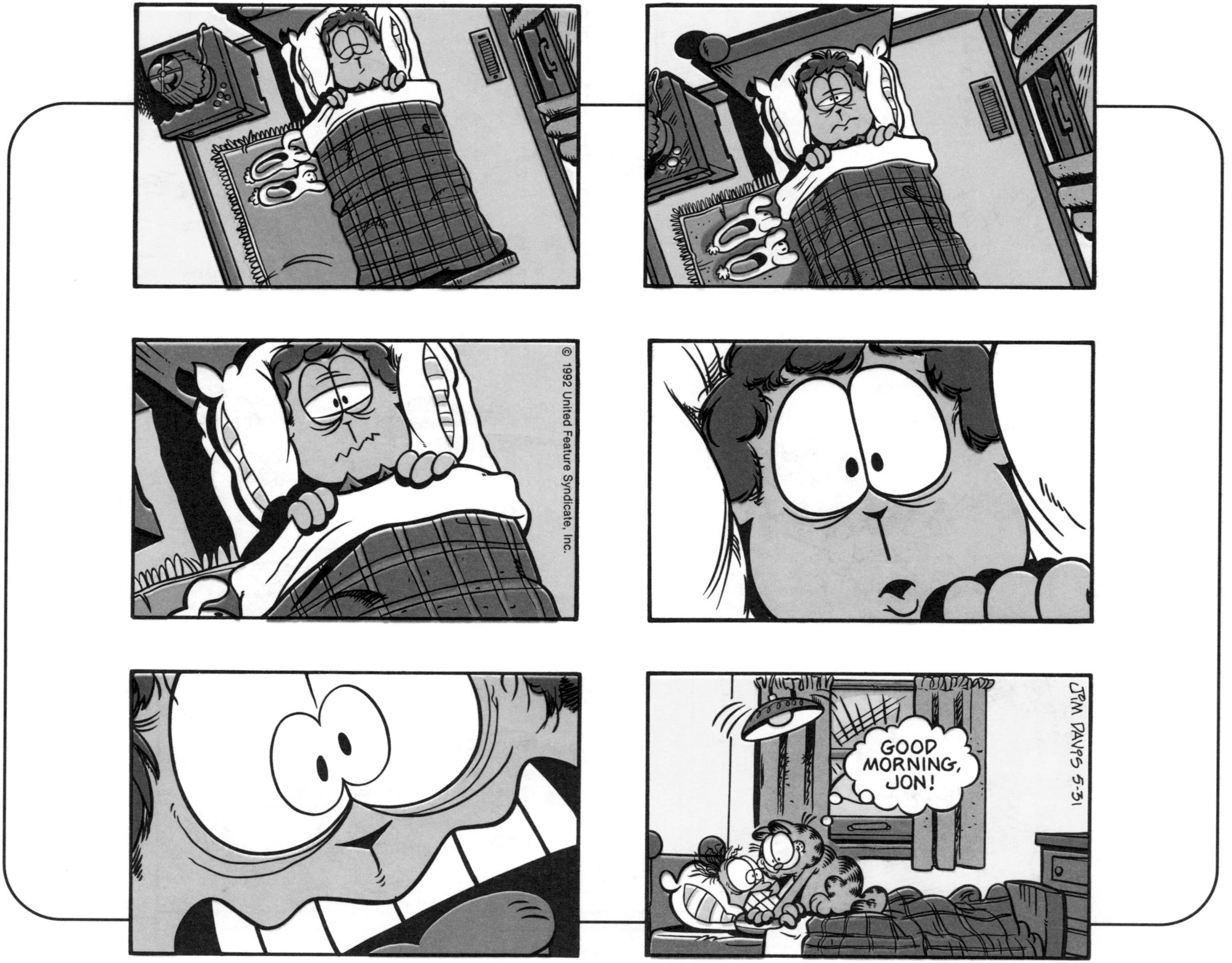
© 1992 United Feature Syndicate, Inc.
GOOD MORNING, JON!
JIM DAVIS 5-31

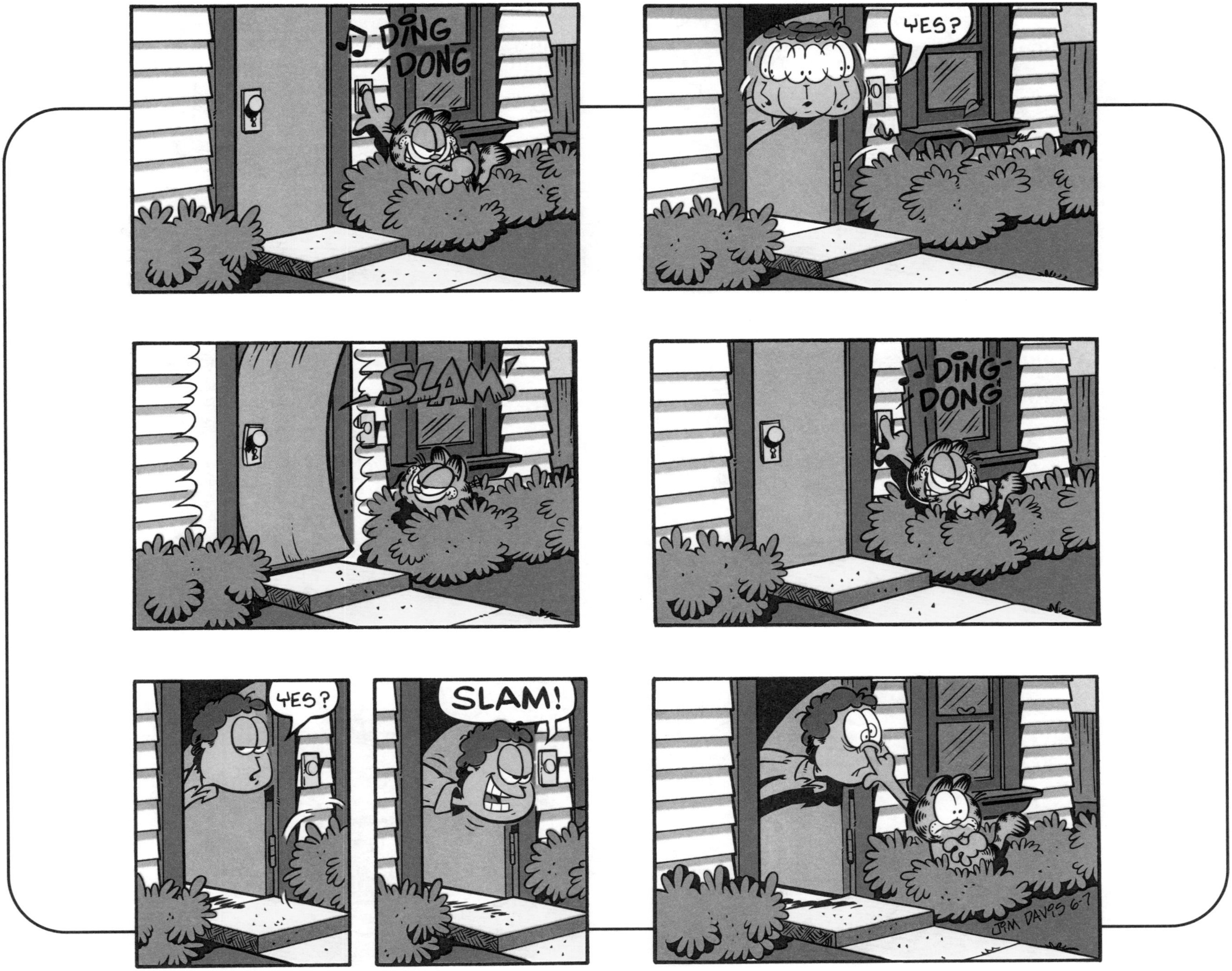
DING DONG
YES?
SLAM
DING-DONG
YES?
SLAM!
JIM DAVIS 6-7

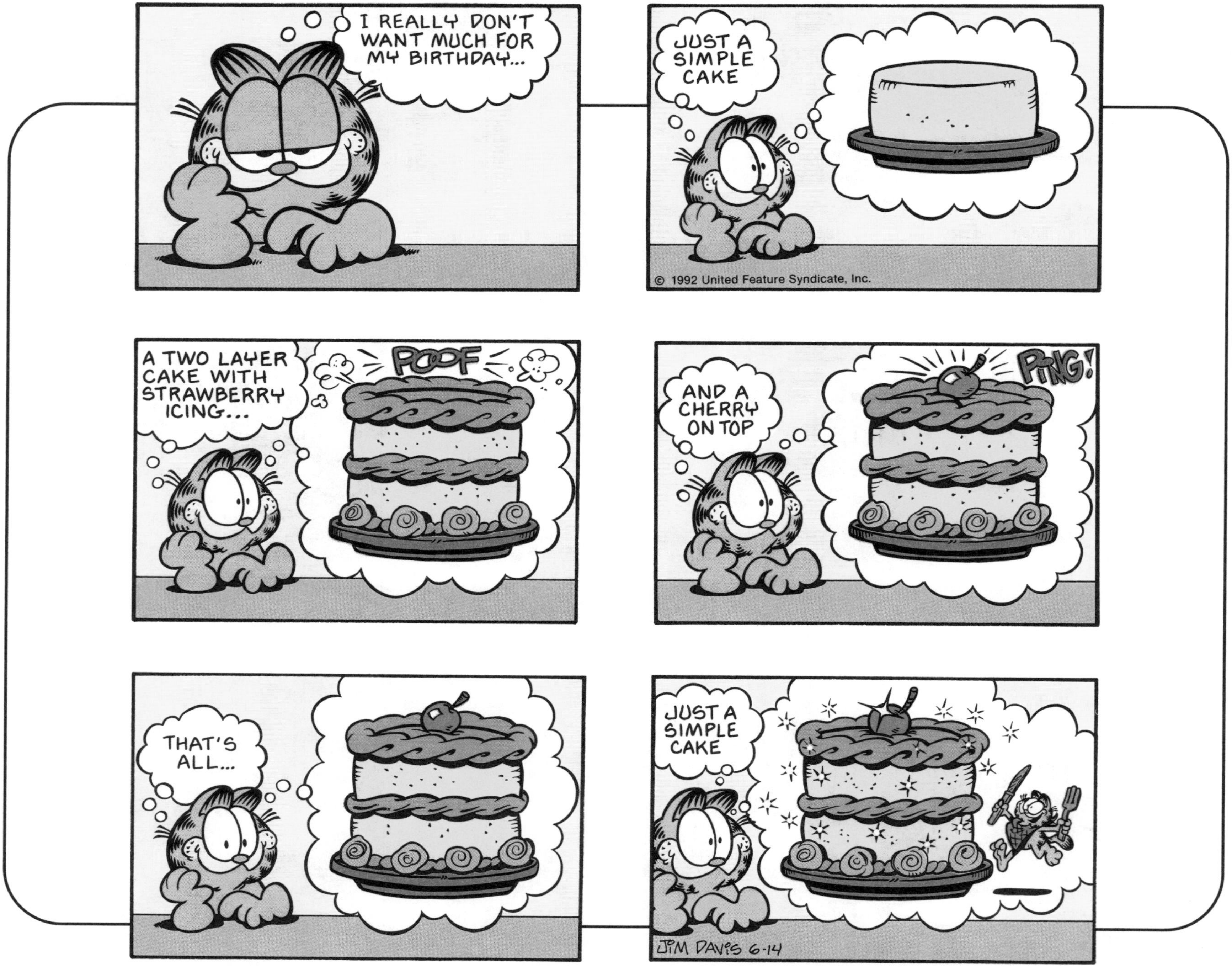
I REALLY DON'T WANT MUCH FOR MY BIRTHDAY...
JUST A SIMPLE CAKE
© 1992 United Feature Syndicate, Inc.
A TWO LAYER CAKE WITH STRAWBERRY ICING...
POOF
AND A CHERRY ON TOP
PING!
THAT'S ALL...
JUST A SIMPLE CAKE
JIM DAVIS 6-14

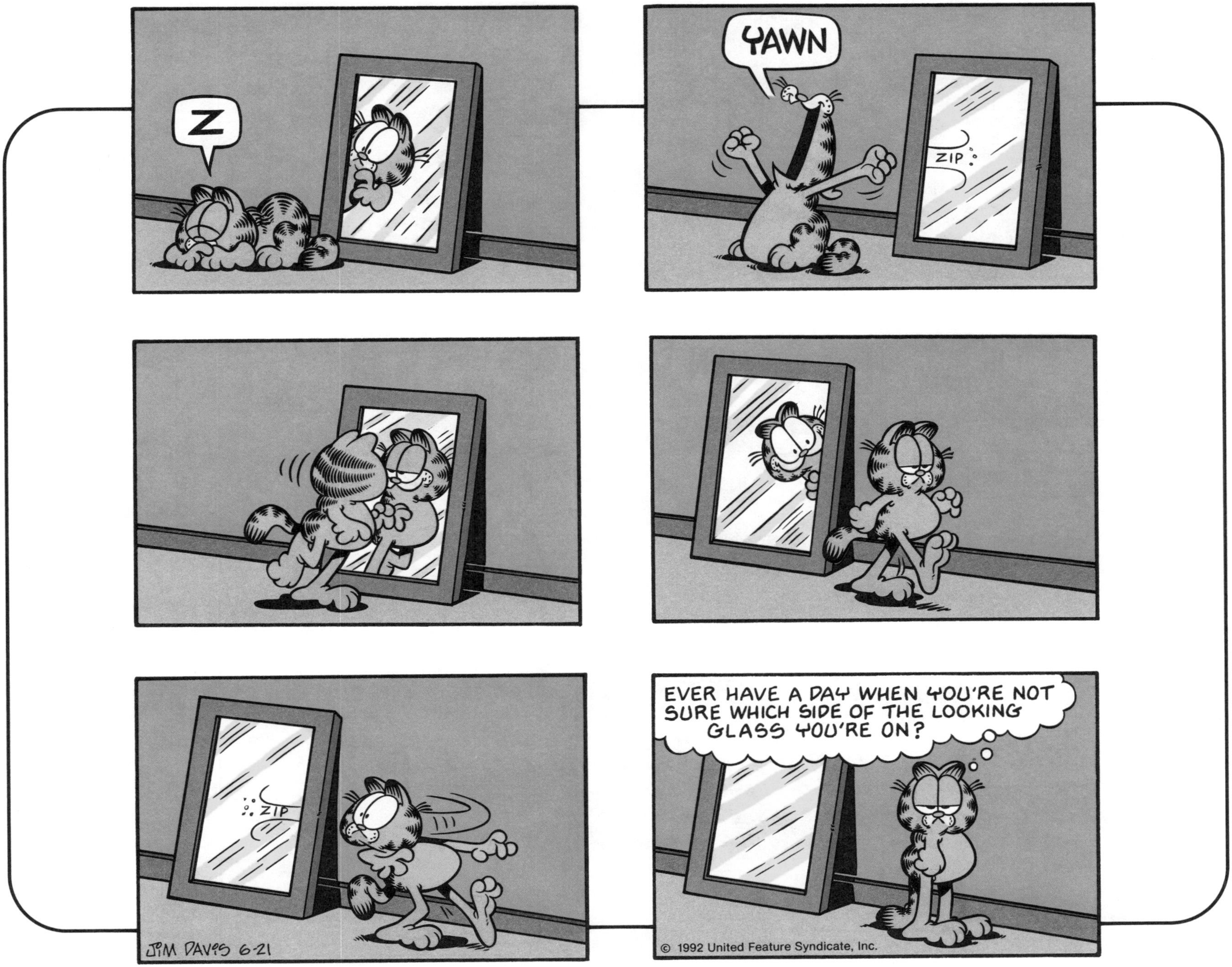
Z
YAWN
ZIP
ZIP
EVER HAVE A DAY WHEN YOU'RE NOT SURE WHICH SIDE OF THE LOOKING GLASS YOU'RE ON?
JIM DAVIS 6-21
© 1992 United Feature Syndicate, Inc.

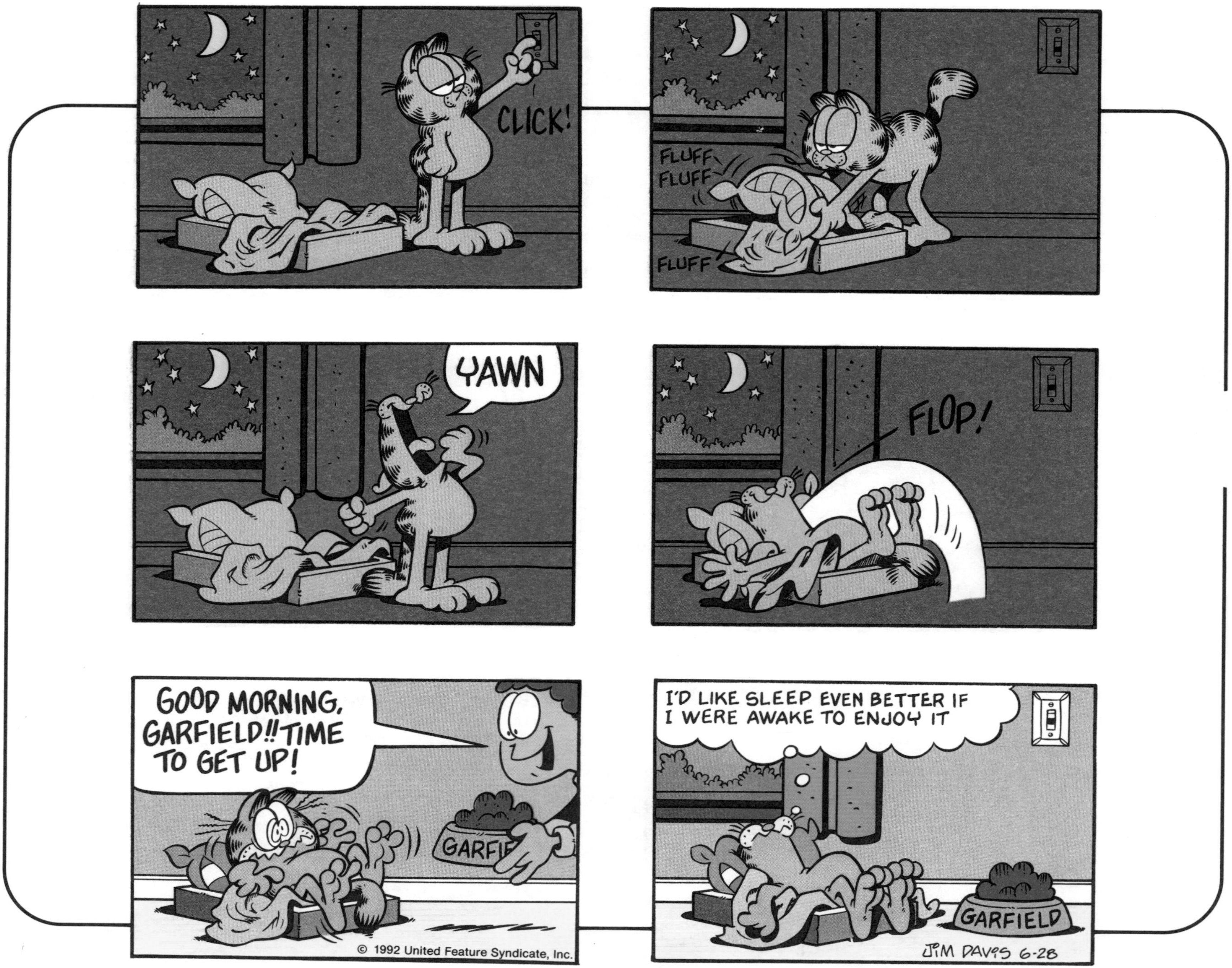
CLICK!
FLUFF FLUFF FLUFF
YAWN
FLOP!
GOOD MORNING, GARFIELD!! TIME TO GET UP!
GARFIE
I'D LIKE SLEEP EVEN BETTER IF I WERE AWAKE TO ENJOY IT
GARFIELD
JIM DAVIS 6-28

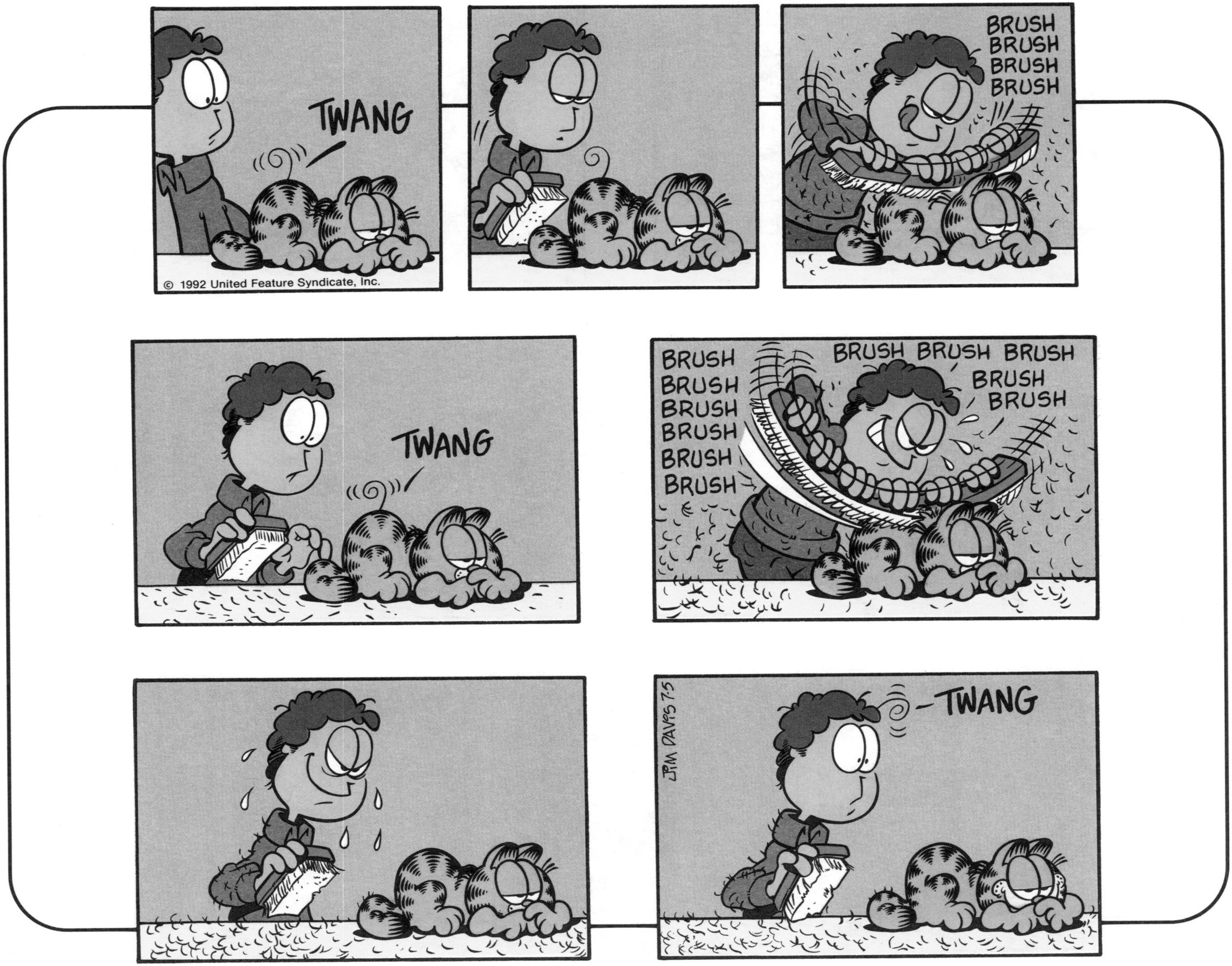

TWANG
BRUSH
BRUSH
BRUSH
BRUSH
TWANG
BRUSH
BRUSH
BRUSH
BRUSH
BRUSH
BRUSH
BRUSH BRUSH BRUSH
BRUSH
BRUSH
TWANG
JPM DAVPS 7-5

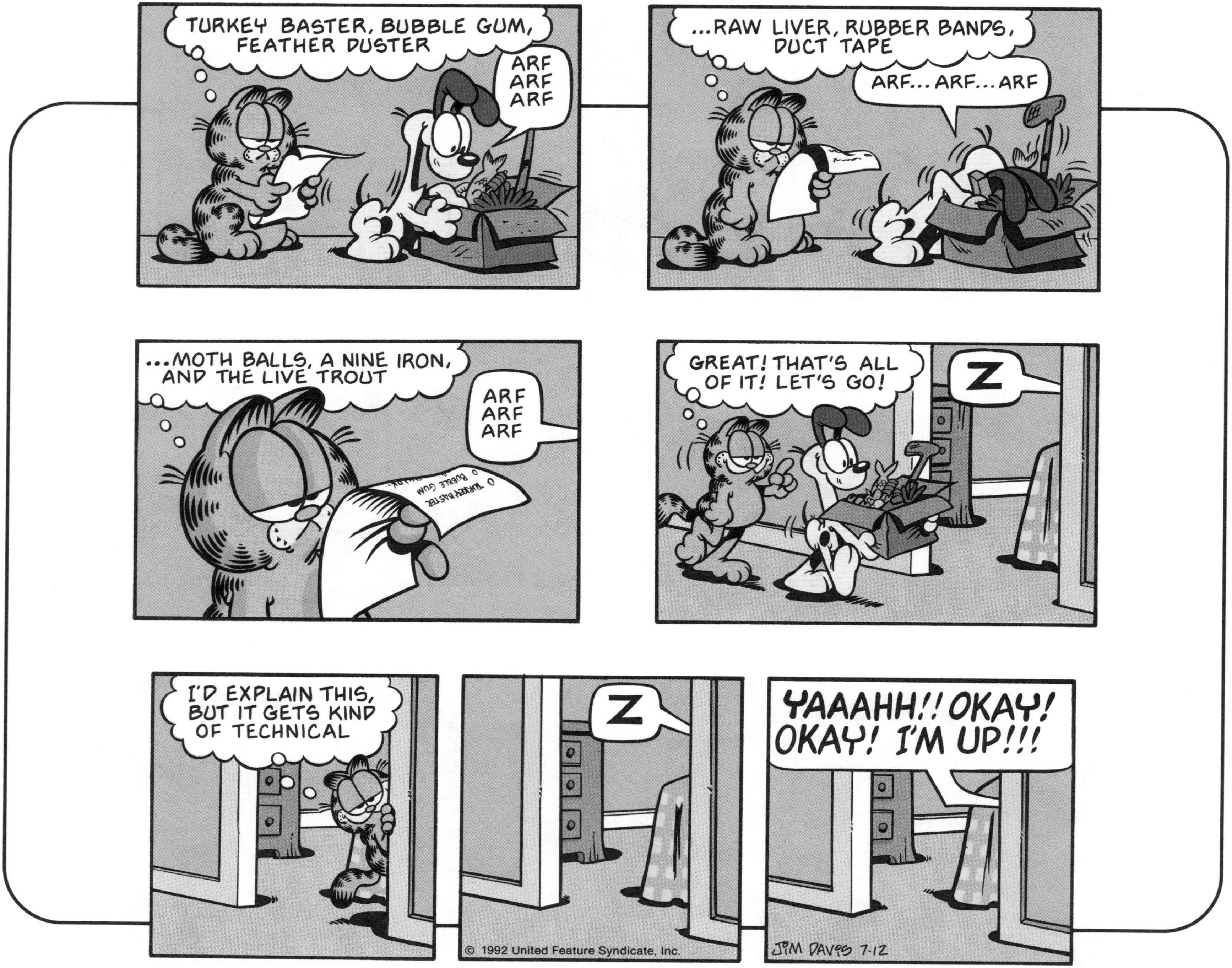
TURKEY BASTER, BUBBLE GUM, FEATHER DUSTER
ARF ARF ARF
...RAW LIVER, RUBBER BANDS, DUCT TAPE
ARF... ARF... ARF
...MOTH BALLS, A NINE IRON, AND THE LIVE TROUT
ARF ARF ARF
GREAT! THAT'S ALL OF IT! LET'S GO!
Z
I'D EXPLAIN THIS, BUT IT GETS KIND OF TECHNICAL
Z
YAAAHH!! OKAY! OKAY! I'M UP!!!
© 1992 United Feature Syndicate, Inc.
JIM DAVIS 7-12

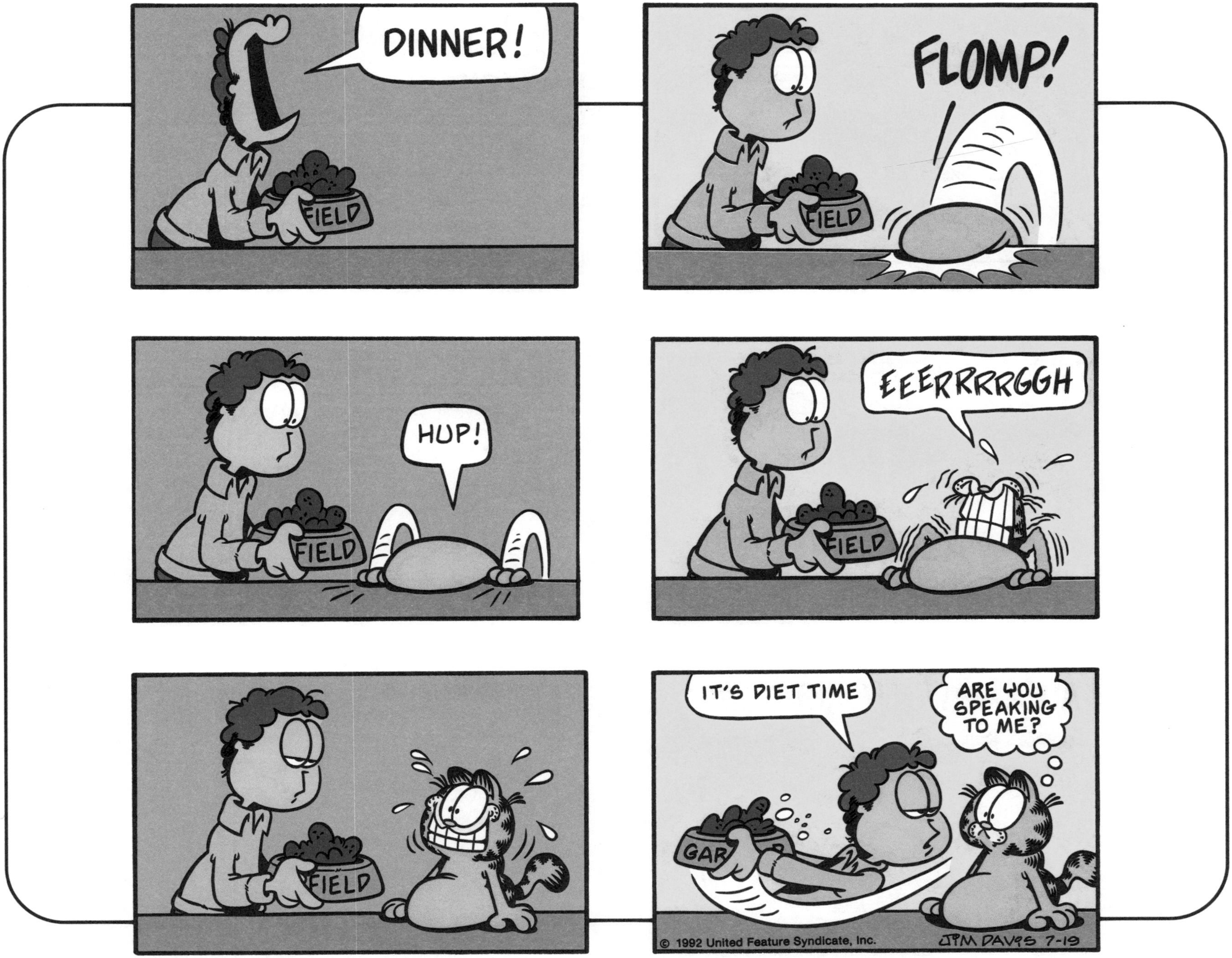
DINNER!
FLOMP!
HUP!
EEERRRRGGH
IT'S DIET TIME
ARE YOU SPEAKING TO ME?
© 1992 United Feature Syndicate, Inc.
JIM DAVIS 7-19

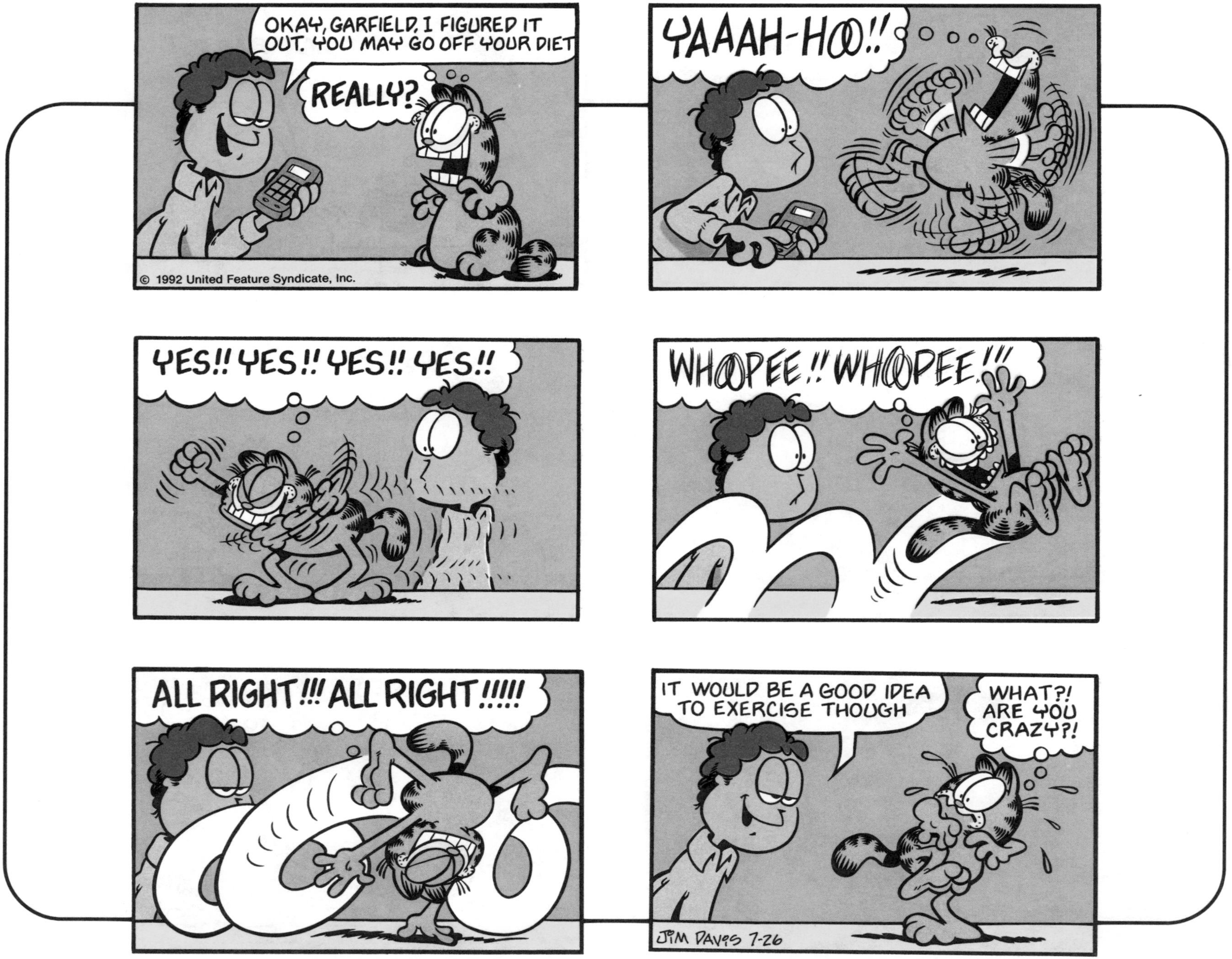
OKAY, GARFIELD, I FIGURED IT OUT. YOU MAY GO OFF YOUR DIET
REALLY?
© 1992 United Feature Syndicate, Inc.
YAAAH-HOO!!
YES!! YES!! YES!! YES!!
WHOOPEE!! WHOOPEE!!
ALL RIGHT!!! ALL RIGHT!!!!!
IT WOULD BE A GOOD IDEA TO EXERCISE THOUGH
WHAT?! ARE YOU CRAZY?!
JIM DAVIS 7-26

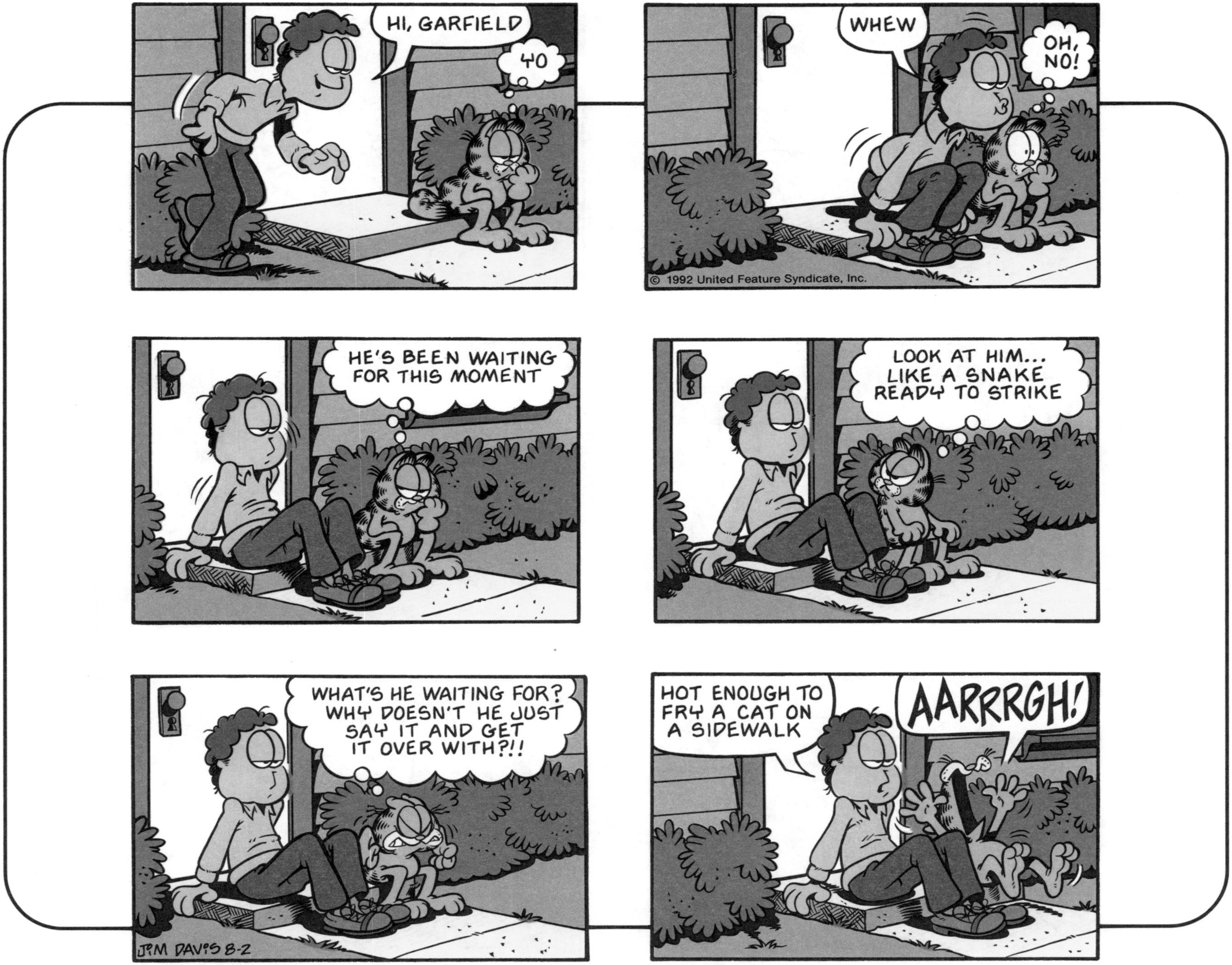
HI, GARFIELD
YO
WHEW
OH, NO!
© 1992 United Feature Syndicate, Inc.
HE'S BEEN WAITING FOR THIS MOMENT
LOOK AT HIM... LIKE A SNAKE READY TO STRIKE
WHAT'S HE WAITING FOR? WHY DOESN'T HE JUST SAY IT AND GET IT OVER WITH?!!
JIM DAVIS 8-2
HOT ENOUGH TO FRY A CAT ON A SIDEWALK
AARRRGH!

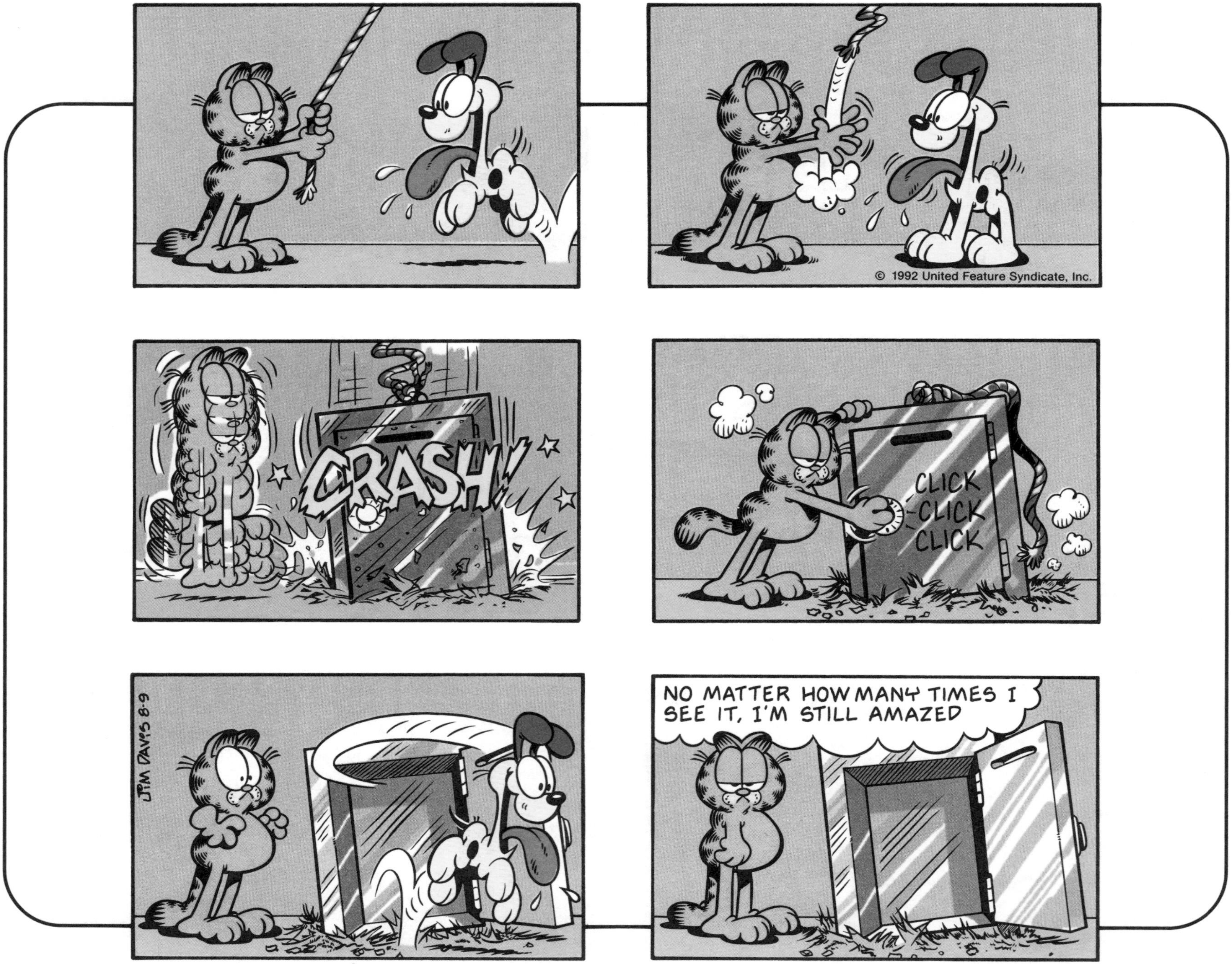
© 1992 United Feature Syndicate, Inc.
CRASH!
CLICK
CLICK
CLICK
JIM DAVIS 8-9
NO MATTER HOW MANY TIMES I SEE IT, I'M STILL AMAZED

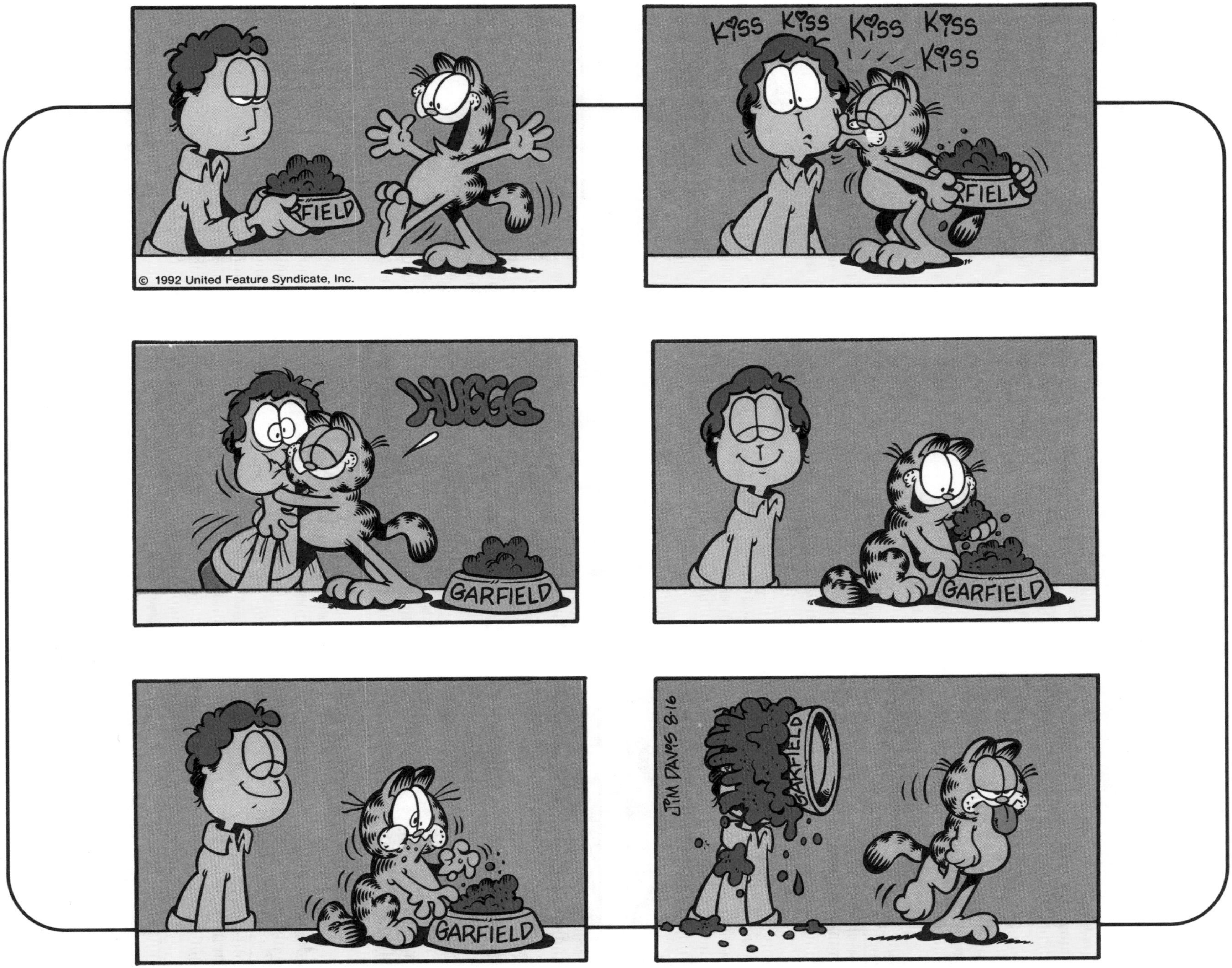
© 1992 United Feature Syndicate, Inc.
FIELD
KISS KISS KISS KISS
KISS
FIELD
HUGGG
GARFIELD
GARFIELD
GARFIELD
JIM DAVIS 8-16
GARFIELD

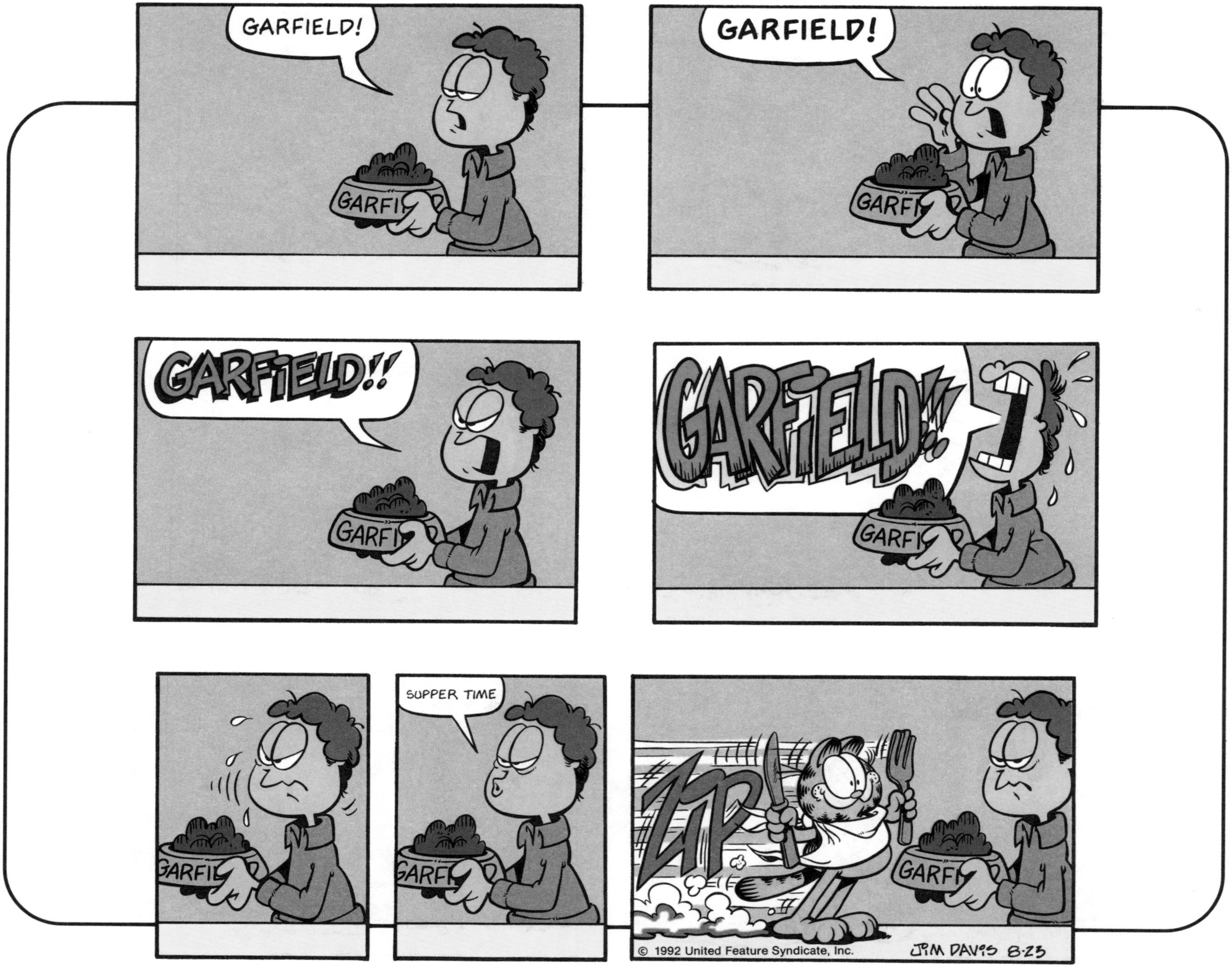
GARFIELD!
GARFIELD!
GARFIELD!!
GARFIELD!!
SUPPER TIME
ZIP
GARFIELD
© 1992 United Feature Syndicate, Inc.
JIM DAVIS 8-23

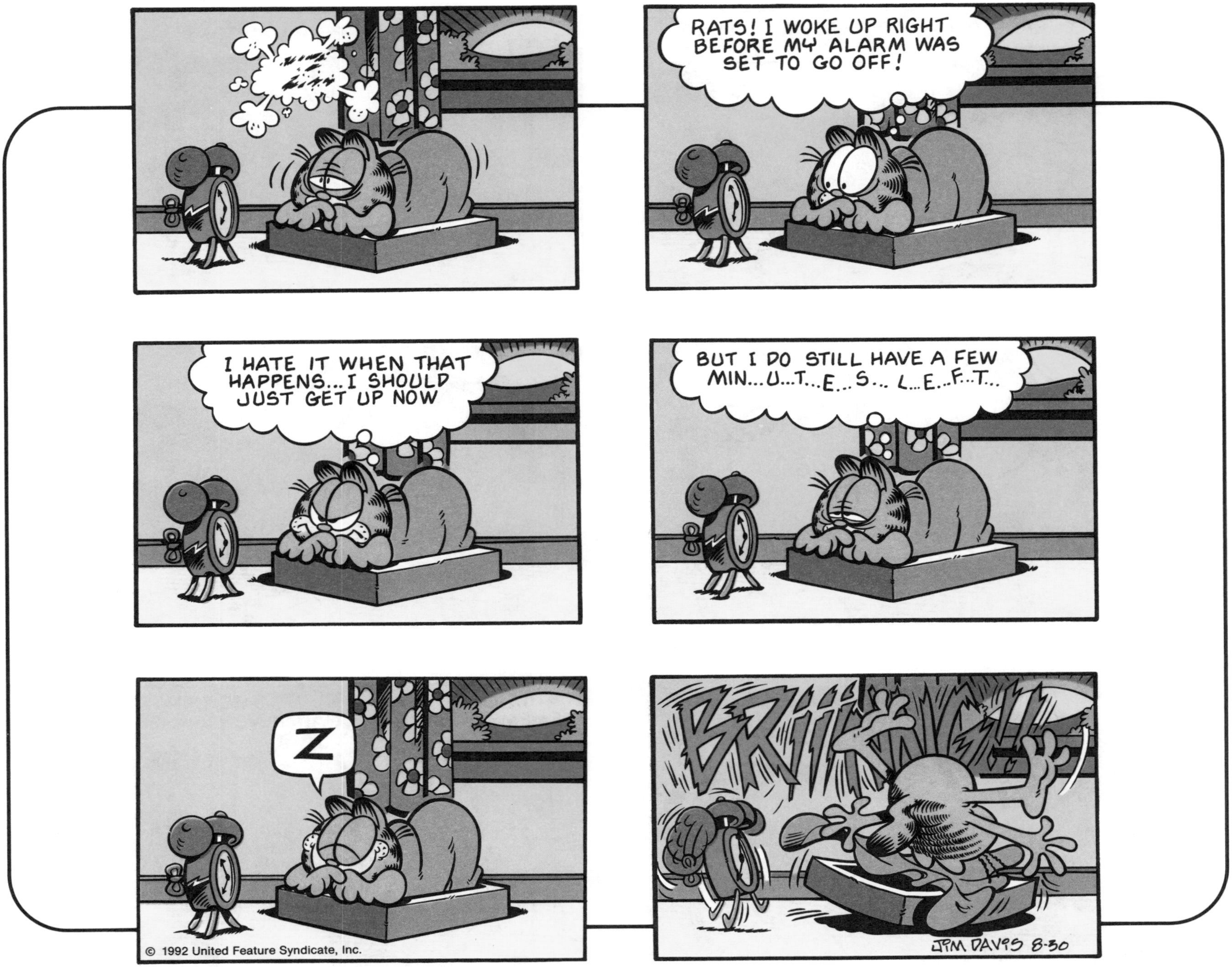
RATS! I WOKE UP RIGHT BEFORE MY ALARM WAS SET TO GO OFF!
I HATE IT WHEN THAT HAPPENS...I SHOULD JUST GET UP NOW
BUT I DO STILL HAVE A FEW MIN...U...T...E...S... L...E...F...T...
Z
JIM DAVIS 8-30

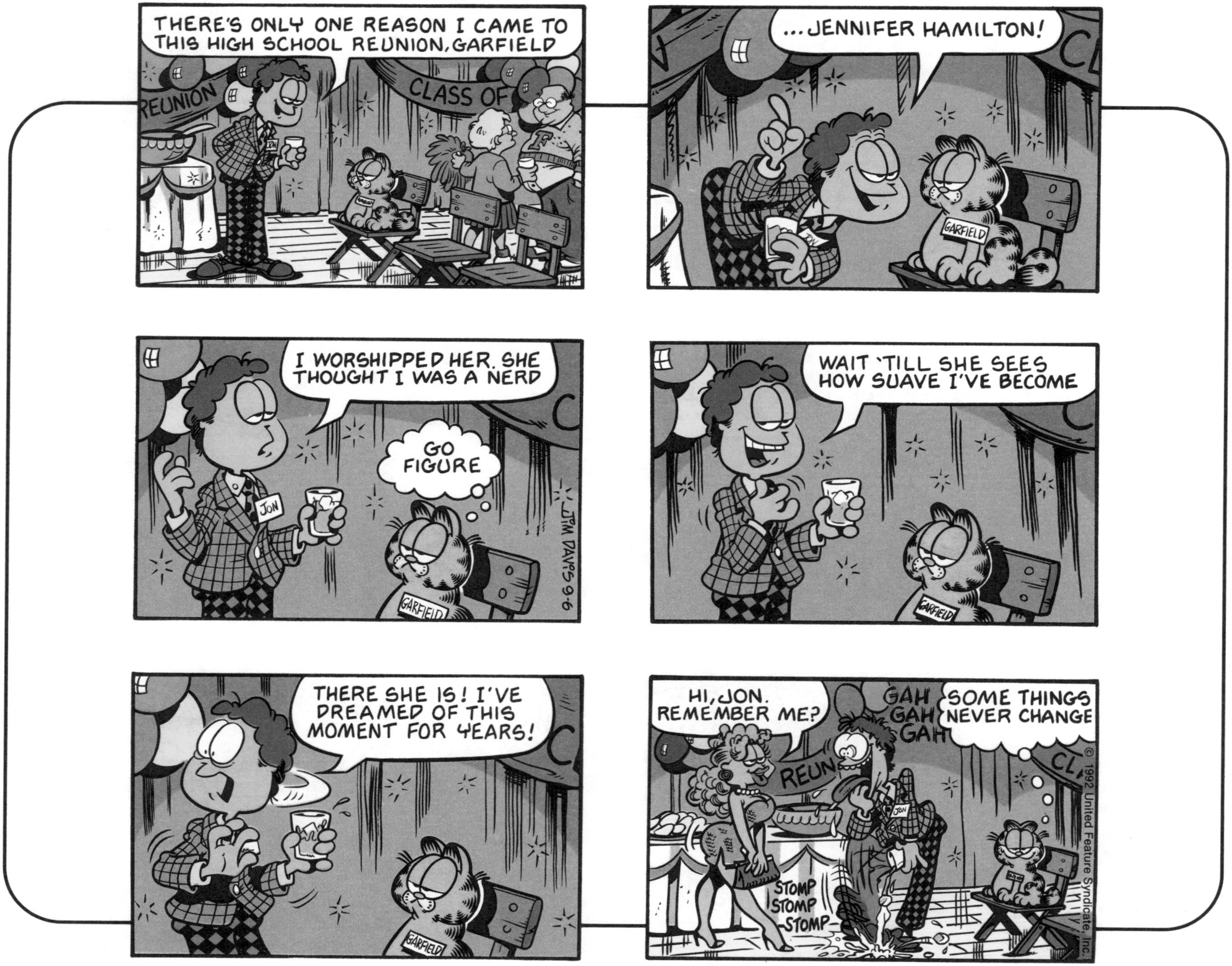
THERE'S ONLY ONE REASON I CAME TO THIS HIGH SCHOOL REUNION, GARFIELD
REUNION
CLASS OF
...JENNIFER HAMILTON!
JON
GARFIELD
I WORSHIPPED HER. SHE THOUGHT I WAS A NERD
GO FIGURE
JIM DAVIS 9-6
WAIT 'TILL SHE SEES HOW SUAVE I'VE BECOME
THERE SHE IS! I'VE DREAMED OF THIS MOMENT FOR YEARS!
HI, JON. REMEMBER ME?
GAH GAH GAH
SOME THINGS NEVER CHANGE
STOMP STOMP STOMP
© 1992 United Feature Syndicate, Inc.

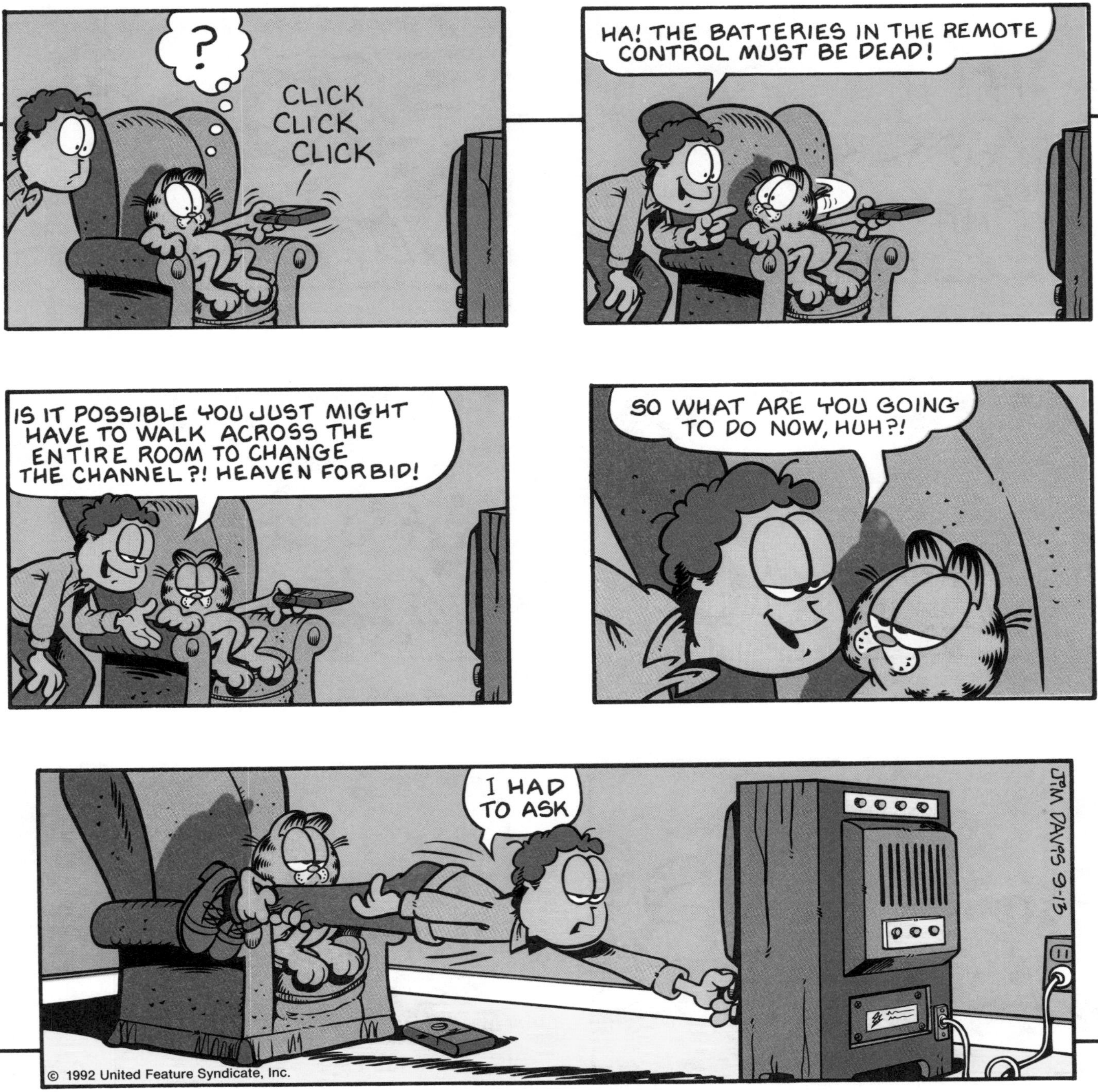
?
CLICK
CLICK
CLICK
HA! THE BATTERIES IN THE REMOTE CONTROL MUST BE DEAD!
IS IT POSSIBLE YOU JUST MIGHT HAVE TO WALK ACROSS THE ENTIRE ROOM TO CHANGE THE CHANNEL?! HEAVEN FORBID!
SO WHAT ARE YOU GOING TO DO NOW, HUH?!
I HAD TO ASK
JIM DAVIS 9-13
© 1992 United Feature Syndicate, Inc.

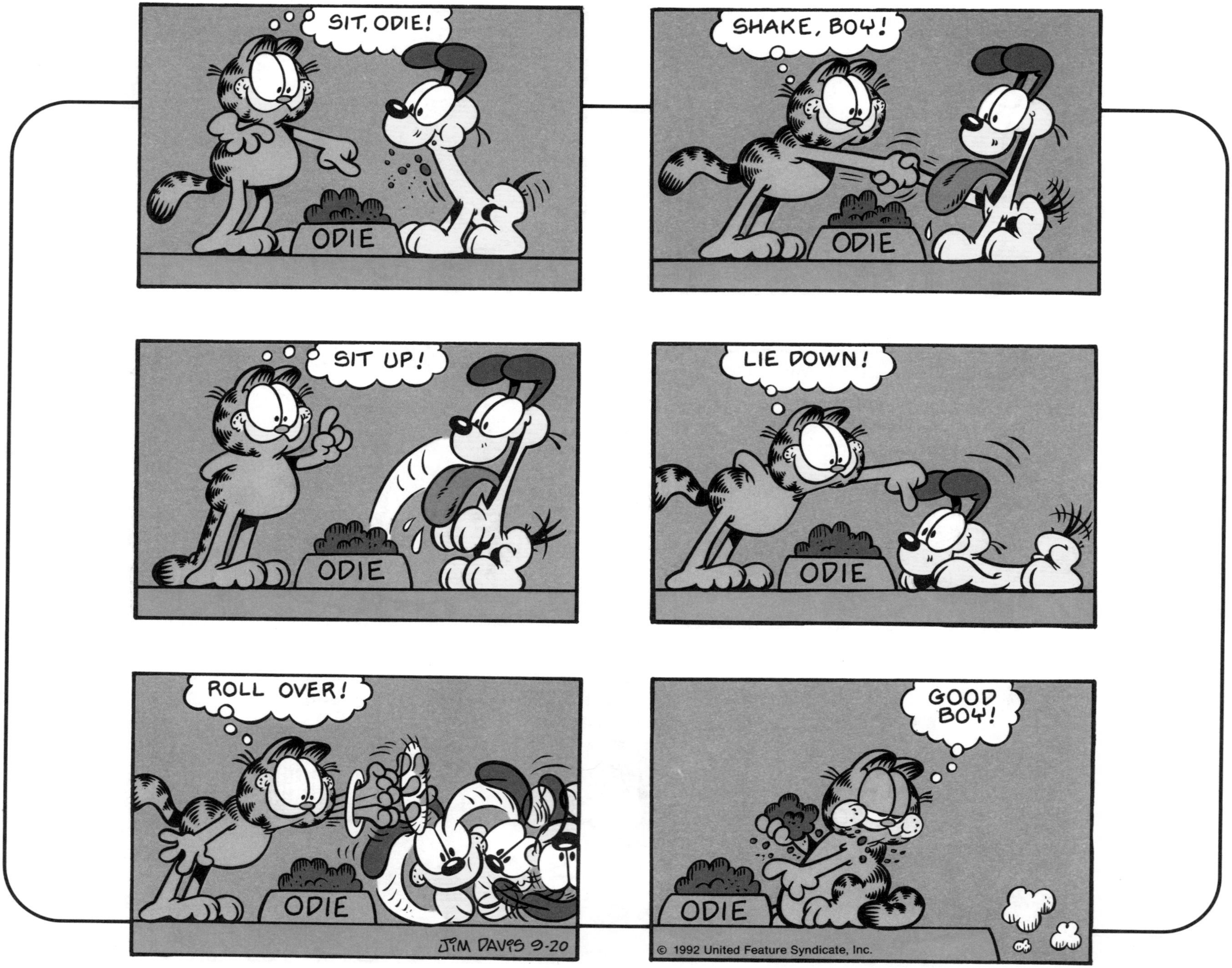
SIT, ODIE!
SHAKE, BOY!
SIT UP!
LIE DOWN!
ROLL OVER!
GOOD BOY!
ODIE
JIM DAVIS 9-20

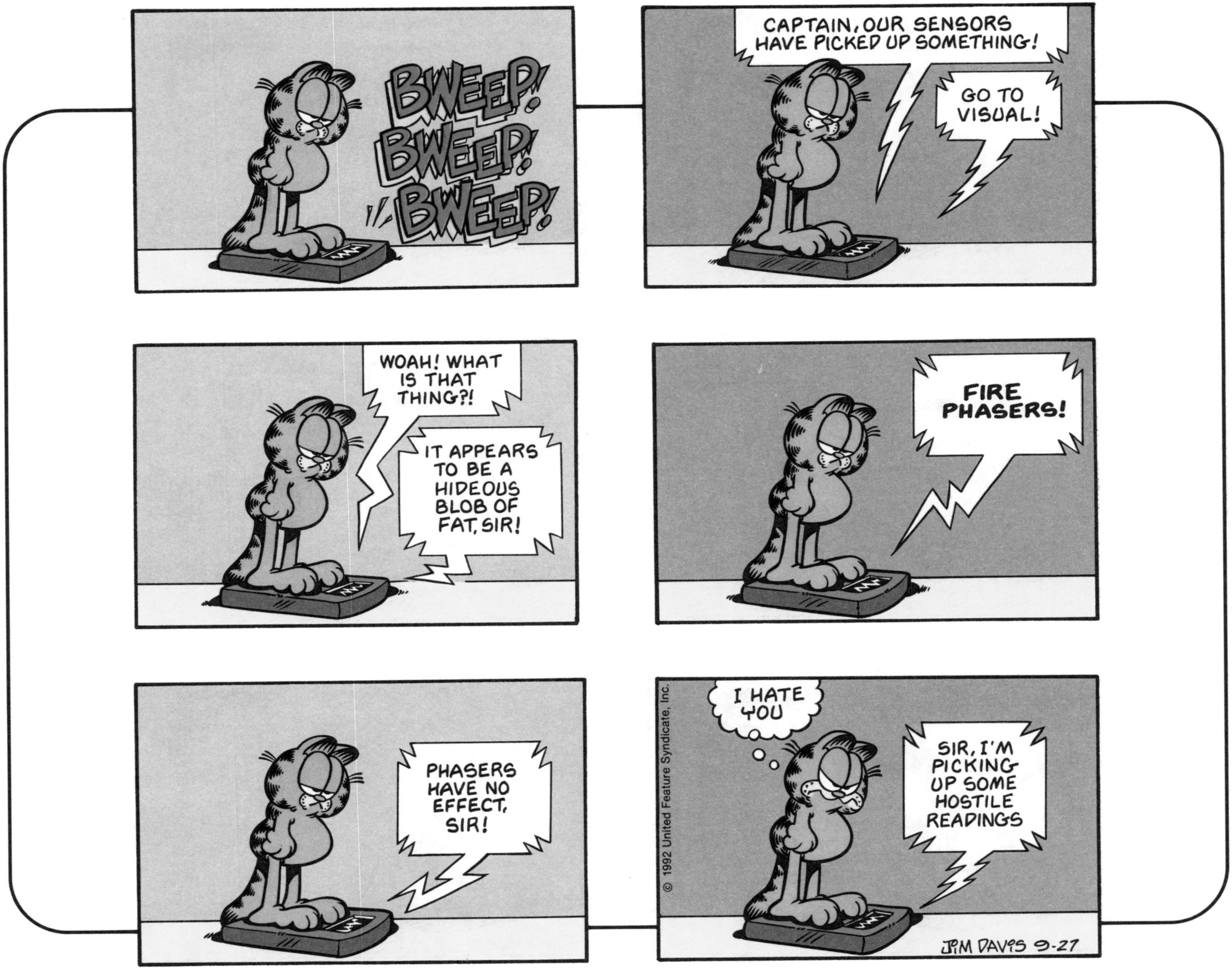
BWEEP! BWEEP! BWEEP!
CAPTAIN, OUR SENSORS HAVE PICKED UP SOMETHING!
GO TO VISUAL!
WOAH! WHAT IS THAT THING?!
IT APPEARS TO BE A HIDEOUS BLOB OF FAT, SIR!
FIRE PHASERS!
PHASERS HAVE NO EFFECT, SIR!
I HATE YOU
SIR, I'M PICKING UP SOME HOSTILE READINGS
JIM DAVIS 9-27

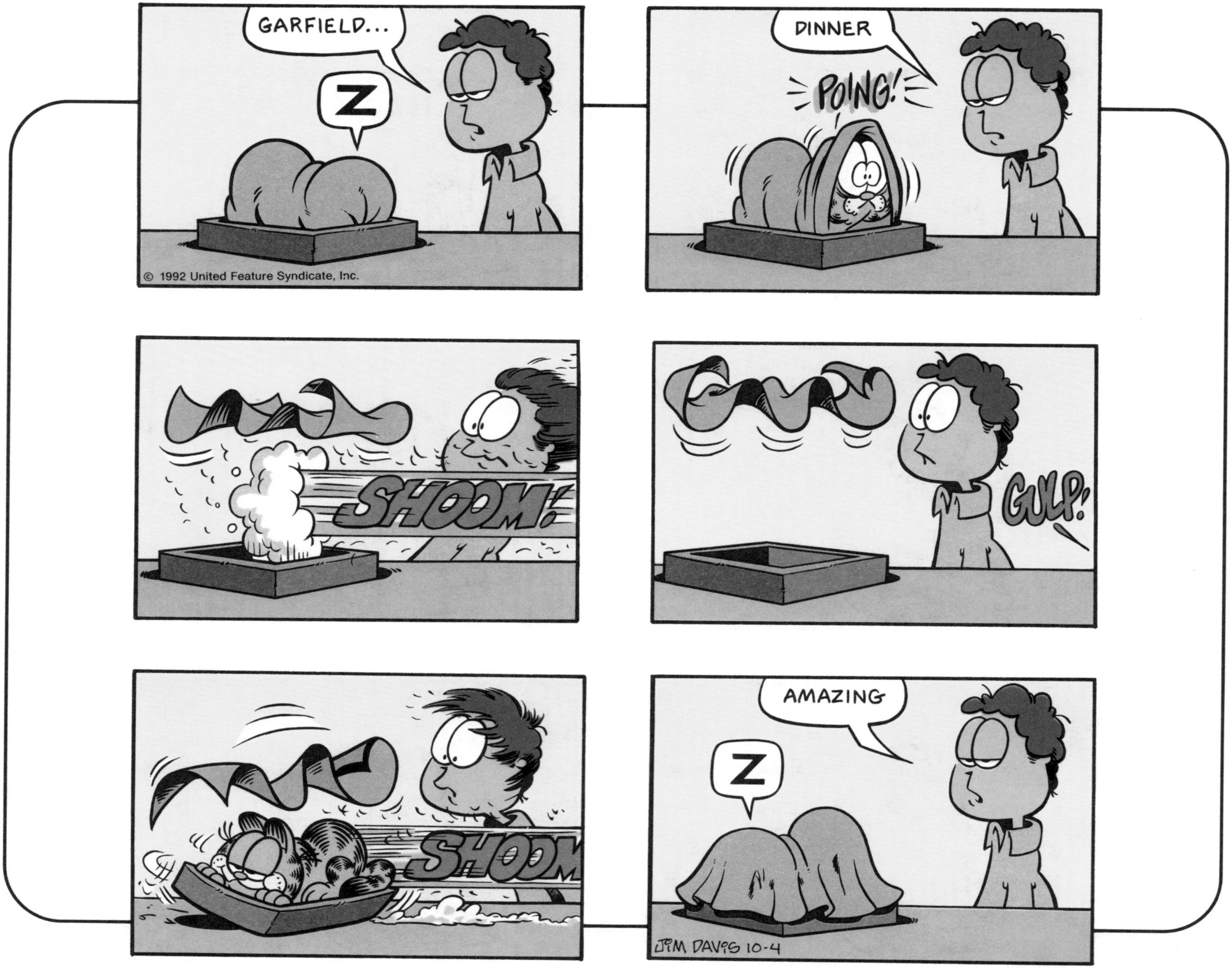
GARFIELD...
Z
© 1992 United Feature Syndicate, Inc.
DINNER
POING!
SHOOM!
GULP!
SHOOM
AMAZING
Z
JIM DAVIS 10-4

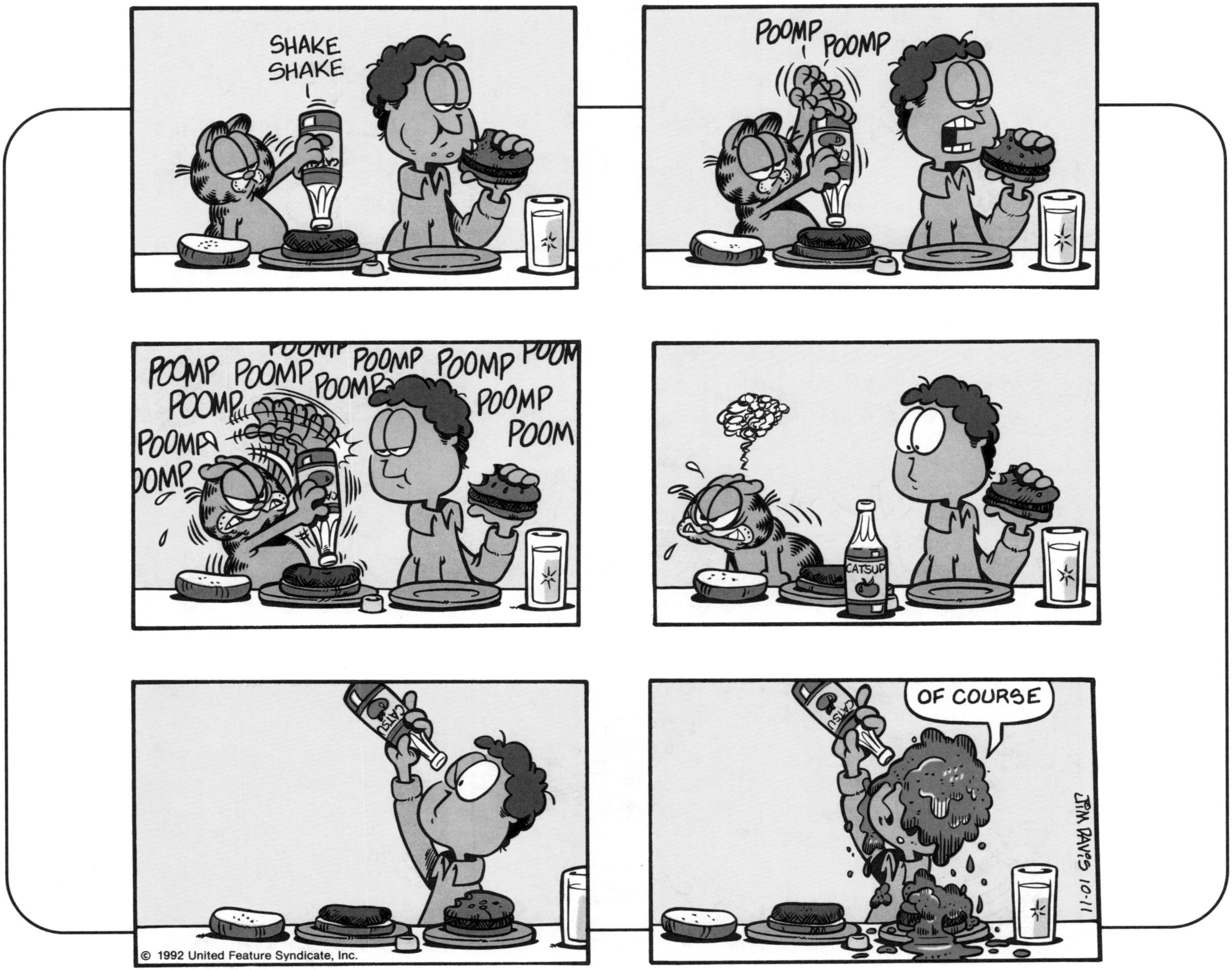
SHAKE SHAKE
POOMP POOMP
POOMP POOMP POOMP POOMP POOMP POOMP POOMP POOMP POOM
CATSUP
OF COURSE
JIM DAVIS 10-11

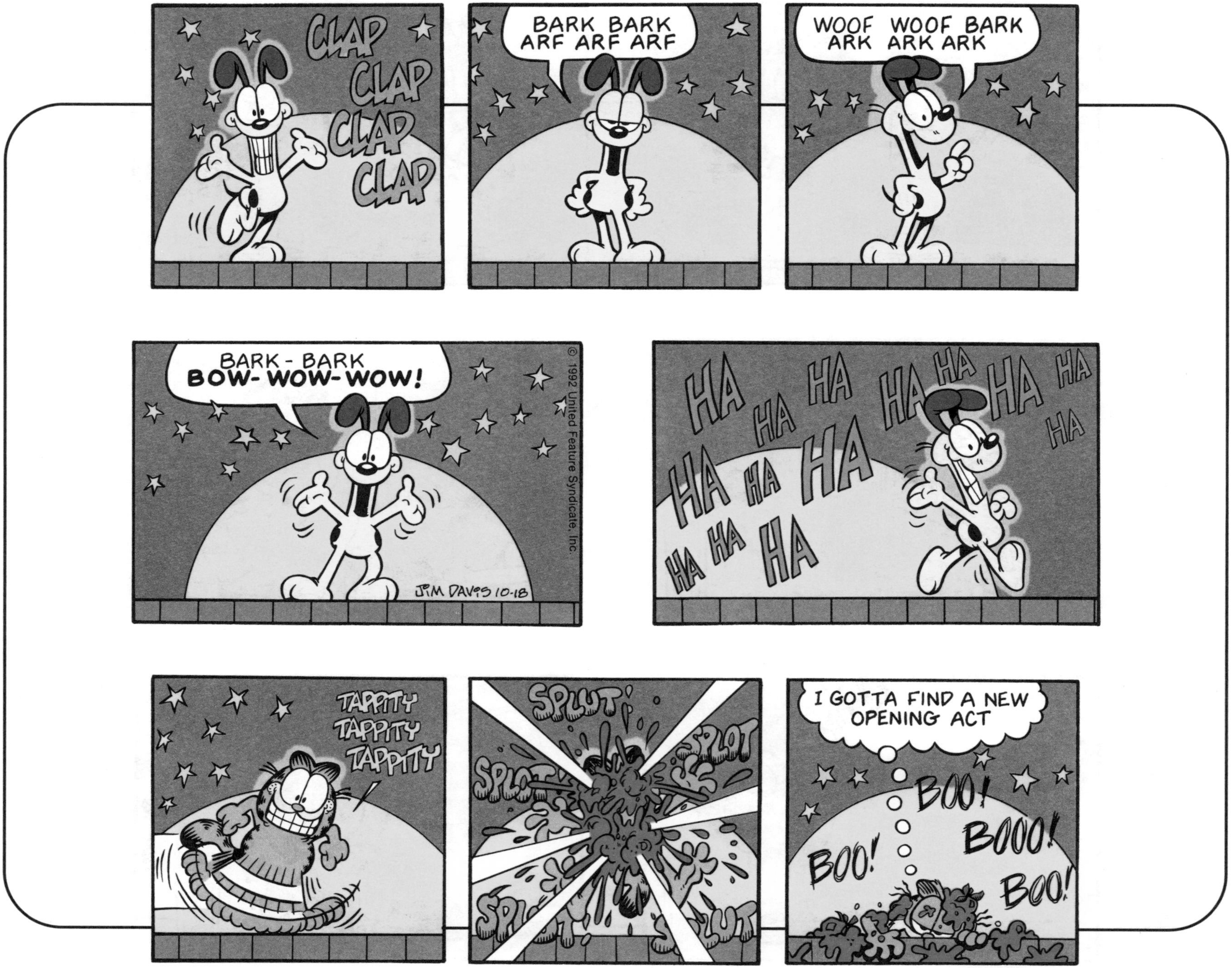
CLAP CLAP CLAP CLAP
BARK BARK ARF ARF ARF
WOOF WOOF BARK ARK ARK ARK
BARK - BARK **BOW- WOW- WOW!**
© 1992 United Feature Syndicate, Inc.
JIM DAVIS 10-18
HA HA HA HA HA HA HA HA HA HA HA HA HA HA HA HA
TAPPITY TAPPITY TAPPITY
SPLUT!
SPLOT
SPLOT!
I GOTTA FIND A NEW OPENING ACT
BOO!
BOOO!
BOO!
BOO!

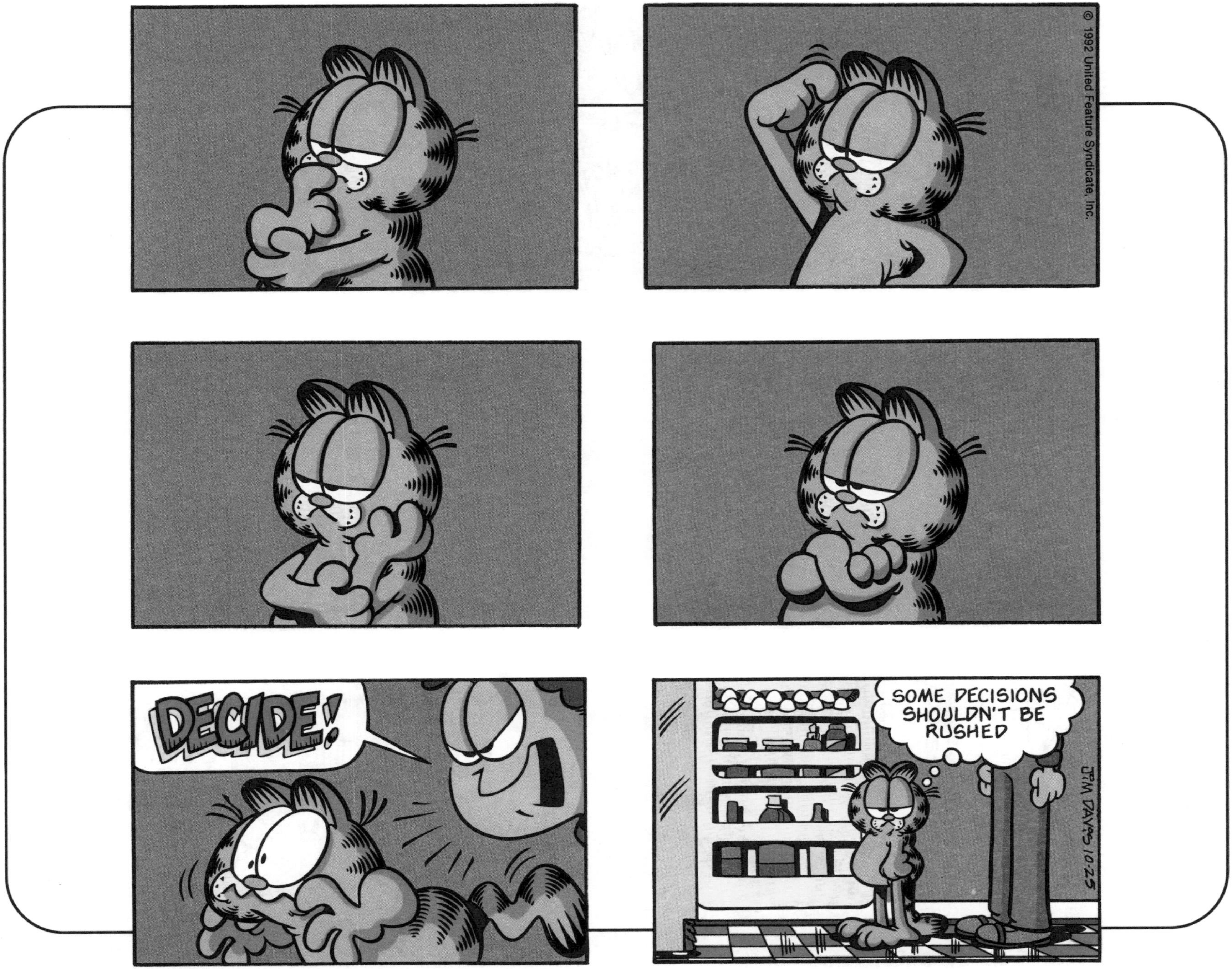
© 1992 United Feature Syndicate, Inc.
DECIDE!
SOME DECISIONS SHOULDN'T BE RUSHED
JIM DAVIS 10-25

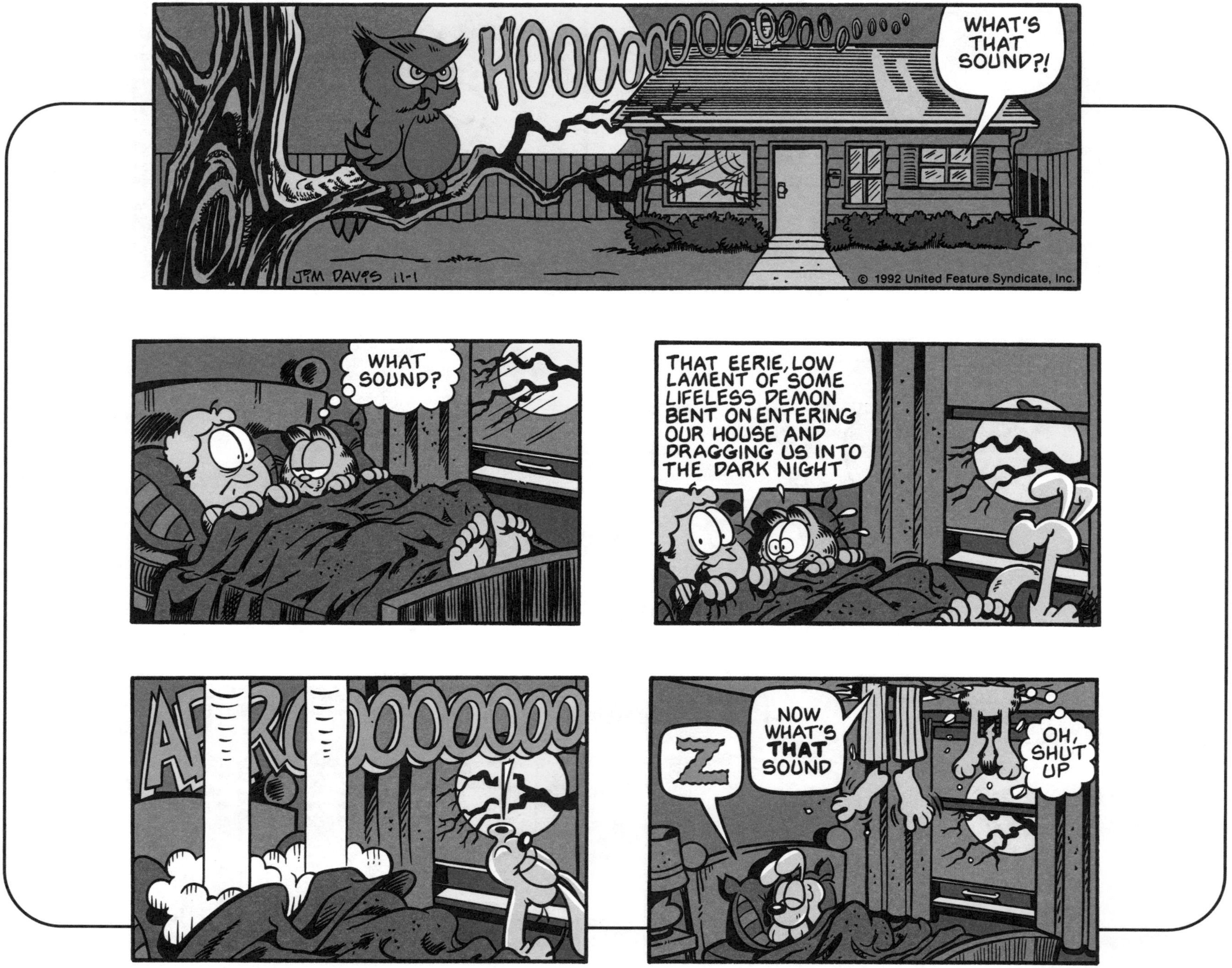
HOOOOOOOOOOOOOOOOOOO
WHAT'S THAT SOUND?!
JIM DAVIS 11-1
© 1992 United Feature Syndicate, Inc.
WHAT SOUND?
THAT EERIE, LOW LAMENT OF SOME LIFELESS DEMON BENT ON ENTERING OUR HOUSE AND DRAGGING US INTO THE DARK NIGHT
AROOOOOOOOO
Z
NOW WHAT'S **THAT** SOUND
OH, SHUT UP

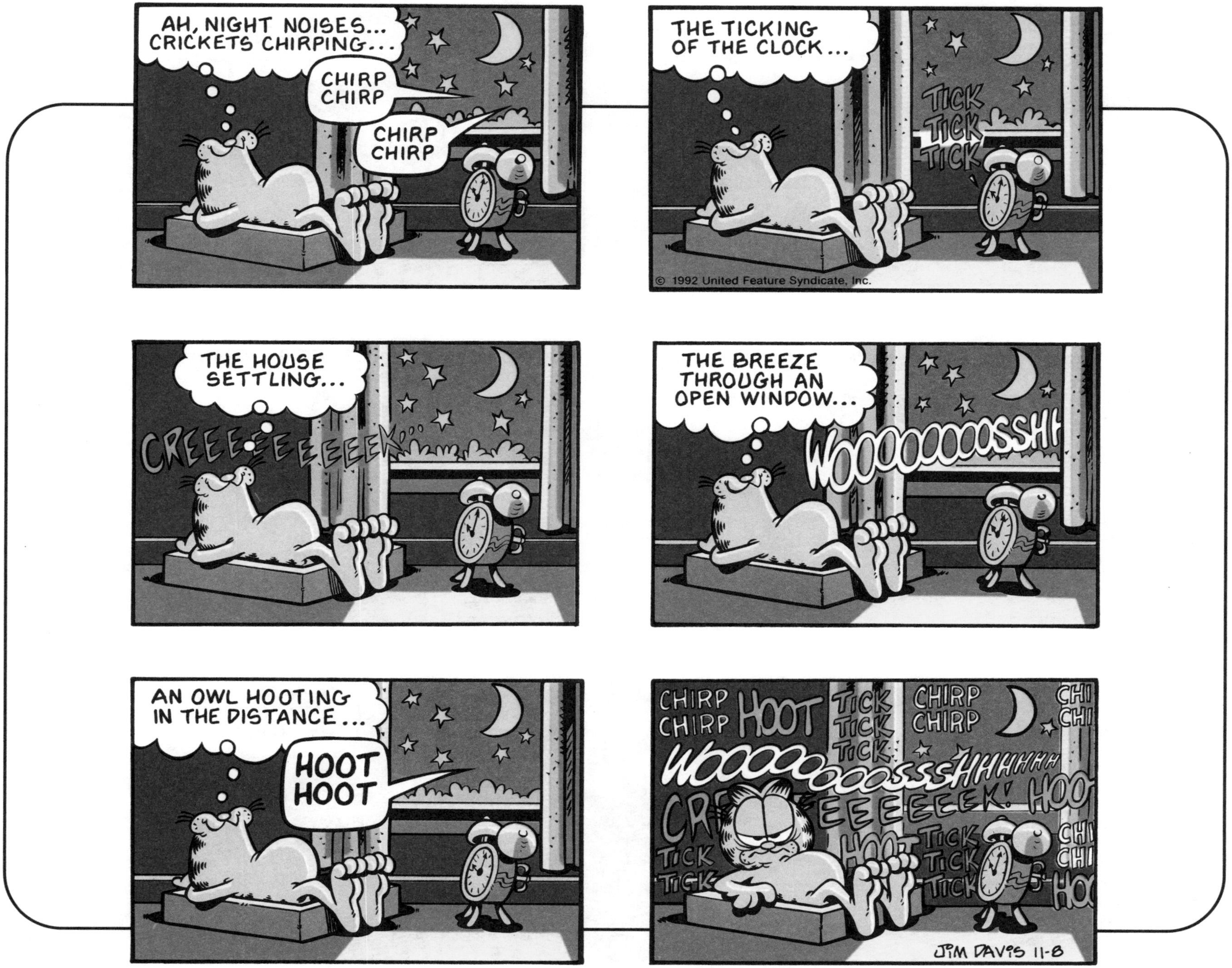

AH, NIGHT NOISES... CRICKETS CHIRPING...
CHIRP CHIRP
CHIRP CHIRP
THE TICKING OF THE CLOCK...
TICK TICK TICK
© 1992 United Feature Syndicate, Inc.
THE HOUSE SETTLING...
CREEEEEEEEEEK...
THE BREEZE THROUGH AN OPEN WINDOW...
WOOOOOOOOOSSHH
AN OWL HOOTING IN THE DISTANCE...
HOOT HOOT
CHIRP CHIRP
HOOT
TICK TICK TICK
CHIRP CHIRP
WOOOOOOOOOOSSSHHHHHHH
EEEEEEEEK!
HOOT
TICK TICK TICK
JIM DAVIS 11-8

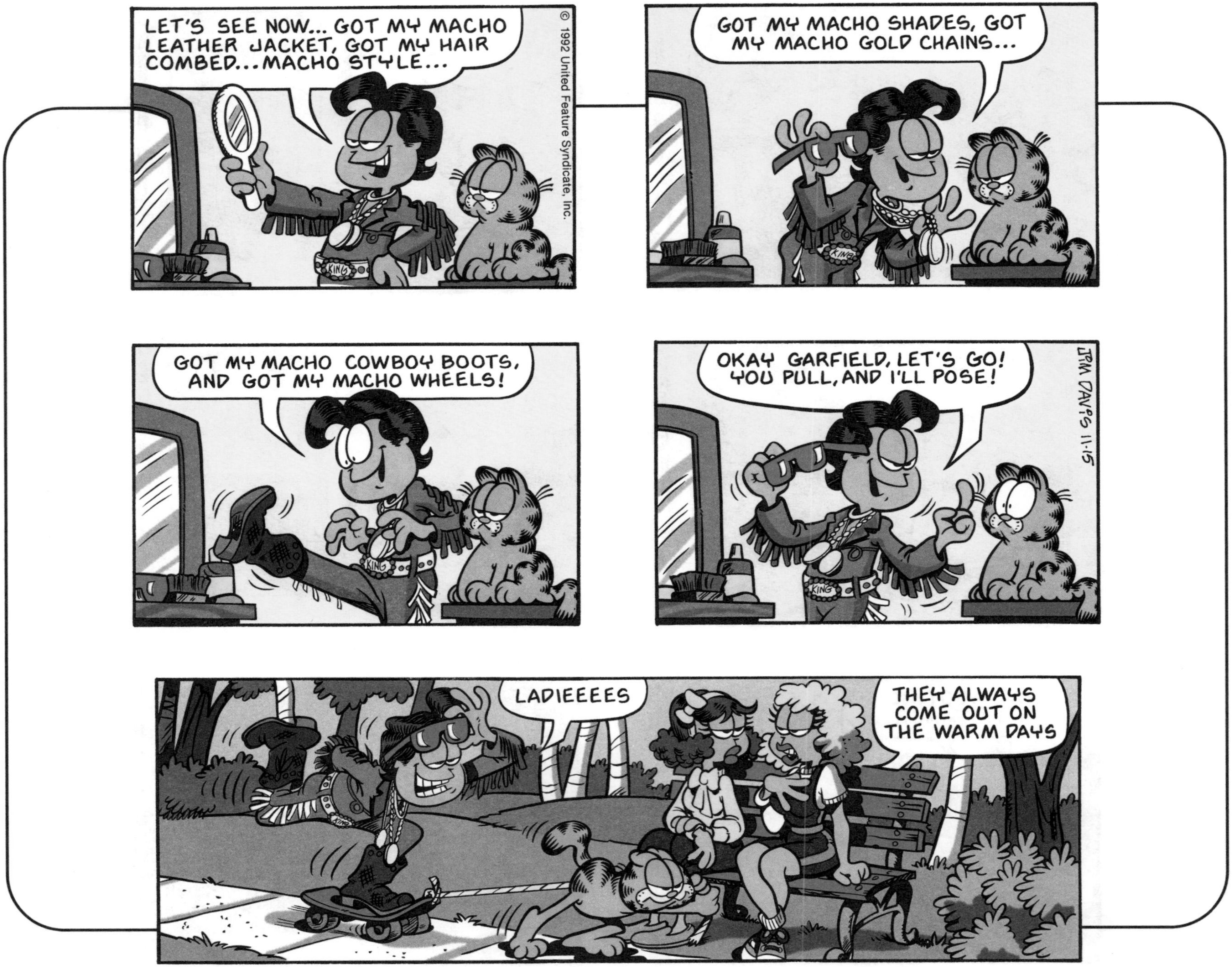
LET'S SEE NOW... GOT MY MACHO LEATHER JACKET, GOT MY HAIR COMBED...MACHO STYLE...
© 1992 United Feature Syndicate, Inc.
KING
GOT MY MACHO SHADES, GOT MY MACHO GOLD CHAINS...
KING
GOT MY MACHO COWBOY BOOTS, AND GOT MY MACHO WHEELS!
KING
OKAY GARFIELD, LET'S GO! YOU PULL, AND I'LL POSE!
JPM DAVIS 11-15
KING
LADIEEEES
THEY ALWAYS COME OUT ON THE WARM DAYS

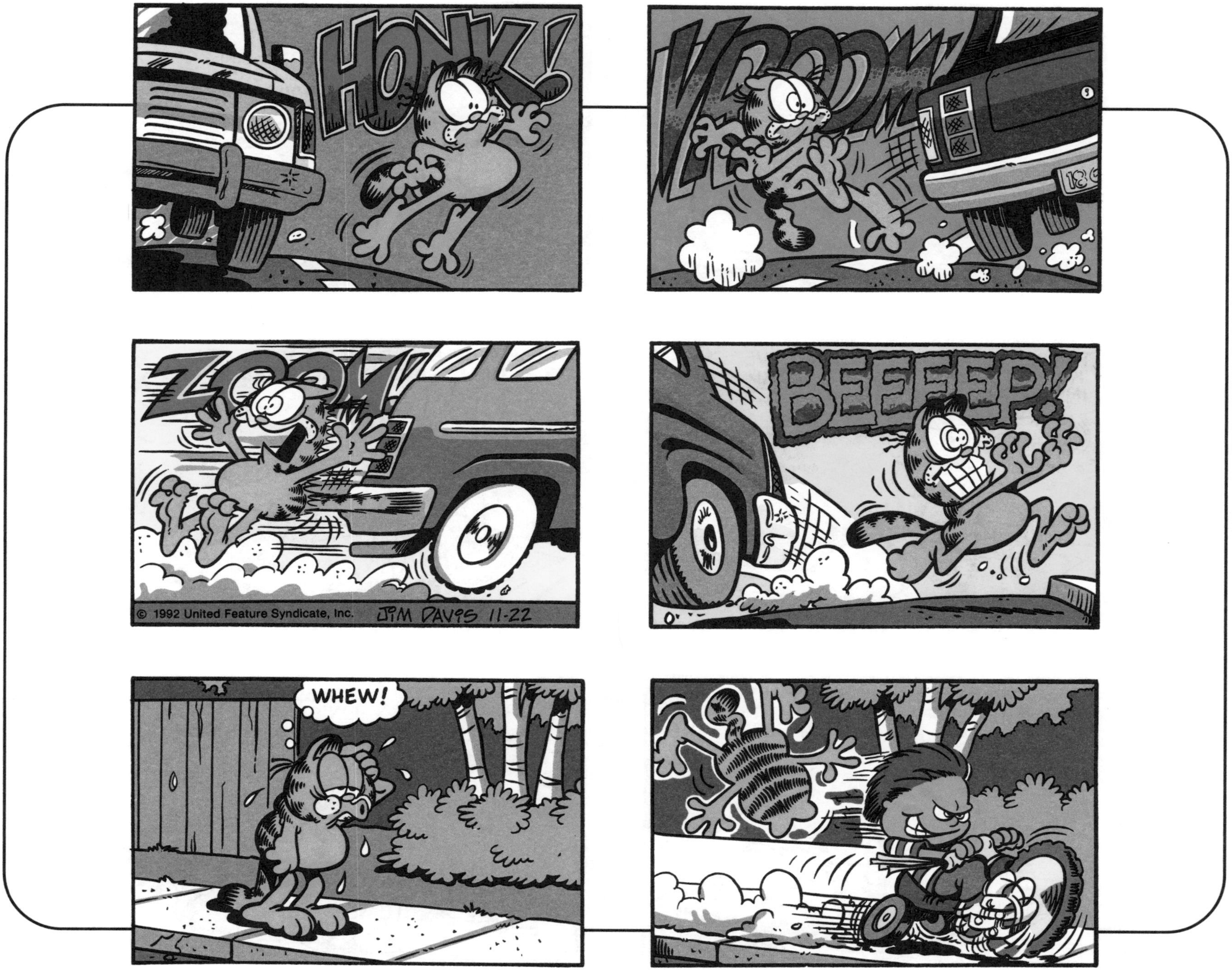

HONK!
VROOOM!
ZOOM!
BEEEEP!
© 1992 United Feature Syndicate, Inc.
JIM DAVIS 11-22
WHEW!

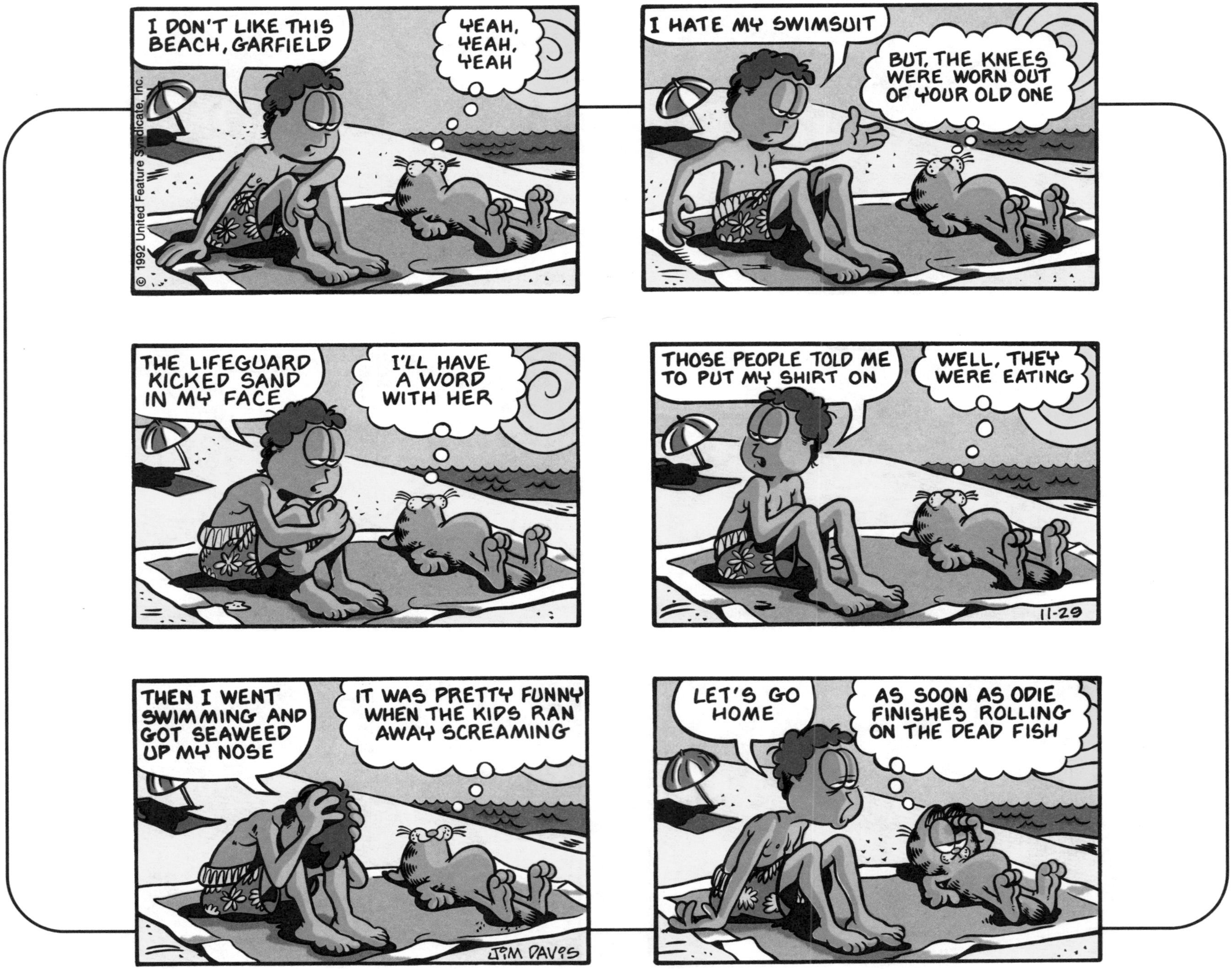
I DON'T LIKE THIS BEACH, GARFIELD
YEAH, YEAH, YEAH
I HATE MY SWIMSUIT
BUT, THE KNEES WERE WORN OUT OF YOUR OLD ONE
THE LIFEGUARD KICKED SAND IN MY FACE
I'LL HAVE A WORD WITH HER
THOSE PEOPLE TOLD ME TO PUT MY SHIRT ON
WELL, THEY WERE EATING
11-29
THEN I WENT SWIMMING AND GOT SEAWEED UP MY NOSE
IT WAS PRETTY FUNNY WHEN THE KIDS RAN AWAY SCREAMING
JIM DAVIS
LET'S GO HOME
AS SOON AS ODIE FINISHES ROLLING ON THE DEAD FISH

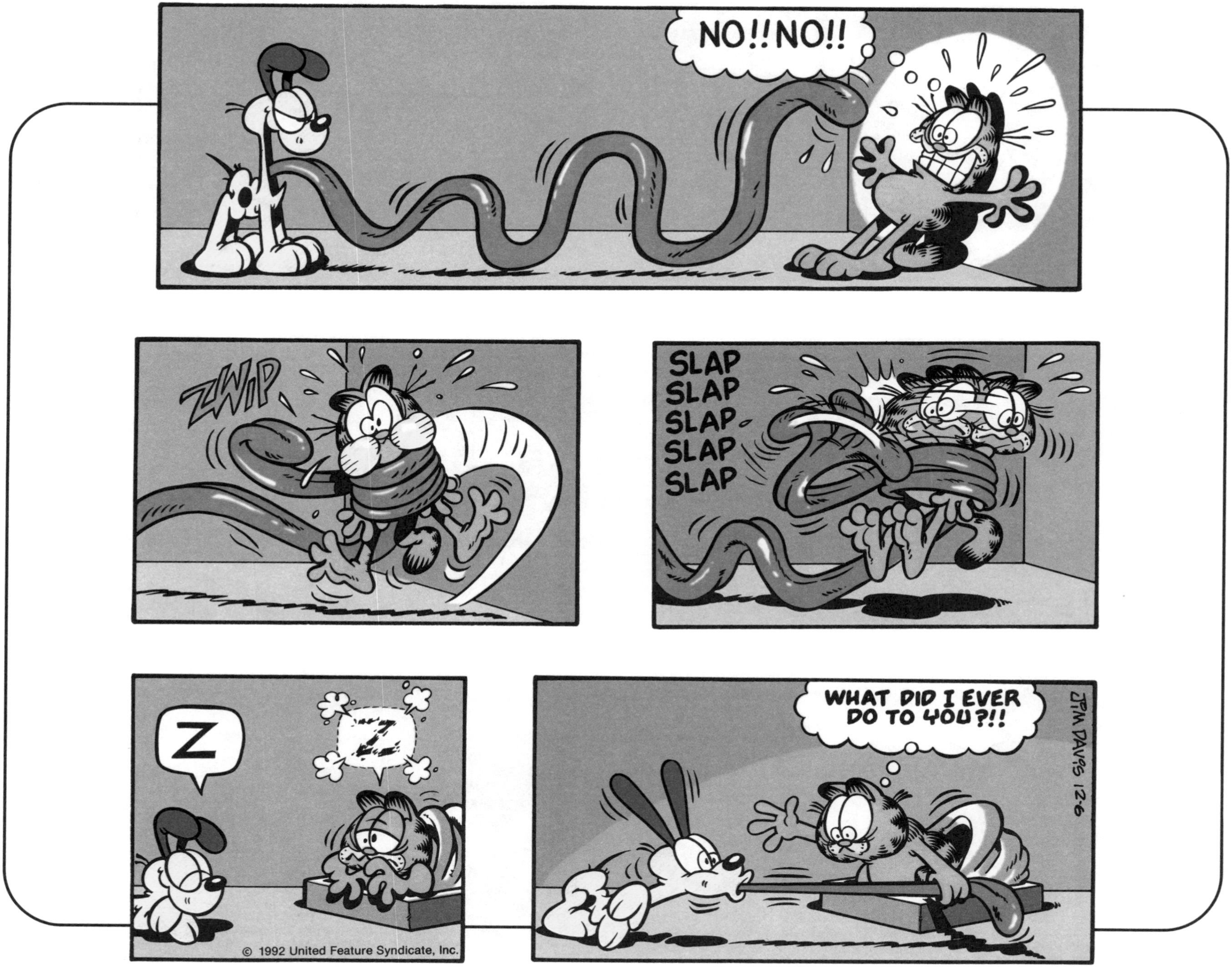
NO!! NO!!
ZWIP
SLAP SLAP SLAP SLAP SLAP SLAP
Z
Z
WHAT DID I EVER DO TO YOU?!!
JIM DAVIS 12-6
© 1992 United Feature Syndicate, Inc.

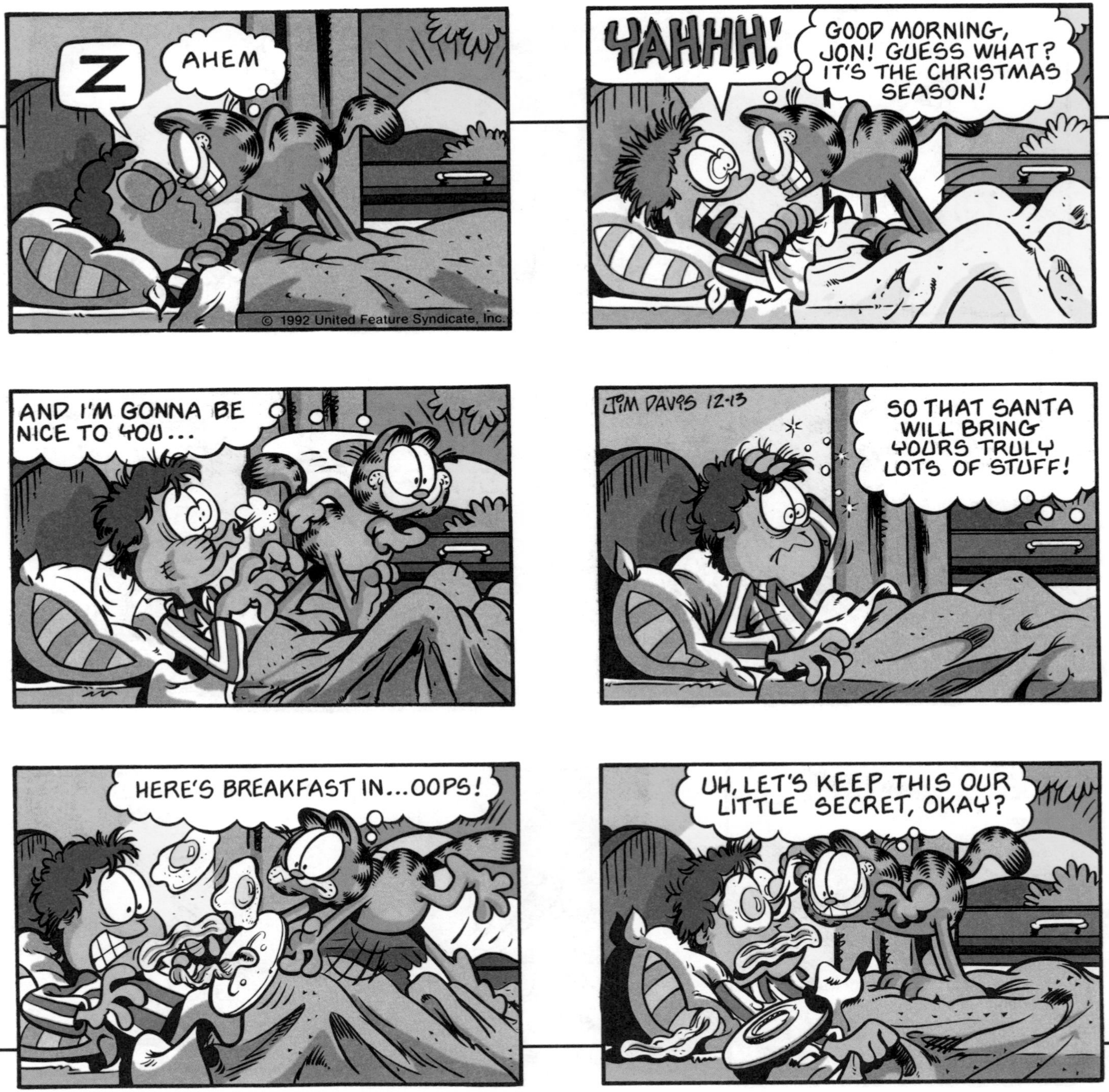
Z
AHEM
© 1992 United Feature Syndicate, Inc.
YAHHH!
GOOD MORNING, JON! GUESS WHAT? IT'S THE CHRISTMAS SEASON!
AND I'M GONNA BE NICE TO YOU...
JIM DAVIS 12-13
SO THAT SANTA WILL BRING YOURS TRULY LOTS OF STUFF!
HERE'S BREAKFAST IN...OOPS!
UH, LET'S KEEP THIS OUR LITTLE SECRET, OKAY?

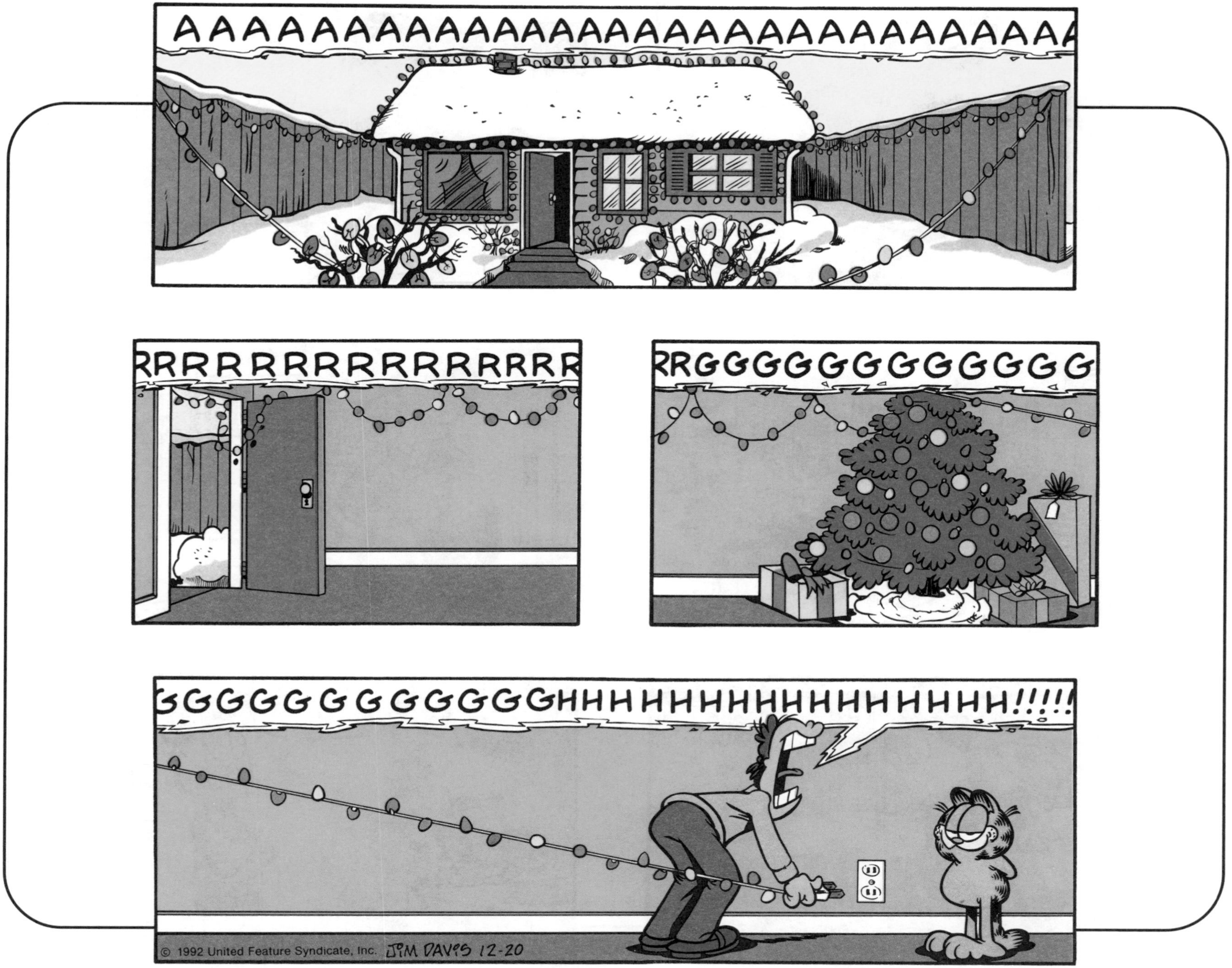
AAAAAAAAAAAAAAAAAAAAAAAAAAAA
RRRRRRRRRRRRRRR
RRGGGGGGGGGGGG
GGGGGGGGGGGHHHHHHHHHHHHHHHH!!!!!
© 1992 United Feature Syndicate, Inc. JIM DAVIS 12-20

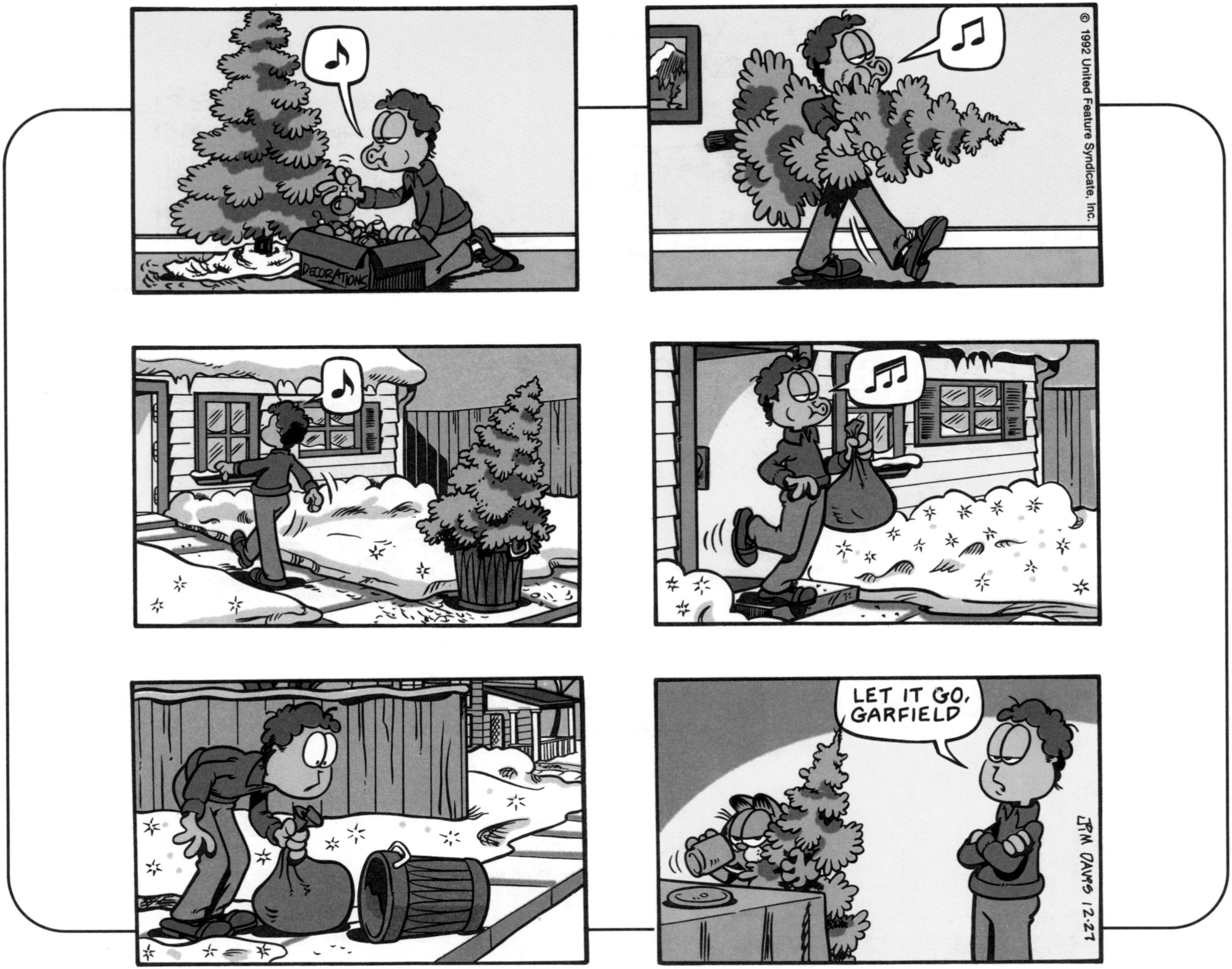

© 1992 United Feature Syndicate, Inc.
LET IT GO, GARFIELD
JIM DAVIS 12-27

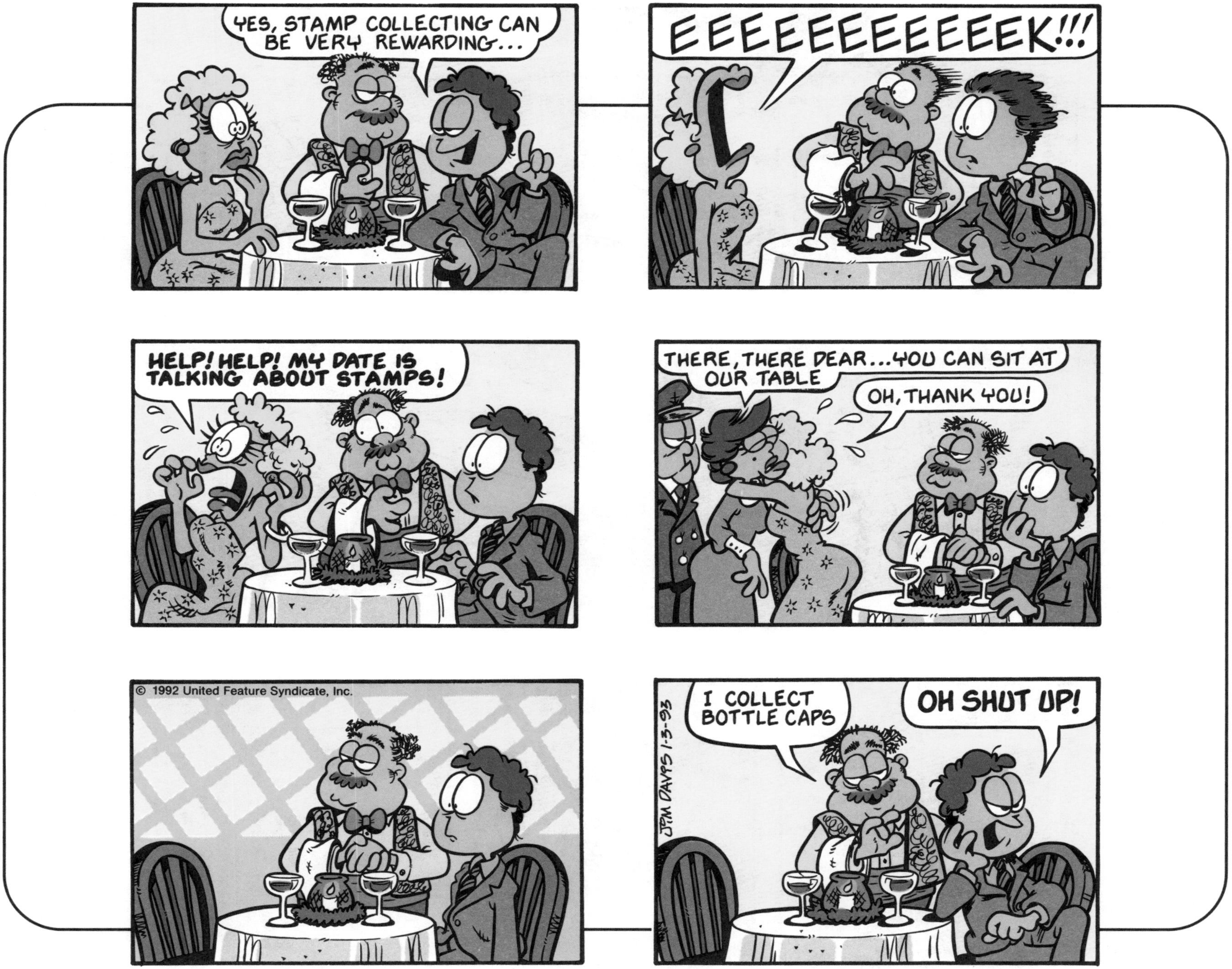

YES, STAMP COLLECTING CAN BE VERY REWARDING...
EEEEEEEEEEEEK!!!
HELP! HELP! MY DATE IS TALKING ABOUT STAMPS!
THERE, THERE DEAR...YOU CAN SIT AT OUR TABLE
OH, THANK YOU!
© 1992 United Feature Syndicate, Inc.
JPM DAVPS 1-3-93
I COLLECT BOTTLE CAPS
OH SHUT UP!

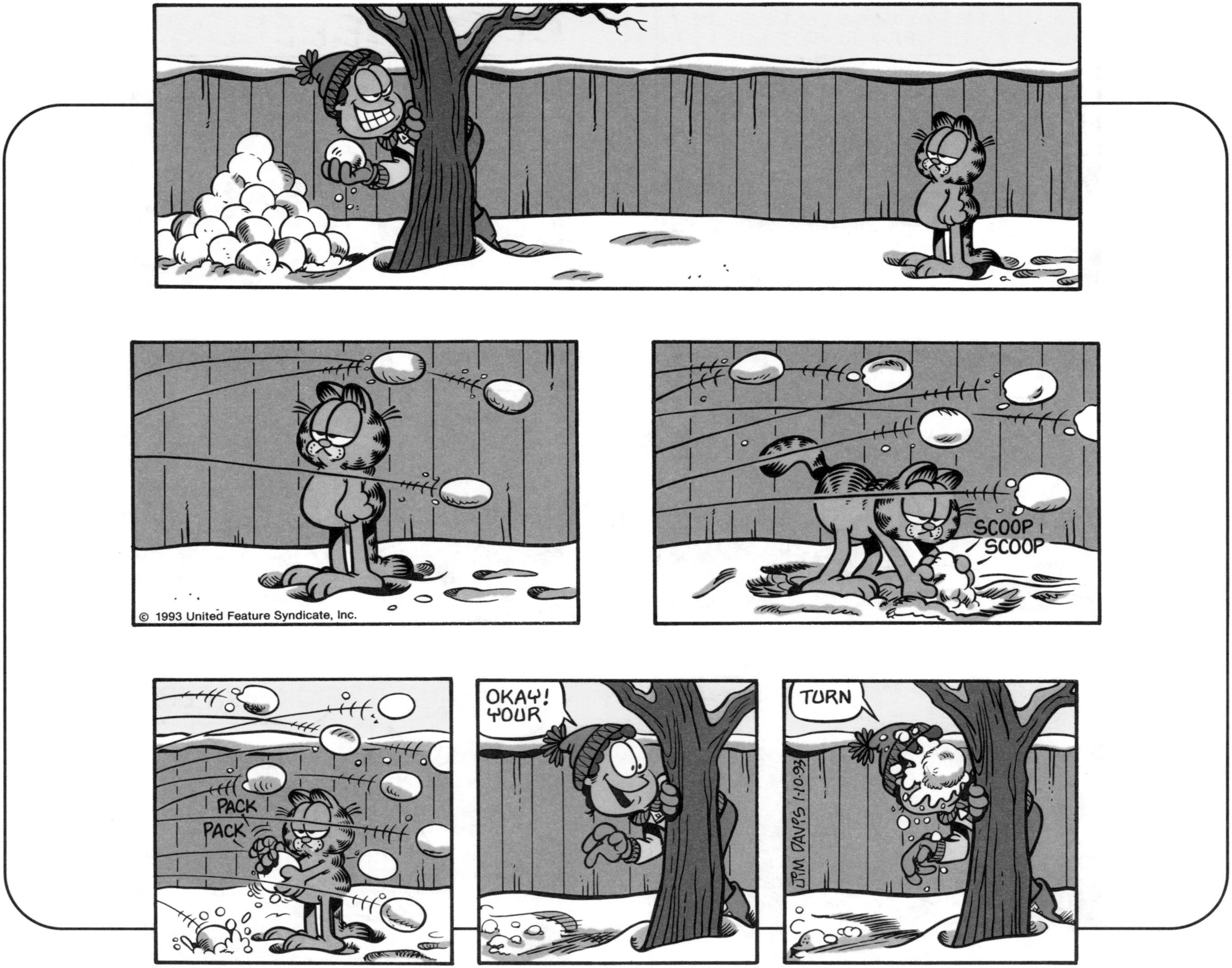

SCOOP
SCOOP
PACK
PACK
OKAY! YOUR
TURN
JPM DAVIS 1-10-93

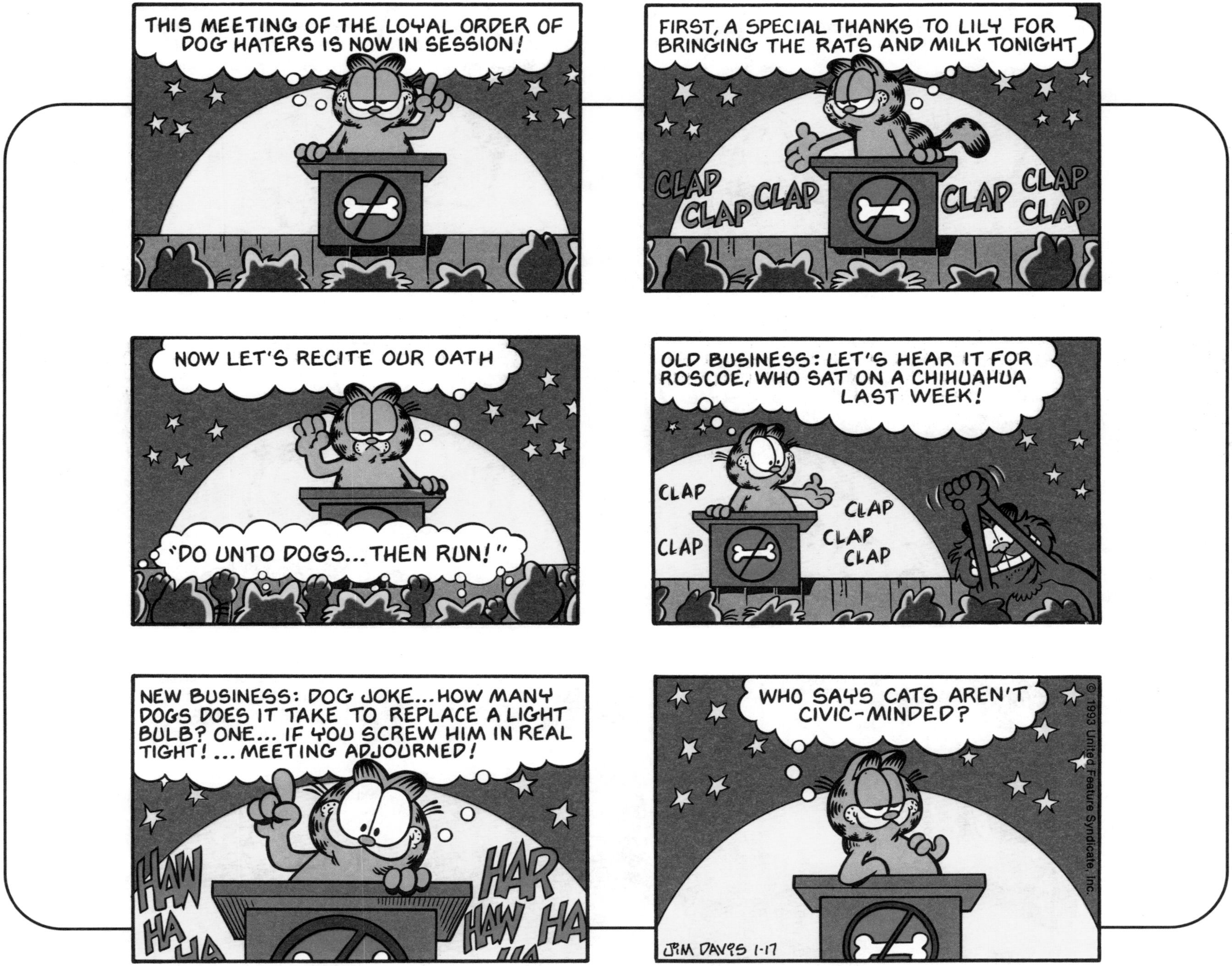
THIS MEETING OF THE LOYAL ORDER OF DOG HATERS IS NOW IN SESSION!
FIRST, A SPECIAL THANKS TO LILY FOR BRINGING THE RATS AND MILK TONIGHT
CLAP CLAP CLAP CLAP CLAP CLAP
NOW LET'S RECITE OUR OATH
"DO UNTO DOGS... THEN RUN!"
OLD BUSINESS: LET'S HEAR IT FOR ROSCOE, WHO SAT ON A CHIHUAHUA LAST WEEK!
CLAP CLAP CLAP CLAP CLAP
NEW BUSINESS: DOG JOKE... HOW MANY DOGS DOES IT TAKE TO REPLACE A LIGHT BULB? ONE... IF YOU SCREW HIM IN REAL TIGHT! ... MEETING ADJOURNED!
HAW HA HAR HAW HA
WHO SAYS CATS AREN'T CIVIC-MINDED?
JIM DAVIS 1-17
© 1993 United Feature Syndicate, Inc.

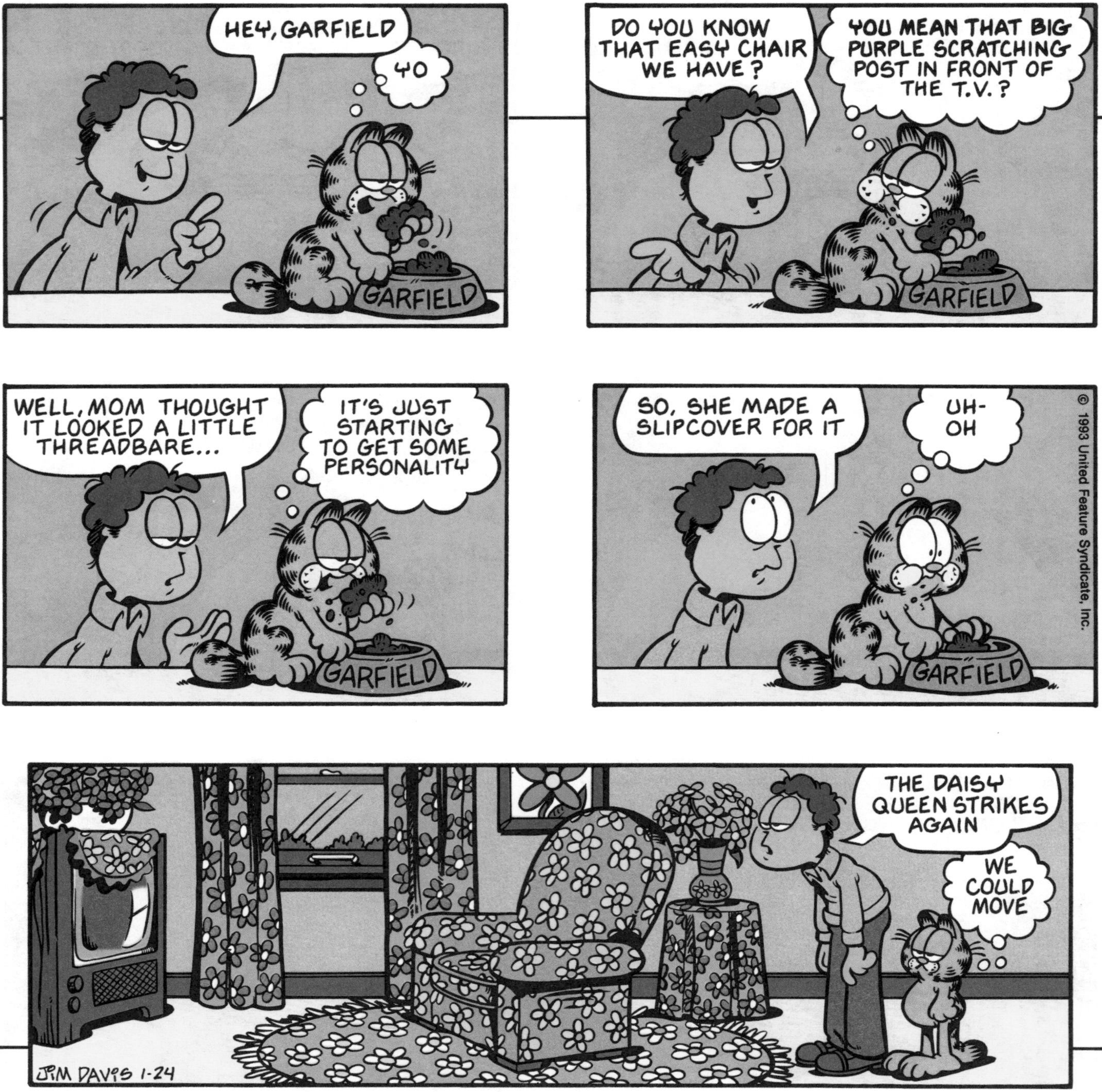
HEY, GARFIELD
YO
GARFIELD
DO YOU KNOW THAT EASY CHAIR WE HAVE?
YOU MEAN THAT BIG PURPLE SCRATCHING POST IN FRONT OF THE T.V.?
GARFIELD
WELL, MOM THOUGHT IT LOOKED A LITTLE THREADBARE...
IT'S JUST STARTING TO GET SOME PERSONALITY
GARFIELD
SO, SHE MADE A SLIPCOVER FOR IT
UH-OH
GARFIELD
© 1993 United Feature Syndicate, Inc.
THE DAISY QUEEN STRIKES AGAIN
WE COULD MOVE
JIM DAVIS 1-24

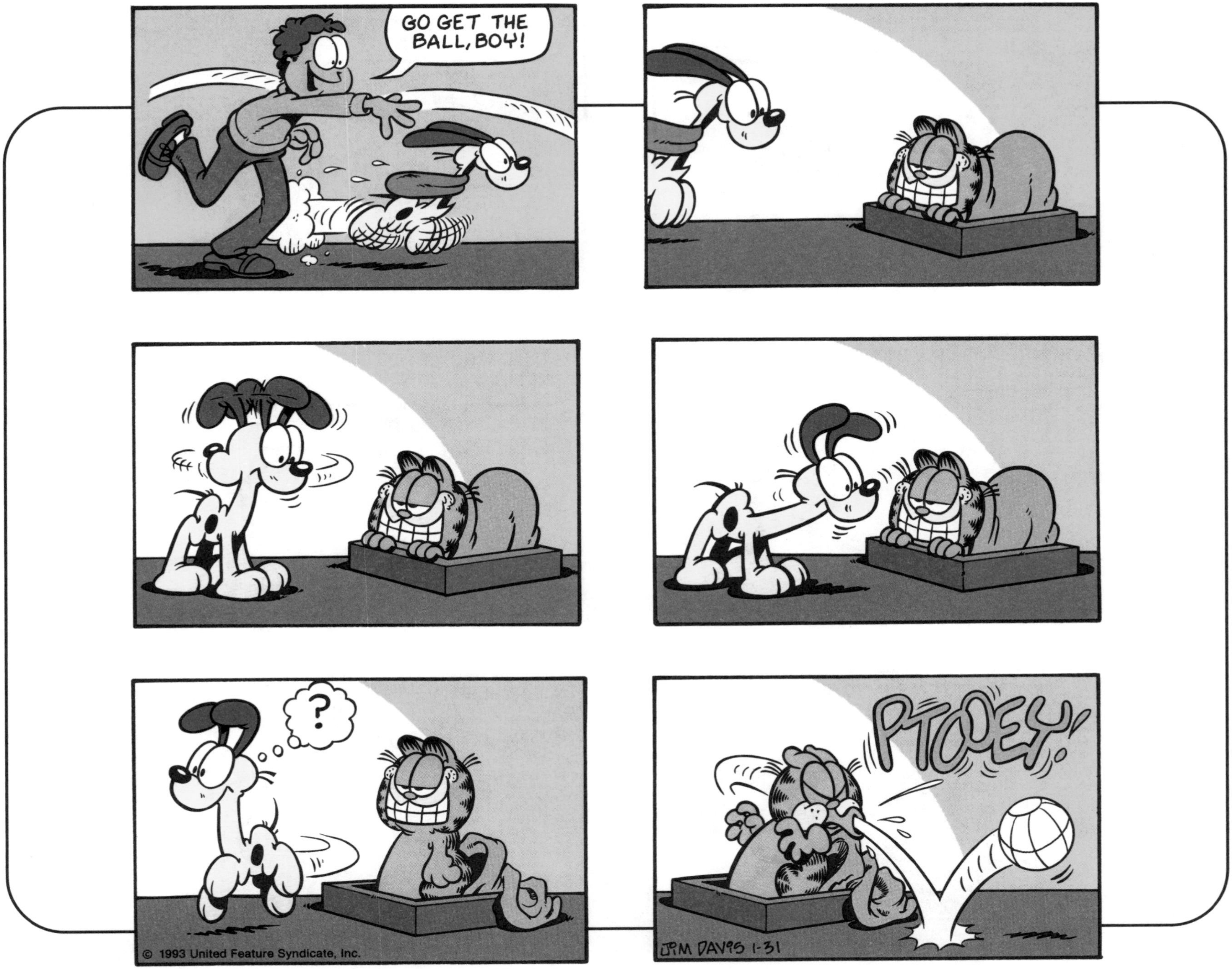
GO GET THE BALL, BOY!
?
PTOOEY!
JIM DAVIS 1-31
© 1993 United Feature Syndicate, Inc.

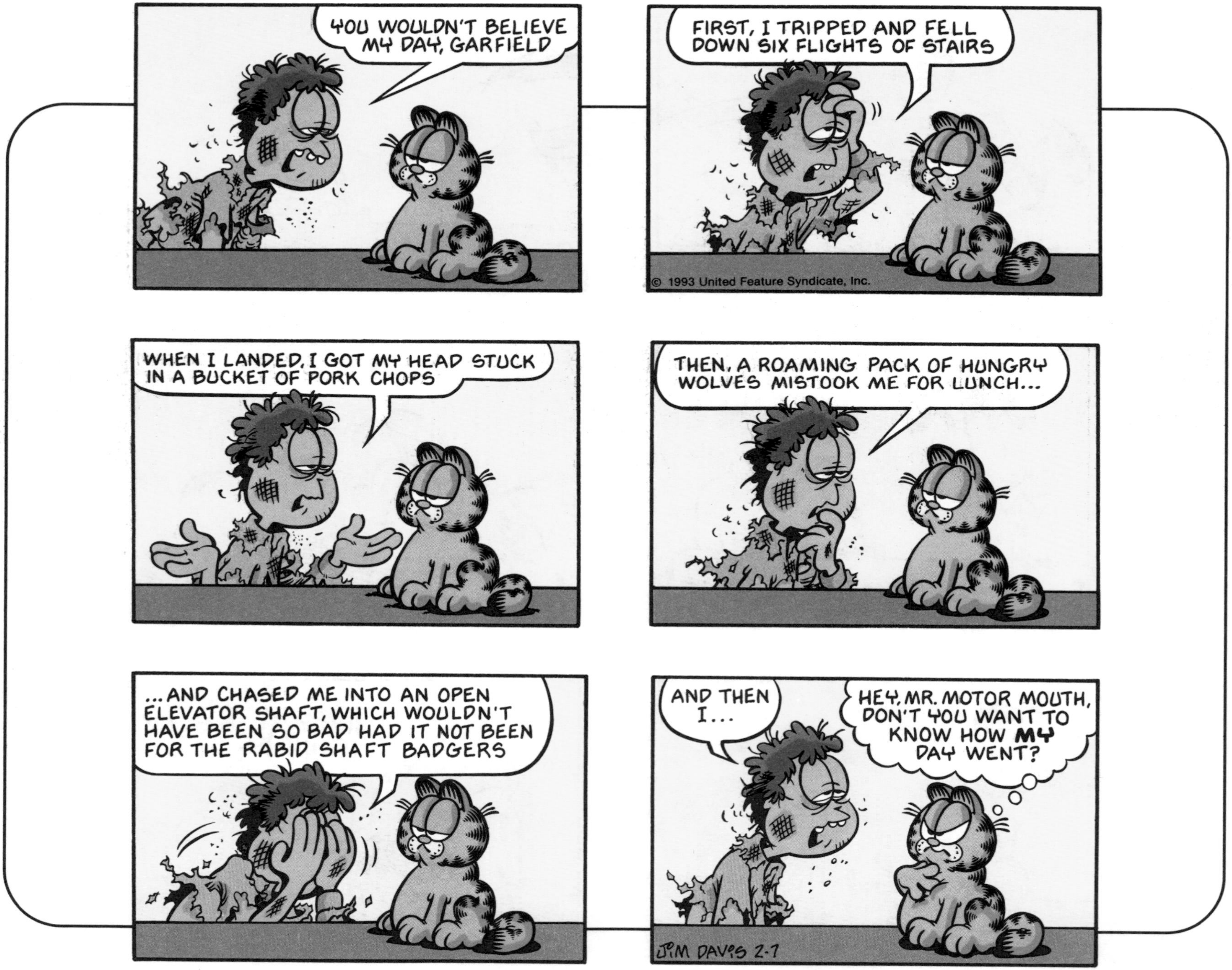
YOU WOULDN'T BELIEVE MY DAY, GARFIELD
FIRST, I TRIPPED AND FELL DOWN SIX FLIGHTS OF STAIRS
© 1993 United Feature Syndicate, Inc.
WHEN I LANDED, I GOT MY HEAD STUCK IN A BUCKET OF PORK CHOPS
THEN, A ROAMING PACK OF HUNGRY WOLVES MISTOOK ME FOR LUNCH...
...AND CHASED ME INTO AN OPEN ELEVATOR SHAFT, WHICH WOULDN'T HAVE BEEN SO BAD HAD IT NOT BEEN FOR THE RABID SHAFT BADGERS
AND THEN I...
HEY, MR. MOTOR MOUTH, DON'T YOU WANT TO KNOW HOW MY DAY WENT?
JIM DAVIS 2-7

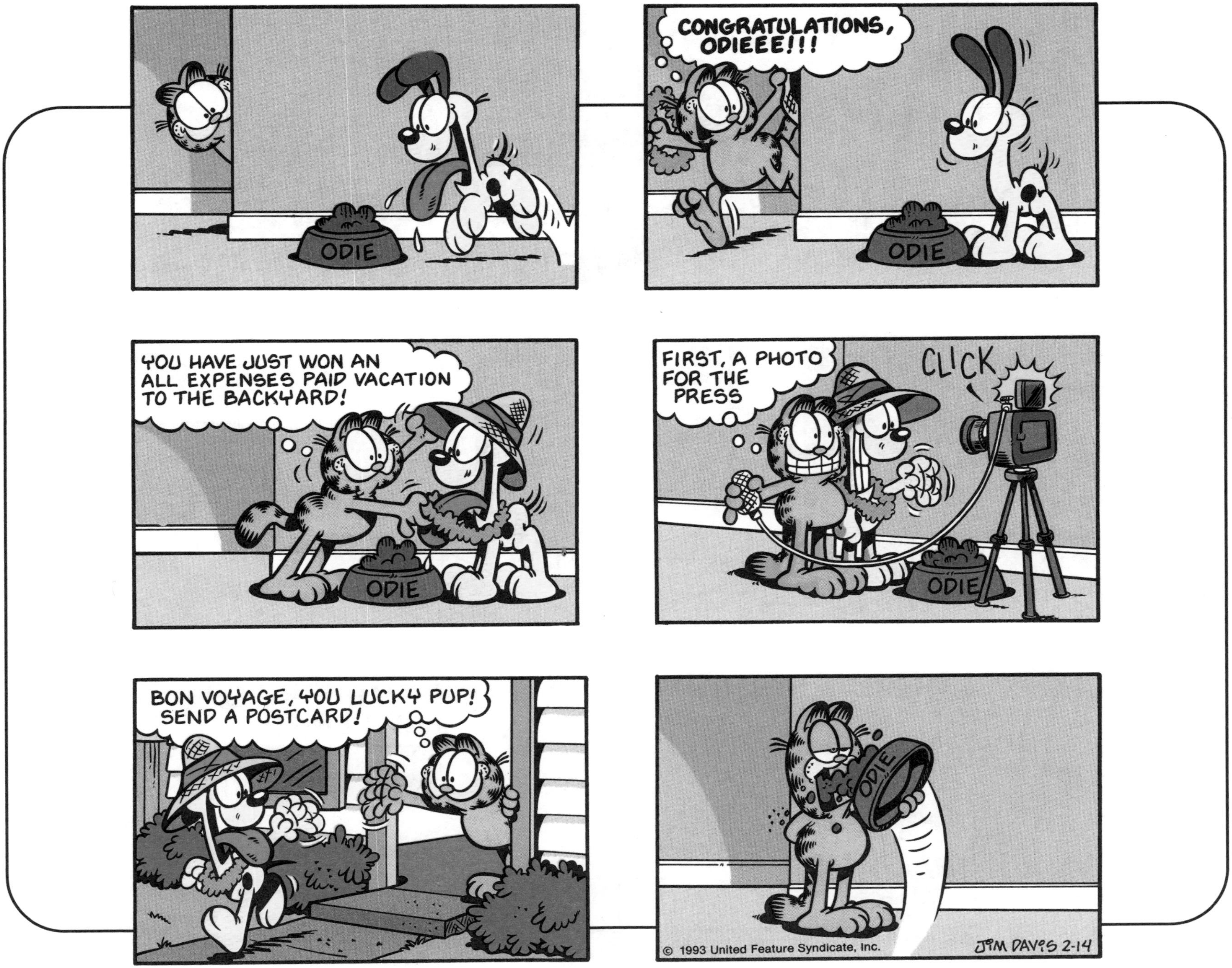

CONGRATULATIONS, ODIEEE!!!
YOU HAVE JUST WON AN ALL EXPENSES PAID VACATION TO THE BACKYARD!
FIRST, A PHOTO FOR THE PRESS
CLICK
ODIE
BON VOYAGE, YOU LUCKY PUP! SEND A POSTCARD!
© 1993 United Feature Syndicate, Inc.
JIM DAVIS 2-14

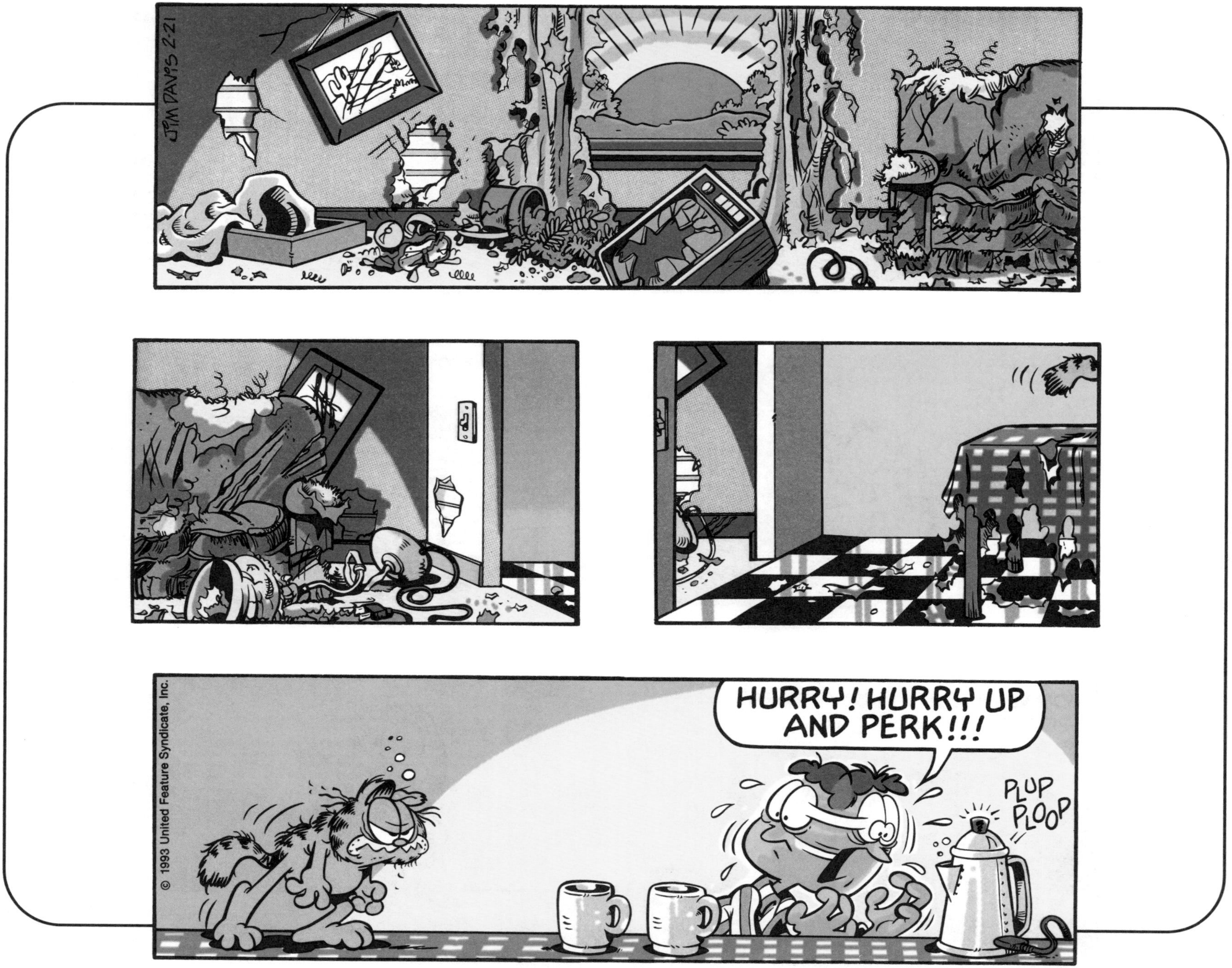
JIM DAVIS 2-21
© 1993 United Feature Syndicate, Inc.
HURRY! HURRY UP AND PERK!!!
PLUP
PLOOP

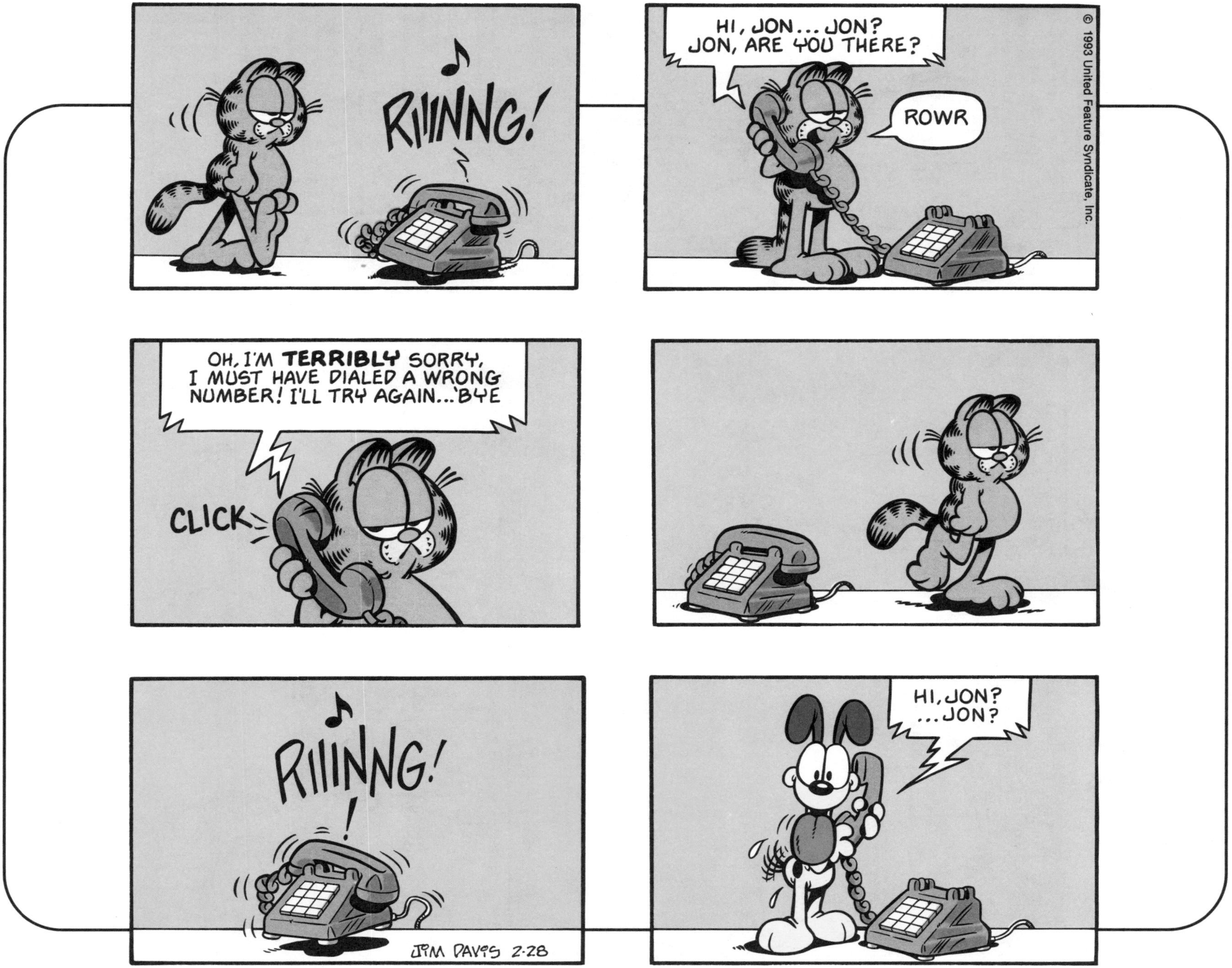
RIIINNG!
HI, JON... JON? JON, ARE YOU THERE?
ROWR
OH, I'M **TERRIBLY** SORRY, I MUST HAVE DIALED A WRONG NUMBER! I'LL TRY AGAIN...'BYE
CLICK
RIIINNG!
JIM DAVIS 2-28
HI, JON? ...JON?
© 1993 United Feature Syndicate, Inc.

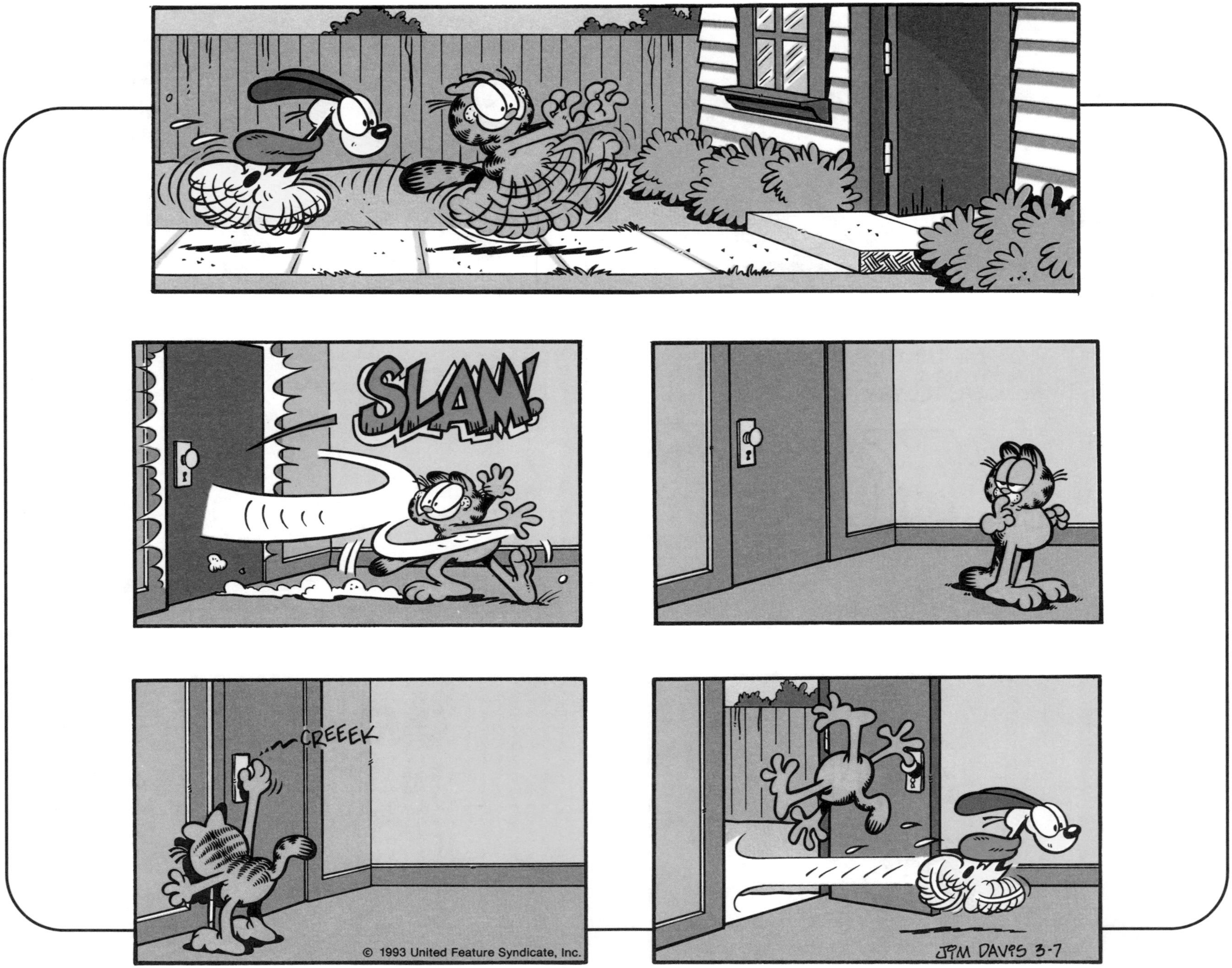
SLAM!
CREEEK
© 1993 United Feature Syndicate, Inc.
JIM DAVIS 3-7

the World According to Garfield

"PEARLS OF WISDOM"

FIRST OF ALL, KNOW THYSELF. THEN, KNOW THY ZIP CODE

AS YOU TRAVEL THE ROAD OF LIFE, REMEMBER TO STOP AND EAT THE FLOWERS ALONG THE WAY

DOGS ARE LIKE NAILS. THEY BOTH NEED A GOOD WHACK ON THE HEAD

THE WISE MAN HEARS NO EVIL, SEES NO EVIL, SPEAKS NO EVIL, AND HAS NO FUN

ANYTHING WORTH DOING CAN BE DONE AFTER NOON

A BIRD IN THE HAND WOULD BE EVEN BETTER IN THE MOUTH

ALWAYS BE YOURSELF... UNLESS YOU CAN BE SOMEONE RICHER

LIFE IS A FOOD CHAIN. FAR BETTER TO BE THE DINER THAN THE DINNER

IT IS A WISE MAN WHO KNOWS THAT CATS KNOW BEST

OBSERVE THE SPIDER, HOW PATIENTLY HE WEAVES HIS WEB. THEN SQUASH THE SUCKER

A LITTLE EGO GOES NOWHERE